The V

CHRISTOPHER DOBSON
AND
RONALD PAYNE

The Weapons of Terror

International Terrorism
at Work

M

First published 1979 by
THE MACMILLAN PRESS LTD
London and Basingstoke
Associated companies in Delhi Dublin
Hong Kong Johannesburg Lagos Melbourne
New York Singapore and Tokyo

Photoset in Great Britain by
Vantage Photosetting Co. Ltd,
Southampton and London,
and printed in Great Britain by
A. Wheaton & Co. Ltd,
Exeter

British Library Cataloguing in Publication Data

Dobson, Christopher
  The weapons of terror.
  1. Terrorism
  I. Title II. Payne, Ronald
  322.4'2   HV6431
  ISBN 0-333-23872-9
  ISBN 0-333-23873-7 Pbk

Contents

1 | Terror: How it Came to the Seventies

An india-rubber ball which, when squeezed in his trouser pocket, detonated a glass flask of dynamite concealed in his jacket twenty seconds later was the primitive yet effective device carried by the archetypal terrorist of literature, 'the Professor'. In Joseph Conrad's novel *The Secret Agent*, written at the turn of the century, this clever university drop-out was pitted against the head of England's anti-terrorist squad, Chief Inspector Heat. It was entirely appropriate that he should have used an academic title; for then as now the feeling of power enjoyed by a terrorist held strong attraction for intellectuals who turned to the gun and the bomb when their political arguments failed to convince. As he himself boasted, 'The Professor' had no future – yet his philosophy goes marching on.

The terrorist with the elaborately contrived weapon in his pocket spoke the truth when he said of England:

It is this country which is dangerous, with her idealistic conceptions of legality . . . to break up the superstition and worship of legality should be our aim. Nothing would please me more than to see Inspector Heat and his likes take to shooting us down in broad daylight with the approval of the public. Half our battle would be won then; the disintegration of the old morality would have set in in its very temple.

He might well have been thinking out loud as the spokesman for a terrorist group today; for his descendants are still intent upon making a violent clean sweep of the 'old morality'; the same battle still rages and it is fought to the same principles of terrorist war by similar people with similar aims. Only the weapons have changed, and they have changed in spectacular style.

The aim of this book is to show how the development of military technology, producing ever smaller and more deadly weapons, has affected the skills of terror and altered its tactics. Although the forces of order also benefit from improved weapons, that is not really the point, for the more often they have to use the weapons, the more easily they provide propaganda for the terrorist cause. The Professor's latter-day men still want to provoke shooting in the street. Security forces want above all else to avoid it and in this battle their improved weapons are psychological rather than military. Commissioner Michael Codd of the New York Police Department, which used to be known as a 'shoot-first force', now says:

There can be no precipitate use of firepower, considering the carrying strength of the average bullet. It can travel further than the limits of where the problem exists, and is a serious danger in the crowded urban conditions under which we live.

Thus the up-to-date bullets of law and order, when used without care, not only travel further, but they strike in the cause of the terrorists they are seeking to overcome. That is why a new squad is in action in New York – the Negotiating Squad under Lieutenant Frank Bolz, who has talked out ninety hostage-takers with the slogan: 'We aim to bore them to death.'

Modern weapons help the terrorists more than they help security forces, whether they be police or soldiers. When the British Army in Ulster was issued with American-made Armalite rifles in July 1977, this same highly efficient weapon had been in the armoury of the Provisional IRA for several years. The rifles were issued in limited numbers to the anti-terrorist military squads, and then only for specific sniping tasks even though Mr Robert Brown, the Under-Secretary of State for Defence for the Army, described them as being 'the best available against terrorism'. The Armalite is light and easy to handle, while its high muzzle velocity gives its .223 calibre bullet devastating penetration power. It is this power which makes it such an effective weapon of terror but makes the Army so cautious about its use. One bullet which killed a soldier in August 1977 passed through him and seriously wounded a young girl.

It is an irony that at about the time these rifles went into service with the British Army the Ministry of Defence gave orders that the standard infantry weapon, the self-loading rifle, was to be modified by the addition of a cam to the selective fire switch so that this automatic weapon could fire only single shots.

For although it is a great advantage for the terrorists to fire rapid bursts because they do not care how many people they injure, the Army's counter-fire has to be restricted so that if possible only terrorists in action are hit. Whenever soldiers wound or kill non-terrorists the IRA is given a rich harvest of propaganda. Even when a gunman is hit, his weapon is spirited away and the terrorists claim him to be an innocent victim. When the Americans used their Armalites on full automatic fire in Vietnam the effect was so destructive that men hit by the hail of bullets were said to be 'blown away'. There can be no blowing away in Ulster, even of an established terrorist, because of the sympathy it would evoke for his cause.

One of the main aims of terror is to make murderers into heroes and so persuade opponents and neutrals that the terrorists' cause is righteous and their actions are justified. Their tactic is to make it appear that it is the authorities who are guilty of brutality and in the wrong. In a topsy-turvy way weapons that are too deadly help to promote this tactic.

The equipment of the terrorist during the nineteenth century was the revolver and the bomb. The revolver was usually bulky and woefully inaccurate except at point-blank range – the KGB still teaches its assassins not to fire until they can almost touch their victims. The bomb was an elaborate affair with a fuse that was often difficult to manage; not until the end of the century were efficient hand grenades in use.

This basic equipment did not change radically until the Second World War when, during the Nazi occupation of

Europe, resistance groups were set up throughout the occupied territories with the support of the Allied governments operating from Britain. We have in our possession an official manual composed by the renowned Sir Colin Gubbins, KCMG, DSO, MC, who ran Special Operations Executive from his headquarters in Baker Street, London. This illustrated pamphlet describes in a variety of languages how to sabotage railway lines and how to carry out attacks on the army of occupation. It was parachuted by the thousand to resistance groups in Europe. Along with it the Royal Air Force dropped supplies of easily assembled Sten sub-machine-guns and the new and very adaptable plastic explosives together with instantaneous fuses and simple detonators.

Even before the war Sir Colin Gubbins, who had earlier seen service in Ireland and in Russia in 1919, composed several manuals on the practice of guerrilla warfare. The first was a common-sensical affair pointing out the need for a friendly population and daring leadership. 'Guerrilla actions', he wrote, 'will usually take place at point blank range as the result of an ambush or raid . . . Undoubtedly, therefore, the most effective weapon for the guerrilla is the sub-machine-gun.'

He then went on to put together the *Partisan Leader's Handbook* for a more popular readership, explaining how to prepare an ambush and blow up a railway engine. He also recommended giving short shrift to informers – kill them. Later he produced a clearly written pamphlet on how to use high explosives, and it was this work which developed into the airlifted guide we have already quoted. It was significant that British soldiers on the eve of the Second World War were already developing such expertise and were also running a number of training courses in forms of subversive warfare for selected civilians – explorers, linguists, mountaineers and men with extensive foreign contacts. The skills of guerrilla warfare were learned by respectable citizens, and modern weapons became virtually household utensils. The practice of terrorism became not only respectable but honourable, and above all, an everyday affair.

Since then much more reliable, smaller and more deadly automatic weapons have been developed. They are compact, easy to conceal and have greater killing power. Smaller amounts of explosives can do greater damage. The great advantage of these developments to those who indulge in terrorism is that one man can carry a great deal of hidden death with him. Paradoxically, one of the results of this increased ability to kill is that the threat of death has overtaken actual assassination as the prime weapon in the terrorists' arsenal.

When Tsar Alexander II was bombed to death by a revolutionary group the process was set in motion which led directly to the Russian Revolution and the wiping out of the Russian Royal family at Ekaterinenburg. When Gavril Princip mortally wounded the Archduke Franz Ferdinand at Sarajevo he did so on the grounds of nationalism. His shots brought about the First World War, destroyed empires and dynasties and led to the formation of the world as we know it.

But when John Kennedy, leader of the world's most powerful nation was shot down by Lee Harvey Oswald who, until conclusive evidence is produced to the contrary must be judged to have acted alone for his own reasons, the world wept but continued on its course. The truth of the matter is that in modern states with an efficient bureaucracy working in a settled infrastructure, the fate of the world does not depend on the life of a single individual. President Johnson was a very different individual to Kennedy but was he any worse as a President? Would Kennedy have been better able to cope with Vietnam? It is at least debatable.

The recent assassinations of Wasfi Tell, Prime Minister of Jordan, King Feisal of Saudi Arabia and Christopher Ewart-Biggs, the United Kingdom's ambassador to Dublin, have been carried out for a variety of reasons: Tell's was for revenge by Black September, Feisal's by a deranged member of his family, and Ewart-Biggs' by the Provos trying to prove that they could strike in the Republic of Ireland as well as Ulster. None was carried out for old-fashioned revolutionary reasons. None has changed the face of the world. The only recent political assassination carried out for true revolutionary reasons by a terrorist group was the killing of the Spanish Prime Minister Carrera Blanco. But even that killing was superfluous, for after the death of Franco Spain was set firmly on the path towards democratic liberty. Carrera Blanco's death neither hastened nor retarded its progress.

So what has developed over the past twenty-five years is that the threat of the deed has become a more effective weapon than the deed itself – especially when the potential victim is not a replaceable politician but a group of people with a high content of women and children whose plight can be displayed on the television screen in the most poignant fashion.

It is here that technical advances play into the terrorists' hands. The developments in weapons mean that one man can now carry the fire power of a platoon and the development of the Jumbo jet has provided the terrorists with the ideal target. The Jumbo is totally under the control of the captain and a handful of men on the flight deck and they are responsible for the lives of several hundred passengers confined within a vulnerable cell flying several miles high. Once terrorists achieve the position of being able to threaten the flight crew they have virtually achieved victory. For unless the authorities give in to the hijackers' demands, the terrorists must be overcome either physically or mentally. The dangers of a shoot-out are apparent – within an aircraft someone is bound to get hurt – and when it is decided to break down the hijackers' will to carry on, the inevitably long drawn out process involves mounting psychological stress for the hostages as well as the hijacker, along with the danger that one of the terrorists may crack and blow everybody to pieces.

It is this element of the unknown, of inherent danger, that makes hijacking so much more effective a tool of terror than assassination. And as aircraft become bigger and more complicated to operate so an armed takeover becomes more dangerous, and therefore more spectacular. In the nature of things the seizure of a Jumbo with 400 people on board attracts greater attention than that of a smaller plane with fewer passengers at risk. Experience has proved that, despite increased security precautions, it is still possible to smuggle arms and explosives on board these giant aircraft. Indeed the more people being processed before a flight, the more likely it is that terrorists can evade the security checks. There have also been instances of ground crew – cleaners and caterers – planting weapons on board aircraft so that their comrades, who pass the security checks 'clean', have their guns and grenades waiting for them.

From an analysis of two decades of hijackings it may be taken that the ideal terror group for the purpose consists of a leader and four or five accomplices. The leader plus one, both armed with automatic pistols and grenades, make their way on to the flight deck, usually from the first-class compartment. It is their responsibility to threaten the captain and flight-deck crew and then give them orders for radio transmission. English is the standard international language for airline operations so the leader at least must speak good English. Somewhere in the main cabin is the explosives man who places his charges at prearranged positions after careful examination of the type of aircraft before the raid – modern hijackers know their aircraft well. The charges must be in position before the aircraft lands at the fuel stop or destination ordered by the leader. The role of the other three or four men and women in the team is to intimidate the passengers and cabin crew by ostentatiously displaying automatic weapons and grenades while the explosive operator goes about his business. They must create an atmosphere of fear.

Most of the early hijackings were regarded sympathetically in the West, for these acts in the years just after the Second World War were the work of desperate political refugees intent on flight from the new tyranny in Soviet-controlled Eastern Europe. All but a handful of the twenty-one hijackings reported fell into this category.

The armed seizure of aircraft for political terror aims was first organised by Raul Castro, brother of the famous Fidel. In 1958 Cuban revolutionaries pirated a Cuban airliner flying from Miami, and it crashed in the Oriente province killing seventeen people. From that modest beginning developed the methodical seizure of more and bigger aircraft, and it was to Castro that there fell the doubtful honour of welcoming to Cuba the first Jumbo jet ever to be hijacked and to mark the occasion in August 1970 he went to Havana airport to inspect it. In the two-year period before that there had been no less than 121 hijackings to Cuba, more than half of them from the United States. Not all concerned acts of political terrorism, for many were carried out by criminals, the mentally unbalanced and by political refugees. Partly because of the criminal involvement Castro became disillusioned with hijacking and over the treatment of passengers who found themselves enjoying the faded delights of Havana: by 1973 co-operation between Cuba and the United States had become so customary that the two governments signed a five-year agreement undertaking to return seized aircraft and ships and to return hijackers for trial and severe punishment. This brought to an end the frantic period of air piracy in that part of the world.

But by that time the Cuban technique of air piracy was being actively exploited and perfected in the Middle East by Arab terrorist movements. The most notable exponents were members of the Popular Front for the Liberation of Palestine (PFLP), the most extreme of the Palestinian movements. It is Marxist in outlook and has an admiration for Maoism and for that extraordinary Communist dictator, Kim Il Sung of North Korea. Defeated in its attempts to raid effectively across the Israeli border, with its bases in Gaza and the West Bank destroyed after the Six Day War in 1967, and thrown out of Jordan by King Hussein, the PFLP looked on hijacking as a modern development of raiding, the traditional form of tribal warfare in the countries of Arabia.

For the Arabs, hijacking came on the scene when they were searching for some way to strike at Israel. The Israeli Army had defeated and humiliated the armies of the Arab states and had then mopped up the guerrillas. The Palestinian cause was going by default. Terrorism and particularly hijacking provided the answer. All that was needed was money and arms. And they had plenty of both. Money was flowing into their coffers from the newly prospering oil states and they had the resources to equip themselves with new weapons for the continuing struggle.

During the 1950s stocks of up-to-date arms and ammunition had fallen into Arab hands. What had happened was that when, at the end of the ill-fated Suez campaign, the Anglo–French forces withdrew from the canal, the British abandoned their bases in the zone. Before Egyptian nationalisation of the canal they had come to an agreement with President Gamal Abdul Nasser that these bases would remain in being after a withdrawal of troops from Egypt so that in the case of a major international conflict they could be re-activated to supply the British Army. At the end of 1956 when the last troops left after the so-called 'police action', the Egyptians took over the installations and found themselves in possession of a huge store of weapons, equipment and ammunition. Small arms and ammunition, Sten guns, SMLE rifles and grenades soon found their way into the arsenals of Arab independence and terrorist movements all over the Middle East. Quantities were passed over to the Algerian National Liberation Front fighting against the French in Algeria, and other supplies went to the Palestinians. For the first time these groups had the military hardware needed to establish training camps and set up guerrilla forces on a lavish scale. It is one of the ironies of the Middle East's continuing wars that these arms, planned to be used by the British to keep the peace, came to form the armoury of those groups dedicated to making war.

However, these weapons from the British bases were not the latest in design. More modern equipment obtained through another act of power politics quickly superseded them. For in the course of his quarrel with the British, and stung by the refusal of John Foster Dulles to finance the building of the Aswan High Dam, President Nasser began flirting with the Russians. Military aid from them included for the first time the highly sophisticated weapons being produced for the Soviet Union by the efficient arms factories of Czechoslovakia. It was the time of the Kalashnikovs. A new generation of weapons was suddenly available in Egypt, and by way of Egypt to the terror groups and liberation movements, so that guerrillas no longer needed to make do with second-hand equipment.

So, frustrated in their attempts to raid into Israel, but with gold in their war chests and modern Russian weapons in their armouries, the Palestinian movements, taking the Cuban and Latin American revolutionaries as a model, moved into the field of terrorism. And what could be more obvious than to strike internationally? The Israelis were international people with Jewish friends and relations in communities in every country in the world. The Arab terrorists, descendants of men who had raided across the deserts to attack the caravans of their enemies, began using their new weapons to attack the airline routes of the twentieth-century world.

The first Palestinian hijacking was on 23 July 1968, when PFLP terrorists boarded an El Al Boeing 707 at Rome Airport and forced it to land in Algiers. This was followed by a number of other attacks on Israeli airliners in Europe, and the campaign continued successfully until El Al began placing guards armed with high velocity .22 pistols on all flights and installing locked bullet-proof doors to the flight decks of their aircraft. These precautions proved their value in September 1970 when Leila Khaled and Patrick Arguello, a Latin American working for PFLP, tried to hijack an El Al aircraft they had boarded at Amsterdam. They were overpowered by armed Israeli sky marshals and Arguello was fatally wounded. Leila Khaled herself did not press home the attack, failing at the critical moment to take the pin from the grenade she was holding. Arguello did pull the pin from his grenade, but it had a weak spring and failed to explode.

Despite this failure other terrorist squads similarly equipped forced a TWA 707 and a Swissair DC8 to land at Dawson's Field, a runway carved in the desert by the RAF at the end of the Second World War, forty miles north of Amman in Jordan. A British VC 10 en route from London to Bahrain was also forced down there and held hostage for the release of Leila Khaled, who was now being detained at Ealing police station after the El Al flight had made an emergency landing at Heathrow. Finally, in this biggest of all series of hijacks, a TWA Jumbo out of Amsterdam was seized, taken to Cairo and blown up.

Five governments became involved in lengthy negotiations with the Palestinians who were of course then able to claim that they were operating on a nation-to-nation basis and that their cause had been officially recognised. But as in so many acts of terrorism the very success of the act brought about a violent reaction. King Hussein of Jordan decided to rid himself of his dangerous guests and unleashed his Bedouin army on the Palestinian guerrilla bases. In sharp fighting the guerrillas, who provided the terrorist groups with their men, weapons and sanctuary, were either wiped out or forced to retreat into Syria and the Lebanon. It was then that Al Fatah, the Palestinian group led by Yasser Arafat, formed Black September to revenge itself on Hussein and to carry on the war against Israel by terror. Black September was responsible for the massacre at the Munich Olympic Games in which eleven Israeli athletes were murdered; the same organisation then mounted an elaborate hijack of a Lufthansa flight to secure the release of their imprisoned comrades. So terrorism bred a terrible retribution and then yet more terrorism.

Although the mass hijack practised in 1970 has not been repeated it is none the less true that big jet aircraft in use all over the world remain extremely vulnerable to attack in the air. A Jumbo with more than 400 people aboard and worth over $20 million can still be held at the mercy of terrorists equipped with simple weapons. In almost every case two weapons have been used for air piracy – the pistol, easily concealed about the person of the hijacker, and the hand grenade. The grenade is the back-up weapon. So long as the terrorist has the courage to remove the pin and hold the lever in his hand, all he has to do if guards threaten to shoot or overpower him is to release his grip on it. Then everyone dies.

Grenades were an important part of the arsenal carried in suitcases by a suicide squad of the Japanese 'Red Army' working with PFLP who carried out a murderous raid at Lod Airport, Israel, in 1972. Their bags were not searched by Air France, and when they disembarked in Israel they simply opened up the suitcases, took out grenades and Czech VZT 58 automatic rifles and opened fire on people in the airport, killing twenty-four and wounding seventy-two others.

Hijacking of aircraft is just one of the methods of terrorist warfare now extensively used. Kidnapping of prominent figures either for a ransom or in order to score some political propaganda point is just as common if less spectacular. It is an ancient technique which again was re-launched by the Cubans. They set the fashion for the political use of the kidnap weapon when in 1958 Castro supporters grabbed the racing driver Juan Fangio. Other Latin American groups of terrorists began to pick on foreign diplomats. When, in 1970, the Guatemalan government refused to accede to the demands of terrorists who had seized the West German ambassador Count von Spreti, the terrorists murdered him.

Inspiration for the Latin American terrorists came from Carlos Marighella, who was a Communist Party veteran already in his sixties when he abandoned rigid party methods in favour of real revolution. 'The only way out for Brazil', he wrote, 'is through armed struggle and preparation for the armed insurrection of the people.' The chapter 'Handbook of Urban Guerrilla Warfare' in Marighella's book *For the Liberation of Brazil* rapidly became the textbook for terrorists operating far away from Brazil – in Japan, the Middle East and Europe. Marighella explained:

The urban guerrilla does have one enormous advantage over the conventional soldier and the policeman: he is defending a just cause, the cause of the people – whereas they are on the side of an enemy the people hate.

Though his arms are inferior to those of his enemy, his moral superiority is incontestable, and it is this which enables him to carry out his major tasks: to attack and to survive.

Of course, when Marighella speaks of the terrorists' arms being inferior he is thinking in terms of heavy weapons for it is usually true that in conventional military terms the forces of order can outgun the terrorists. The point is that with the range of weapons – including hand-held rockets with the explosive power of an artillery shell – now available to terrorists who have the funds or influence to acquire them they can develop their own tactics. This makes them into formidable opponents who cannot easily be defeated.

No specially complicated weapons are needed for political kidnapping: anything will do – a pistol, a knife, a bludgeon, even a mere threat – as long as it is strong enough to overcome a man's mental or physical resistance. What is new in the technique is the exploitation of the act through television by the kidnappers. Terrorism enjoys high ratings on the TV screens and the terrorists revel in massive exposure – a far cry from the old days of secret cells and passwords where exposure usually meant death, and was to be avoided at all costs.

During the bargaining phase – or as it is now more grandly called, the negotiation phase – of a kidnapping, a vast audience is involved as well as the principals, and the kidnappers' temporary importance is elevated in direct ratio to the number of viewers. The best example of the use of publicity by urban guerrillas was the Olympic Games massacre at Munich in September 1972. International attention was already concentrated on the games when the Palestinians struck and television cameras serving virtually every country in the world were on the spot to register this cruel assault. Through the wonders of satellite television the murderers had an audience of 500 million people. The fact that they could hardly have believed that Israel would give in to their demands did not matter. They achieved what they had really set out to do: they had made the rest of the world aware of the Palestinian cause.

Much less publicised is the urban guerrilla tactic of bank robbery, much favoured in Latin America and imitated elsewhere. Almost every group in the terrorist movement has resorted to it – the Algerian FLN, the Irish, the Baader–Meinhof gang in Germany. Stalin himself was a renowned bank robber in his terrorist days. Its advantage for the revolutionary with a pistol or two in the armoury is that it can be carried out swiftly, that it supplies funds for the movement while at the same time giving him the ideological satisfaction of believing that he is striking a blow against the capitalist system. Marighella himself wrote in 'Handbook of

Urban Guerrilla Warfare': 'Bank raids are the most popular form of action ... we have almost made them a kind of entrance exam for apprenticeship in the technique of re-volutionary war.' The only drawback was that they might confuse ordinary customers unfavourable to the idea of losing their money and possessions. For this very reason the instructor advised his followers not to behave like bandits, which in the circumstances is advice not always easy to follow.

Because it carries little risk for the terrorist, bombing is a popular tactic. This method has the disadvantage that be-cause entirely innocent people are often killed by indiscriminate use of the shopping-bag bomb and the even more lethal car bomb, the bomber incurs the wrath of the public. It is after bomb outrages that calls for executions are most frequently made, but even that can serve the terrorists' purpose of creating martyrs.

The making of bombs is one craft which has greatly advanced since the beginning of the twentieth century, and terrorists have made full use of improved methods to employ bombs for political purposes. There is no mystery about the components of any kind of bomb – a high explosive charge weighing anything from a few ounces for a letter bomb to hundreds of pounds for a car bomb. Modern explosives in good condition are easy to handle and safe until they are set off by a detonator, usually a metal tube containing more sensitive explosives such as fulminate of mercury. The deto-nator explodes if crushed, but the heat of a flash can also set it off, and a flash can easily be produced in several ways. Chemical action can be used, or an electric current passed through a filament, or a percussion cap like those used in firearms. These basic methods place a wide range of possible bomb devices at the disposal of terrorists skilled in their use. In a later chapter we shall go into details about the workings of various kinds of bomb devices and explain how difficult it is for anti-bomb squads to disarm such devices. The impor-tance of these technical developments is that they have affected the operational methods of urban guerrillas by giving them a wider range of action and a greater choice of targets. A skilled explosives man can send a letter bomb through the post to kill one person. He can equally well destroy an aircraft when it reaches a selected height by using an altitude fuse which sets off the bomb at that point. In November 1974 the IRA placed two time bombs using cheap watches as timers in two crowded Birmingham pubs. They killed 20 people and wounded another 180.

Bombs, even the most sophisticated kind, are well-established terrorist arms. Now there are signs that the same terrorists who have made unscrupulous use of them are graduating to even more powerful weapons. In 1975 'Carlos', Ilich Ramirez Sanchez, the most notorious of all present-day terrorists, opened fire with a Russian rocket launcher (unsuccessfully) on an El Al plane at Orly Airport near Paris. In a similar operation a few days later at the same airport, another unsuccessful attempt was made to destroy an aircraft. There can be no doubt that heavier modern weapons are already in the arsenal of urban guerrillas for their war on society.

Italian police – tipped off by the Israelis – raided a flat leased by a group of Arabs in Ostia, near Rome, in 1973 and there they made a most alarming discovery. For not only were the Arabs members of PFLP, they were also armed with two SAM 7s – the Russian hand-held anti-aircraft missiles – with which they were preparing to shoot down an El Al airliner as it approached Leonardo da Vinci Airport: the flat was directly beneath the flight path to the airport. It would have been a simple target for a weapon designed to shoot down supersonic fighters and which did so many times during the Yom Kippur War. Later, British police made raids near London Airport and the Army was called out in search of similar weapons following a tip-off that the Palestinians had smuggled SAMs into England. Other rocket weapons were captured at Nairobi Airport when the Kenyans arrested a joint PFLP–Baader–Meinhof commando group who were yet again planning to shoot down an El Al airliner.

Weapons such as the SAM are made available to terrorists by friendly governments, particularly that of Colonel

Gaddafi of Libya – it was proved that the Rome SAMs came from his armoury, in which massive stocks of modern Russian weapons are stored. Before the advent of SAM-type weapons it would have been very difficult for terrorists to set up anti-aircraft guns powerful enough to shoot down a Jumbo. But hand-held missiles guided by infra-red devices now make it possible for men to carry them to an airfield perimeter on the back seat of a hired car or, from the roof of a strategically sited rented flat, to shoot down a £10 million airliner carrying hundreds of passengers.

What of the future? Will terrorists eventually turn to the use of even more devastating weapons in order to blackmail world governments and to make their propaganda points? The science of mass killing has made great progress since 'the Professor' invented his rubber ball and flask device in the Conrad novel. Chemical weapons capable of poisoning a city's water supply are available in most countries. Nuclear materials are to be found, bought or captured in the ever increasing number of countries with nuclear weapons or power generators. It sounds melodramatic to suggest that a determined terror group might make its own nuclear bomb, and threaten to detonate it unless its political demands were agreed. Yet it is perfectly possible for a physicist to make such a device – a university student in America has produced the plans of a workable nuclear device. We shall examine the possibilities in a later chapter, but first, in order to appreciate the dangers of the weapons of terrorism, it is necessary to examine the kind of people who use them.

2 | Terrorism: The Reasons Why

What really makes a terrorist? Some come to it by chance, some by design, for 'wide is the gate and broad is the way' that leads to this particular form of destruction. The ranks of the urban guerrilla armies include many types, idealists as well as criminals and psychopaths. And yet, despite their differences, they have a unifying factor: they have all come under the influence of those political thinkers who preach that violence is essential to make the world a better place 'for the masses'. The criminals and psychopaths use the philosophers to provide them with an easy, glib rationalisation of their actions while the idealists are deluded by their gurus into thinking that violence provides the only true road to salvation.

As the anti-colonialist wars in several parts of the world came to an end in the 1950s and 1960s the concept of a Third World composed of the poor and miserable countries came into being and acted as a magnet for the interest and compassion of young people in the Western world and in Japan, the only truly industrialised nation in the East, who identified with its struggles and with the poverty of less fortunate people in their own countries. The feeling grew among young intellectuals that rich countries should do more for the poor, and that in the West we should feel guilt for our past colonial exploitation and pay for that guilt through massive programmes of aid – the paradox being, of course, that many of the newly liberated countries have fallen into tribal dissension, corruption and inefficiency and are far worse off than they were under colonialism.

It was in this atmosphere of revulsion against the luxuries

of life that capitalism has brought to the middle classes of the developed world, that the philosophers of terror began writing their volumes of theory – and in some cases of practice – about the efficacy and morality of guerrilla and urban guerrilla warfare. The inspiration was Latin American, for Castro's triumph in Cuba had impressed everyone; he had shown how a small band of guerrillas could overthrow the regular army of a dictator and he and his companions became immediate heroes in the universities. Before long the students of Europe and America began devouring the new literature of subversion.

Among the earliest and most influential of the new wave philosophers was Frantz Fanon, a black doctor born in Martinique who took over as head of the Psychiatric Department of Blida Hospital in Algeria as the war between the Arabs and French began there in 1952. He became a supporter of the National Liberation Front but did not live to see it achieve independence, dying of leukaemia shortly before independence in 1962. Though not a violent man himself, Fanon was consumed with hatred for colonialism and racial oppression, and he made a mystique out of violence. 'Violence alone, violence committed by the people and educated by its leaders, makes it possible for the masses to understand social truths and gives the key to them,' he wrote in a book entitled *The Wretched of the Earth*.

Not only was violence a means of ending colonial rule, he argued, but was also an improving element in itself, 'a cleansing force'. 'It frees the native from his inferiority complex and from his despair and inaction; it makes him fearless and restores his self-respect.'

Fanon justified such beliefs by the premise that European affluence was in itself scandalous because it derived from robbery of the very soil of the Third World and from slavery. An immense debt had therefore been built up which must now be repaid, and it justified the armed struggle by the wretched of the earth against deportations, massacres, forced labour and slavery, 'the principal means used by capitalism to augment its reserves of gold and diamonds, its wealth . . .' A Marxist in theory, Fanon felt nothing but scorn for the working class in the West, for it had simply accepted the benefits of latter-day colonialism. During the Algerian war he even had harsh words for Jean-Paul Sartre, whom he otherwise admired. Simone de Beauvoir reported: 'He could not forget that Sartre was French and he blamed him for not having expiated that crime sufficiently.'

The violent preachings of Fanon are important because they began to set a pattern of thought among leftward-looking intellectuals in the Western world. This helps to explain the process by which students turned to terrorism. His books instilled that sense of guilt, that feeling that the Third World of the ex-colonies had right on its side, which has provided so much support for international terrorists. The Germans of the Baader–Meinhof groups and before them the French students, whose revolt in Paris in 1968 coincided with a climax of anti-Americanism over the war in Vietnam, drew inspiration from Fanon's impassioned pleading on behalf of the colonially exploited and oppressed. He helped set the scene for international terrorism by justifying resort to it as a legitimate way of attacking injustice.

If the inspiration of latter-day terrorism came from Fanon and his Algerian experiences, the tactics of the modern style were made in Latin America. The founding father of this school of violence was Carlos Marighella, who practised what he preached, running a revolutionary group in Brazil. In his chapter 'Handbook of Urban Guerrilla Warfare' in *For the Liberation of Brazil* he wrote:

Bank raids are the most popular form of action. In Brazil they are very common; we have almost made them a kind of entrance exam for apprenticeship in the technique of revolutionary war . . . In this particular activity, revolutionaries have two types of competitors – bandits and right-wing counter-revolutionaries. This to some extent confuses ordinary people, and therefore the guerrilla will try to make clear the purpose of his action, in two ways: he will refuse to behave like a bandit, either by misguided violence, or by taking money or personal possessions from customers who may be in the bank; and he will back up his expropriation by some form of propaganda – writing slogans attacking the ruling classes and imperialism on the walls, handing out pamphlets, or giving people leaflets explaining the political purpose of what he is doing.

This passage gives the flavour of the naive and extraordinary advice handed out by the master. Yet it was taken seriously not only in Latin America but also by the European bands. Baader–Meinhof terrorists, who on several occasions left copies of the Marighella handbook in their abandoned cars, specialised in bank robberies. Moreover, on one occasion in Berlin they attempted to carry out the helpful advice to placate the customers of banks under attack by offering them chocolate covered cakes known as 'Negro Kisses'. They even left behind a box of these delicacies for the bank employees they had been threatening to kill only a few minutes before. The armed raiders, two men and two women, then made off with DM 100,000. It is not surprising that Andreas Baader once remarked that he found the gathering of money stolen from banks 'a particularly pleasing experience'. The terrified customers at the Berlin bank made no comment on their feelings.

In Britain, the Angry Brigade, a much less effective group which shared many ideas in common with Baader–Meinhof, and by no means unacquainted with the works of Marighella, made their money more modestly by stealing cheque books and credit cards. But shortly before the ringleaders were arrested they began planning raids on post offices and banks, justifying themselves with the thought that respect for the law should never be more than a tactical consideration.

In Brazil, Marighella's suggestion was carried through by his followers more ruthlessly, and in less than a year they lifted the best part of half a million pounds from banks in Rio and São Paulo. But in the course of their 'entrance exams' a number of Brazilian comrades were taken by the police. In order to rescue fifteen of them from prison, Marighella's group in September 1969 kidnapped the United States ambassador in Brazil, Charles Burke Elbrick, and held him hostage. The government gave in to their demands in order to avoid bloodshed and diplomatic embarrassment. Encouraged by this victory the terrorists went on to other acts, gradually escalating their demands for the release of more prisoners. Five were handed over for the life of the kidnapped Japanese consul, forty more for the West German ambassador and finally seventy for the Swiss ambassador. In the end the lesson was learned by the government of Brazil that it did not pay to give in to terrorist blackmail. But the successes of the hostage-takers also showed that from their point of view the advice of Carlos Marighella was sound. In 'Handbook of Urban Guerrilla Warfare' he wrote:

We can kidnap and hide policemen, North American spies, political figures, or notorious enemies who are a danger to the revolution ... To kidnap figures known for their artistic, sporting or other activities who have not expressed any political views may possibly provide a form of propaganda favourable to revolutionaries, but should only be done in very special circumstances, and in such a way as to be sure people will accept it sympathetically.

Kidnapping American personalities who live in Brazil, or who have come to visit here, is a most powerful form of protest against the penetration of US impérialism into our country.

That the tactical precepts of Marighella were taken seriously by followers throughout the world is proved by a glance at the subsequent activities of the international groups. The Palestinians turned to hostage taking, and the murder of diplomats and distinguished foreigners; Baader–Meinhof and the Moluccans in Holland took hostages and demanded either the freeing of prisoners, or the publication of political communiqués in return for their lives. 'Carlos' went so far as to hold hostage the entire ministerial strength of OPEC, the international oil body and possibly the most powerful group of men in the world. In every case, the terrorists accepted the dictum of Marighella that the duty of a revolutionary is to make the revolution. They were no doubt flattered by his outline of the personal qualities of an urban guerrilla – courage and initiative, good tactics and a good aim with a gun, the use of skill and cunning. They amount to what used to be called in the British Army 'OLQ' – Officer-like Qualities.

Although Marighella was killed in 1969 in the wave of repression which the actions of his supporters had provoked, his ghost is still with us in the form of his teachings. His book became the standard work for ambitious terrorist leaders, and when it was translated into French in 1970 the French government forbade its distribution and sale. About the same time it was published in Berlin and later a German terrorist said about it, 'You find quite concrete instructions: the urban guerrilla must be fit, and must read this and that, and learn to do this and that.'

His military theories are neither sensational nor very new, but his book did help to popularise the term 'urban guerrilla'. He declared that urban guerrilla warfare started in Brazil in 1968. But the theories are heavily derivative from Chairman Mao's instructions to the Communists on how to take over China from the Nationalists.

When such tactics were applied in Latin America by people like Che Guevara they met with far less success. Conditions in the assorted republics of that continent were different from those prevailing in the Far East. Because Mao had formulated the principle that Communist guerrillas could strangle the cities from the countryside and had, moreover, proved it in battle, the 'encirclement of the city by the countryside' became holy writ. But in Western industrialised societies, and in many parts of Latin America, the great majority of people live in cities. In such places it is hardly possible for the country minority to 'strangle' the city majority.

Even at the time that Marighella was first in action, counter-insurgency forces with new techniques and good training were in the process of destroying rural guerrillas in Latin America. Guevara, who planned to provoke American military intervention in Bolivia and so create a perpetual war like that in Vietnam, had over-reached himself. Rural guerrillas had also failed in Brazil.

The rural *foco* – or focus – advocated by Guevara was a guerrilla-occupied base for activity in the countryside into which recruits theoretically poured to form a miniature revolutionary state. In Latin America the rural guerrillas were unable to win the support which theorists believed would be forthcoming from farmers and peasants. What Marighella did was to adapt the *foco* principle to urban activities, and so the terrorists came to town. It was in the towns that enthusiastic converts such as students and intellectuals were most at home and there they stood a better chance of suvival.

In Latin America the turning point in the terrorist campaigns came with the death of Che Guevara in Bolivia in 1967. In the early 1960s insurgent movements had spread rapidly in Guatemala, Brazil, Peru and other countries in the hemisphere. Their inspiration came from Cuba, where Fidel Castro set about using his island base to encourage revolutionary movements on the continent. As well as providing the know-how and the weapons Castro furnished the example. Tyranny and capitalist imperialism symbolised by the United States were the enemy. 'I was born in Argentina, I fought in Cuba, and I began to be a revolutionary in Guatemala,' was how Che Guevara summed up his autobiography. It was this Spanish–Irishman who became not only the theorist but also the wandering missionary of revolution in Latin America. He was an occasional student and perpetual traveller who learned the theory of subversive warfare, and then in 1960 became famous by writing *Guerrilla War*. Cuba was his only successful campaign in the field. Despite his meticulous writing on the subject his advice was derivative, and in action he made mistake after mistake. What he did manage to do was to provide fashionable trimmings of political theory and philosophy.

As the Guevara cult grew he exerted great influence on more capable guerrilla leaders and on the terrorists as well, although he himself favoured guerrilla war as opposed to terror raids. He once warned against the dangers of terrorism which hindered 'contact with the masses and makes impossible unification for actions that will be necessary at the critical moment'. He saw the need to win the support of local populations in order to get recruits, and there was about him a knightly aura of the social reformer in arms who fought only with the support of the oppressed people.

The Guevara cult and the ideas of the man were spread to Western Europe by his admirer Regis Debray, the French intellectual and philosopher. What was attractive for Europeans in the Guevara theory was the adapted doctrine of proletarian internationalism. Parties and political programmes seemed less important to the revolutionary than the fighting itself, for from the armed clash political beliefs would eventually emerge. The message was, destroy first, see what happens later. And that message caught on among the European students and intellectuals.

When Guevara went off questing for more action once Cuba had been liberated, it was already too late for him in Latin America. The guerrillas were being outfought and outmanoeuvred by counter-insurgency forces who had themselves learned the Cuban lesson. An enthusiastic though blundering commander, he fought his forlorn battles in Bolivia until the autumn of 1967 when the Bolivian Eighth Division, some of its troops disguised as peasants, surrounded Guevara and his band in the Santa Cruz district. Guevara, himself wounded, was finally captured leaning against a tree. They took him to the tiny village of La Higuera and it was there that General Joaquin Zentano Anaya, then a Colonel, received orders from La Paz to shoot the captured guerrilla leader.

His death in such romantic circumstances generated a whole new mythology and it was not long before 'Che Guevara lives' became the rallying call for leftist rebels throughout the world. His name still lived in 1976 when the ill-fated Entebbe raiders announced that they were called the 'Che Guevara–Gaza Group', taking the name at one remove from a Palestinian terrorist who styled himself the Che Guevara of Gaza.

The face on the tee-shirt is now known everywhere. The worry is that Guevara has now been adopted as an unofficial hero by the rigid old Communist Parties he hated; and that he is now idolised by them as well as by the fringe revolutionaries.

Dashing posters of Che in full guerrilla regalia appeared everywhere and it almost seemed as though everybody under the age of twenty-five wanted to be a guerrilla. What was less obvious at the time was that already such irregular forces, defeated in Latin America, were transforming themselves into urban guerrillas, that is to say town terrorists. It was not long before like-minded groups in different parts of the world and in Europe particularly turned from national to international targets. It was a natural development for these terrorists to strike first against soft American targets, diplomats and advisers and then businessmen, in revenge for the strength of US influence in South America. It was the US Army and the CIA who had helped to train the counter-insurgency forces which destroyed revolutionary hopes.

The new radicals in American and European universities approved of the action for they found it easy enough to identify with the man in the beret who died for a cause in the Bolivian mountains. Emotionally at least, students who occupied buildings in London or Berlin, who fought the Chicago police at the Democratic Convention there, were the spiritual followers of Che. In one way or another they were intent on using different degrees of violence to change the established order.

A new nihilism based on rash though high-minded principles was emerging. Regis Debray, the French disciple of Che Guevara who made him more famous after his death than he had been in life, was sentenced in Bolivia for aiding the guerrillas, and his lengthy defence of his own actions and of guerrilla war were widely read. He served only three years of a thirty-year sentence.

Who should lead the revolution was the question he posed when writing on the subject. 'The irony of history has willed . . . the assignment of precisely this vanguard role to students and revolutionary intellectuals, who have to unleash, or rather initiate, the highest forms of class struggle.' And he continually stressed the need for armed struggle. Such statements conspired to spread the idea among the young radicals that they should take up arms against the system. In his introduction to Debray's *Strategy for Revolution*, Robin Blackburn summed it all up:

Along with other guides to guerrilla strategy, Debray's writings have helped a new style of revolutionary politics to spread from the Third World back to the metropolitan heartlands of imperialism. The sort of immediacy which the *foco* strategy can achieve has also been attained in the actions of the revolutionary movement of Europe and North America – in factory and university occupations, black uprisings, squatters' movements and so forth.

The other philosopher who inspired similar thoughts in the universities was Herbert Marcuse, born in Berlin in 1898, a theoretician and sociologist who had become Professor of Political Thought at the University of California. He belonged to the Frankfurt school of philosophy whose supporters had already made the connection between Western prosperity and Third World misery. On the one hand, they said, there was material plenty and 'choice' which gave an illusion of freedom; on the other was the war in Vietnam, black ghettos in the United States, and the sufferings of peasants in Bolivia and Uruguay. To shorthand this contrast they spoke of 'consumption terror' or sometimes 'consumption fascism', which was already halfway to justifying the use of terror to overthrow the system which brought it about.

The Frankfurt philosophers busied themselves confirming and justifying feelings abroad in the rioting 1960s. Moreover the Marcusian argument that Western power elites had provided a surfeit of material needs by creating artificial demand for a superfluity of goods appealed most to the radical chic groups (known in Germany as the *Schili*) as well as to students. Most of them were middle- and upper-class people feeling guilty because they in particular were so well provided with worldly goods. And nowhere did this take hold so firmly as in West Germany where the economic miracle had brought such a cornucopia to people who less than twenty-five years before had been so impoverished by war that a woman could be bought for a carton of cigarettes.

Marcuse also preached that the scientific and technological revolution had changed the structure of the working class, thus altering classic Marxist assumptions. A new technologically-based society had emerged in the West bringing an alliance between big business and the working class, which was no longer revolutionary or intent on overthrowing the established order. 'The people, previously the ferment of social change have moved up to become the ferment of social cohesion. . .' This development created a situation in which only what he called the 'outsiders' were the true revolutionaries. These outsiders were those forced from the system because they were unemployable in it; those persecuted for their colour; the exploited masses of the Third World; and the students disgusted by comfortable consumerism in the West.

Marcuse had observed that in the 1960s many young people were already in revolt against their elders and their ways. He encouraged them in what he called the 'great refusal' to take part in the rat race. He codified and offered an explanation for their discontent and made a flattering suggestion that they were the vanguard, 'the most advanced consciousness of humanity'. Their mission was to lead the powerless and ignorant substratum of society in revolutionary uprising. They were urged not to commit themselves to a society whose interests required the peaceful continuance of its ways; and when legal methods failed, to resort to illegal ones.

The German philosopher from California provided a complete though devious justification for student aggression by telling them that they were no more free than those who lived in totalitarian states east of the Berlin Wall. They enjoyed only an illusion of freedom because the consumer society foisted upon them comfort and luxury.

In the United States, where Marcuse had as great a following as he later won in Europe, the same ideas were current. But there the student movement concentrated on the Vietnam war and its consequences. Students and radicals protested against its cruelties, though more against American than against Vietnamese cruelties. They also attacked the universities themselves because they were used both for military research and for recruitment to the forces. Students simultaneously expressed their Third World guilt complexes and sympathy for fellow outsiders by demanding Black Studies in the universities and an end to colour discrimination. The big monopolies were also a target in their attacks on ostentatious wealth and exploitation.

The same themes were obvious as student revolt spread to

Europe. Nowhere was the movement more active than in the Free University of West Berlin, whose students went through the whole range of fashionable war cries as the SDS – the Socialist Student Union – gave its support to every campaign from 'ban the bomb' to 'Americans, get out of Vietnam', 'racial equality and 'help the Third World'. The proximity of East Berlin and its Communist oppressions originally drove East Germans to seek freedom in the West to demonstrate against their red masters, but when the flow dried up after the building of the Berlin Wall the students, lacking the experience of the refugees, moved leftwards.

The German universities were still fairly stuffy, crowded and old-fashioned places. Though the Free University, established after the Second World War, was the most modern of them, this did not prevent it from becoming a focus for trouble. It was the place for demos, sit-ins, talk-ins and all the other 'happenings' which became so familiar in the 1960s. All these events became indelibly stamped upon the personalities of those who later took to terrorism in Germany.

One event in particular had a powerful effect. In 1967 the Shah of Persia made a state visit to West Germany and undertook the ritual pilgrimage to West Berlin, its beleaguered outpost. The students seized upon him as a natural enemy, the representative of oppression in the Third World. In the course of the demonstration the police clumsily went into action and one officer opened fire on the crowd and killed a mild demonstrator named Benno Ohnesorg, a 26-year-old Protestant student from Hanover. This killing horrified the demonstrators and left its mark on the whole student movement.

A comparable incident took place in 1970 in the United States when National Guardsmen opened fire without warning on students rioting at Kent State University in Ohio in protest against President Nixon's invasion of Cambodia. They killed four students and wounded ten. Although Nixon dismissed the incident as an inevitable consequence of 'the resort to violence' – violence of the young that is – it provided for young people throughout the Western world a perfect example of violence by the state.

Both the Berlin affair and the Kent State University slaughter convinced student radicals that the state and the authorities were the violent oppressors and that they were justified in answering state violence with revolutionary violence.

Coincidentally it was while Marcuse was visiting the Free University on 13 May 1968 that a dramatic protest movement similar to the German one was at its climax in Paris. There thousands of students were marching behind the red flags of Communism and the black flags of anarchy. The revolution had begun in protest against the over-crowded and archaic universities of France. But as the barricades went up on the boulevards and clashes with riot police developed, it became obvious that French students were determined to follow through the idea that they should give a lead to the sluggish workers by marching to overthrow capitalism.

For a short while the ecstasy and the excitement of that revolution did spread to the workers, who although they resented the students and their ways, did go on strike and did in many cases occupy their workplaces. It began to look as though General de Gaulle's Fifth Republic would be destroyed. Then, largely through his extraordinary energy and the counter-magic of his personality, the Republic was saved. The terrified bourgeoisie rallied to his cause, troop reinforcements were brought back from Germany and significantly the workers abandoned their occupations of factory and office in return for more money and better conditions.

May 1968 was the high water mark of student revolt. The Red Bases which had been set up in the Sorbonne and at Nanterre, the new branch of the University of Paris, failed to make a successful revolution, but they had created a new mythology. It had briefly united the new radical themes: violence preached by Fanon; the *foco* theory of Guevara and Debray tried out in the streets rather than the jungles; and the student vanguard of Marcuse's outsiders. Yet at the end of it the world did not seem to have changed all that much. The predictions of Marcuse had come to pass. After ritual strikes and noises of revolution the workers returned to the pleasures of 'terror consumption'. Perhaps they really were invincibly ignorant in the matter of revolution and really were in league with the capitalists. After the heady excitement of the barricades the young revolutionaries savoured bitterness and disappointment. There was no further point in supporting the classic Communist Parties, far less the old-fashioned socialists. They needed something more extreme and this was their justification for turning to terrorism.

This then was the process which made young students into terrorists. However, it would be wrong to think that all terrorists are intellectuals fighting for idealistic motives. The ranks of the IRA, for example, are filled with men who are neither intellectual nor idealistic, men like Anthony Clark, a Liverpool labourer who was arrested after a crude incendiary bomb he planted in a store exploded prematurely and set him on fire. In court he described his recruitment by the PIRA, the Provisional Irish Republican Army. 'Two Belfast men called on me. They asked me if I fancied planting some bombs when they were talking about the Irish troubles. I said I would have a go.'

Harry Duggan, a baby-faced IRA gunman captured in London after being besieged in the Balcombe Street flat with three other terrorists in possession of an arsenal of weapons, took his first steps on the road to murder six years before, when he began going to Provisional Sinn Fein meetings. He came from a village called Feakle, and had become an apprentice in a chipboard factory where his father worked as a carpenter. His father thought he was good at his job and had no idea that he had become a gunman for the Provos. He was rated by the Provisional Army Council as 'a very useful man', and at a time when his mother in Ireland was saying that he had always been a good boy at school, he was selected to go on a terror mission to London. The group he belonged to killed Ross McWhirter, editor of the *Guinness Book of Records*, and blew up an eminent cancer specialist in a London street.

Duggan started his career at Irish political meetings where loquacious Provos denounced the British and their evil ways, and before long he was out on the banks of the river Shannon practising with .22 rifles and specially adapted Webley .38 revolvers. But he was still described by friends as a decent boy who, at the age of twenty-three looked as if he should be singing in the local church choir.

The IRA gave him money and a smart suit and sent him to kill in London. There he joined up with Hugh Docherty, a 25-year-old brought up in an Irish ghetto called Toryglen, a high-rise development area of Glasgow. Raised in bigotry in an isolated community in an alien country, Docherty had moved into terrorism as naturally and easily as he might have fallen into crime.

These three men are typical of the IRA, a world apart from Baader–Meinhof and the Japanese Red Army. Although some of the clichés of international terrorism have entered the limited vocabulary of the IRA and there has been some operational contact between the international groups and the IRA, that organisation remains an insular movement, content with its own myths. One of the oldest of the terrorist movements, it has a justified reputation for strict discipline. In the first eight months of 1977 its kangaroo courts carried out no less than eighty-two 'kneecappings' in which punishment is inflicted by shooting in the back of the knee.

'Kneecappings' are inflicted for a variety of offences from trying to keep part of the haul from post office and bank raids to showing reluctance to remain on duty with an 'Active Service Unit'. It is not the only form of punishment – recently there have been cases of fingers being cut off with razors and one case of castration has been reported. Any attempt to work with the security forces is, of course, rewarded with death, the victim being hooded and shot through the head. Thus, IRA terrorists are kept in line through fear.

But apart from its harshness, the movement depends on the kind of patriotic fervour which inspires some of its hit men. Many are those who have moved into the terror business for sentimental reasons. And probably as many Irishmen have gone off gun in hand through the influence of whiskey and black porter, hymned on by the catchy traditional revolutionary songs, as through any hard-headed political conviction or true revolutionary philosophy. As one IRA mother told a television interviewer, speaking of her son who had killed a British soldier, 'He is a patriot fighting for his country.'

Between the start of the terror campaigns in Ulster in 1969 and the end of 1978 the IRA killed 490 members of the security forces and 1400 civilians. It accomplished all this with the active support of only a small percentage of the population, and without achieving any real political aim.

It is not without interest that when intellectuals and middle-class revolutionaries from outside have tried to aid the cause of the IRA they have been treated with suspicion and contempt. To Irish hit men, the kind of terrorists who would be welcomed by, for example, the German Red Army Faction are simply an embarrassment. When Dr Rose Dugdale, an English sympathiser, was arrested for terrorist actions – including bombing a police station with an explosives-filled milk churn from a hijacked helicopter – which both she and the IRA admitted were in support of the Provos, David O'Connell, a senior member of the leadership, showed no sign of enthusiasm for her help. He admitted that some Provos were involved in the operations with Dr Dugdale, but they had become so without the approval of the Provisional Army Council.

In this respect the IRA are by no means typical of present-day terrorist movements, most of which have international support and strong transnational links. The IRA is a much more earthy group, more suspicious of outsiders and unwelcoming to the student revolutionaries to be found in most similar movements. It even keeps at arms' length the Breton nationalist fighters who share similar aims to itself.

The only acceptable outsiders giving support to the IRA are Irish–Americans. Here again the link is sentimental and symbolised by all those Irish of Boston and New York who take part in St Patrick's day parades and dig into their pockets to support those on 'the ould sod', fighting against the British. Over the last few years, and largely because the Southern Irish government has gone out of its way to inform leaders of Irish–American opinion about the true face of Irish terrorism, the number of dollars flowing into IRA funds has fallen. From a total of $600,000 in 1972 it fell to $150,000 in 1977. William V. Shannon, the US ambassador to Dublin, explained the matter very well in an interview in *The Times* early in 1978. He said that Irish–Americans like himself and Senator Edward Kennedy had come round to the view that if Britain were to give in and withdraw from Ulster, 'there might well be even more violence'.

When it started in 1969 the civil rights issue burst into flames, and Irish–Americans tended to think it was the final act of the drama which began in 1916. To start with there was an instinctive desire to rally behind the Irish, to kick the British out and reunite the country . . . But as the guerrilla war has ground on, people have become much more conversant with the realities and complexities of the situation in the North.

If American support for the Provisionals waging urban guerrilla warfare in the British Isles continues to decline the terrorists may eventually have to turn towards the trans-national terrorist groups which could help to provide them with modern weapons and money. But so far the IRA has remained aloof. It has, moreover, never made use of techniques common elsewhere such as hijacking aircraft, though hostages have been taken. Until now the IRA has stuck very much to the old ways.

Because it fights a traditional cause of some antiquity the Irish Republican Army attracts a higher proportion of mature terrorists to its colours than almost any other. For similar historical reasons Irish terrorists tend to be more working class and decidedly less intellectual than is the case with other 'liberation' movements.

The original IRA was formed to fight in a patriotic cause against an occupying army. Thus it had more in common with the Spanish guerrillas who fought against Napoleon, and with the Algerian National Liberation Front struggling against the French who ruled their country.

It is often accepted as fact that the terrorist activities of the old IRA won the establishment of the Republic of Southern Ireland. The claim is rejected by many Irishmen in the south, including Conor Cruise O'Brien, a former minister in a Dublin government. In a lecture on 'Liberty and Terror' at St Antony's College, Oxford, he argued, 'Basically our state owes its existence to the known and attested demand of a majority of its inhabitants for self-government and to the recognition, in Britain and the world, of the legitimacy of that demand. That demand was repeatedly expressed at the polls: it was also expressed by violent means.'

Even when the democrats had negotiated the setting up of the new state with Lloyd George in 1921, they then had to defend it against the pure Republicans and the continuing gunmen. Michael Collins, who had successfully negotiated with the British, was assassinated the following year by the IRA because he had agreed to compromise over the six largely Protestant counties in the north which remained part of the United Kingdom. From 1922 onwards the IRA was fighting against the government of the Republic of Ireland, and against the Irish Catholics who elected it.

In the 1960s the IRA began to acquire a political flavour of Marxism; that was largely through the influence of one man, David O'Connell, on its leadership. But within a few years it became clear that most members, including those active in terrorism, were not interested in political ideology so much as in the basic nationalism of their cause. The Provisional IRA which took over activities in the north was simpler in its philosophy.

What attracts apprentice killers to its cause is the very simplicity of the movement's basic aims, which may be summed up as 'get the army and the British out of Northern Ireland'. Their ostensible aim is to allow the Irish government in the south to rule over the whole. What they really want is to destroy the democratic government of Dublin as well, and to sever connections with Europe of the Common Market, as well as with England. The Provisional IRA has in its mind a rather woolly concept of creating a *new* Ireland. As Dr Conor Cruise O'Brien remarked in his Oxford lecture, 'The achievement of that new Ireland would I think require two rather basic changes for the island of Ireland: a new geographical location and a new population. These may prove difficult either to negotiate or to extort by political force.'

The basic aim of the IRA is separatist and nationalist. Here we have an important divide in the aspirations of terrorist movements in the modern world, for it is important to distinguish between those movements in Europe, America and Japan who use their form of warfare to make international revolution and overthrow the present system; and those who, like the Irish, are concerned with establishing power in their homeland. In this respect the Irish have something in common with the Israelis who succeeded in setting up their own state through use of the terror weapon: indeed the Israeli Prime Minister, Menachem Begin, was once leader of the 700-strong force of terrorists known as Irgun Zvi Leumi.

The two outstanding examples of what may be called 'territorial' terrorists are the IRA and the various branches of Palestine liberation forces. But the Palestinians, unlike the Irish, are much more willing to accept the aid and support of outsiders and conduct their campaigns worldwide. In fact after Munich, when every Arab in Europe was marked down as a potential terrorist, they came to rely on international groups to carry out their missions. In addition they provided training, weapons and money for these groups of ideological terrorists who at first glance have little reason to be involved in the underground war between Arabs and Jews. Into this category fall members of Baader–Meinhof, the Japanese Red Army and the 'Carlos' network.

For all that, the various Palestinian organisations, which are the best publicised of all guerrilla and terrorist groups, remain fundamentally interested in territorial aims. To them Palestine means the whole of Palestine, and they want to recover that land from Israeli possession and to control it themselves. However their campaign has been a long one, and in the course of it various brands of revolutionary Marxism have impressed themselves upon individual leaders. A distant aim of world revolution is in the minds of numerous Palestinian terrorists and this does give guerrillas from that part of the world something in common with the intellectual terror groups of Latin America and Europe.

It may well be that if the Arab oil powers, and the 'confrontation' states financed by them, namely Egypt and Syria, finally accept an international political settlement of the Palestine problem, the radical Palestinian movements will turn their attacks on those countries with the aim of producing revolutionary governments in them. Already there have been terrorist attacks, sometimes sponsored by Colonel Gaddafi of Libya, against the Egyptian government. The leadership of this trend which takes Palestinian terrorism out of its purely territorial role and involves it in international revolution rests with men like Dr George Habash and Wadi Hadad, who until his death in April 1978 was his chief of operations. They ran the most active and ruthless group, the Popular Front for the Liberation of Palestine (PFLP).

PFLP is fiercely committed not only to the destruction of Israel but also to creating a Marxist–Leninist revolution throughout the Arab world. And after it has disposed of the 'feudal' Arab states, then it intends to terrorise in the cause of world revolution. That is why Dr Habash's men are so ready to provide bases and training for international movements working in the same cause and to make use of their members. Habash's philosophy is that there is no point in classic military operations against Israel, only terror can be effective. PFLP spokesman Bassam Abu Sherif, himself badly scarred by an Israeli parcel bomb, told Dobson at PFLP headquarters in Beirut in 1973: 'We intend to attack imperialist and Zionist interests wherever we find them in the world. They are legitimate targets.'

There can be little doubt that the effectiveness of PFLP operations led to the birth of Black September, established originally to take revenge for the destruction of the guerrilla movement in Jordan by King Hussein, but expanded after its success in killing Wasfi Tell, the Jordanian Prime Minister, into an international organisation which proved its savagery by carrying out the massacre at the Munich Olympics.

Another Arab terror group is a breakaway from PFLP. Known as the Popular Democratic Front for the Liberation of Palestine, it is led by a revolutionary named Naif Hawat-meh. Like several other splinter groups it comes under the umbrella of the Palestine Liberation Organisation led by Yasser Arafat, who is recognised at the United Nations as the respectable statesman of the Palestine cause. But he also leads the politico-military organisation known as Al Fatah ('The Struggle') which itself controlled Black September. Arafat, seeing that he was making more headway through the Council Chamber than by terrorism, has ordered Black September to cease operations. He is an excellent example of a leader in transition from terrorism to political leadership.

All these leaders are clever and mostly well-educated men. Many have been influenced by the international theorists of terrorism, its aims and methods, whose doctrines we shall outline. If Marighella and Che Guevara are known as the philosophers and writers of revolution by subversive war-fare, they are the terrorist warlords. Through their influence and petrodollar resources they are in a position to get the most modern weapons for their own followers. They also supply supporters in the groups of brother terrorists. From the great arsenal of Soviet weapons bought by Colonel Gaddafi, supplies of advanced and heavy weapons trickle through the hands of Palestine groups to other terrorists in the West willing to use them in the cause. There is a danger of more anti-aircraft missiles, bazookas and new grenades filtering through to guerrilla movements worldwide in this way.

In this process yet another of the warlords of terror, code-named Carlos, still plays a large part. He is an interest-ing case history for in his own career he has brought together a number of the threads which weave into the fabric of international terrorism. This plump and affected 29-year-old was born Ilich Ramirez Sanchez, one of the three sons of a Venezuelan Communist lawyer who made his millions through property dealing. The old man chose as first names for his sons the three names of Lenin, and he arranged the education of Carlos with care. The young Ilich was packed off to Cuba to learn the political and martial arts in Fidel Castro's brave new world. One of his instructors was a well-known Russian KGB man, and it seemed only logical that he should progress to complete his studies in Moscow at the Patrice Lumumba University. With such an upbringing it was inevitable that he should make his career in terrorism after bringing himself up to date with the latest techniques in guerrilla warfare under the tuition of Arab instructors at the Palestinian camps in the Middle East.

Carlos worked on behalf of the Palestinians in Europe and elsewhere. He was organisationally in touch with Baader–Meinhof groups in Frankfurt and in Hamburg but he first came to wide public attention when, in order to escape arrest in Paris, he shot and killed his own fellow terrorist Michel Moukharbel and two officers of the French DST. He wounded a third inspector of this special police unit. Even before that 'Il Gordo' (The Fat One), as he was known, had plotted in London where he had attempted to kill a prominent member of the Jewish community, Mr Teddy Sieff of Marks & Spencer. But it was not until he led the squad of Arabs and German Red Army Faction members who seized as hostages the eleven ministers at the Vienna conference of OPEC, and removed them in a getaway plane to Algiers, that his full persona emerged publicly. On the aircraft he spent hours in the company of that shrewd judge of character Sheikh Zaki Yamani, the Saudi Arabian Minister of Petroleum. Carlos by turn threatened to kill him and poured out confidences, clearly anxious to tell somebody the story of his life, or at least his life as he chose to see it.

He was acting out the role of a grand spokesman, a diplomat of terror. But he could not resist using melodramatic language – 'You will have heard of me already; I am Carlos. You can tell that to the others,' he proclaimed, according to Sheikh Yamani over Saudi radio and in conversation with Payne. Carlos dressed dramatically for the occasion in a long trenchcoat with a beret *à la* Guevara, but tilted threateningly forward. He affected a thin fringe of beard, the badge of the anarchist which also conveniently hides a double chin. As weapons he carried a Makarov automatic pistol and a sub-machine-gun.

When his German girl accomplice told him she had just

killed two people, he smiled and said, 'Quite right, I killed one myself.' To Sheikh Yamani he spoke happily of putting pressure on the Austrian government, he boasted of his power and of his sexual exploits, but the political content of his words rang false to Yamani. Carlos claimed mockingly to be a democrat who consulted his fellow terrorists before making any decision. But Yamani noted that Carlos 'is not a committed Communist . . . does not believe in the Palestinian cause or in Arab nationalism but . . . [considers] them as factors which might be exploited to help spread the international revolutionary movement'. Here we have a very precise description of the international terrorist. We are also indebted to Sheikh Yamani, one of the few men who has spent long hours with a talkative terrorist leader and lived to tell the tale, for this summing up:

If a criminal were to deserve the admiration of non-criminals, then Carlos would stand high in the list of those who deserve such admiration. For in addition to his intelligence and outstanding ability . . . many of us believe that he was able to combine all sorts of contradictions by grouping enemies in one force, whatever their aims and intentions. In one operation he served them all. . . .

That is the picture of a successful terrorist warlord who achieves a measure of fame and fortune by the skill with which he carries out his raids. Such men are ready to use even the most devastating weapons for self-glorification in the ostensible cause of imposing their ill-thought-out philosophies.

3 | Terrorists: Behind the Mask

'George Washington was a terrorist. To describe a man as a terrorist is a term of honour.' So spoke one of the Baader–Meinhof defendants after his arrest in Germany. The thinking behind this statement is that acts of violence are not criminal when carried out in opposition to the force used by a state which is itself deemed to be criminal by the terrorists concerned. The German Red Army Faction believed that the American war in Vietnam was an 'unjust' one, and that in this respect it might be compared to the eighteenth-century English war against the American revolutionaries.

One man's terrorist is another man's freedom fighter. While that may be true with respect to historical movements opposing national tyranny when no other means were available, it is more difficult to sustain it considering terrorist movements in the last decade which have cut across recognised national and ideological boundaries. In the cases we have already considered, Ireland and Palestine, there are obvious, though confused, territorial aims for the violent movements involved. But many of the groups now most active kidnap and kill to achieve objectives which are international, doctrinal and revolutionary for revolution's sake. Their campaigns involve guerrilla and terrorist leaders who, unlike the guerrilla troops of the Irish and the Palestinians, have received better than average education and often come from prosperous families. They can afford the intellectual luxury of launching themselves into violent politics without the pressures of poverty to drive them on.

In the case histories so far considered only the leaders are persons of superior education. Dominant terrorists and the theorists who inspire them have the conviction that they can impose their beliefs on others. But for every one who goes on to become leader of a powerful politico-terror movement, for every one who eventually becomes head of state or prime minister, there are thousands of common soldiers of terrorism. They can expect only death, imprisonment or disillusion. They are the infantry of subversive warfare.

Little is recorded of their personalities, or even their fate. Yet only by examining flesh and blood examples is it possible to discover what makes such a terrorist, and to decide why young men and women forsake their studies and abandon their careers in order to take to the political maquis. Fortunately those terror groups which operate in Europe and in Japan are now better known, and their personnel can be examined in greater detail. The best documented are Baader–Meinhof, the Japanese Red Army, the Red Brigades of Italy and minor groups of the same sort in Britain and the United States – the Angry Brigade and the Weathermen. All share roughly the same emotive political convictions. 'One of our tasks is to lay bare and liberate the type of man who wants revolution, who must have revolution because otherwise he would fall apart,' wrote Herbert Marcuse in one of his lectures (in *Five Lectures*). In another context that is our task too, and it is certainly true that some have indeed fallen apart.

Take the case of Hans-Joachim Klein. Born in 1947 he became involved with the Red Army Faction in Germany by way of friends with whom he lived in a Frankfurt commune. This commune was connected with a revolutionary publishing enterprise called Red Star. There, he met Klaus Croissant, who sympathised with the Baader–Meinhof gang and became one of their defending lawyers. Croissant later fled to France to escape charges of helping the terrorists plan operations even while they were imprisoned. He was extradited in hurried circumstances by France and at the time of writing is awaiting trial.

In Frankfurt Klein met Carlos, and it was as one of Carlos' men that he took part in the raid on the OPEC conference in

Vienna. He was shot in the stomach during the raid, and although he was badly wounded the gang took him with them to Libya where he received treatment from a German doctor before disappearing into the terrorist underworld.

Early in 1977 he sent a remarkable letter together with a set of his fingerprints to prove the letter's authenticity and a Czech-made pistol and ammunition to the West German magazine *Der Spiegel*. Klein declared that thinking about the Vienna affair during the two months it took him to recover from his wound had brought him to the decision to give up terrorism. His letter told of his disillusion:

What I heard in a month about the way in which revolutionary violence would bring about a fairer and more humane world made me sick. This was a cause for which I would have gone into the streets. Both my own experiences and the plans I heard about at that time gave me food for thought. That was the most important thing that happened to me . . . I haven't changed from Saul to Paul, but from Saul I have changed back to a person with sensible political thinking and behaviour . . . For this I had to pay a hell of a price.

In Germany although some have turned aside in horror from the movement they once supported, and although the leaders, Ulrike Meinhof, Andreas Baader and Gudrun Ensslin, have taken their own lives in despair in their prison cells, the movement they launched still exists and kills.

In the beginning it was hope and humanity which inspired the young recruits to the Red Army Faction, for they were imbued with the enthusiasms of the New Left for reforms of the universities and of society in general. But the movement continued after the universities had carried out the reforms for which the students had fought. It was still intellectual and its members were almost all middle class. Indeed, except for one ecstatic moment in the course of the Paris revolution when the masses seemed to be following, the workers had never shared the revolutionary spirit of their betters. In Germany most of the early supporters were to be found in the ranks of clergymen, doctors, professors and journalists.

Then protest turned to violence, for it was not enough simply to march and shout slogans. The first stages of violence in Germany had to do with the Third World and in particular the war in Vietnam. Andreas Baader and his 'revolutionary bride', Gudrun Ensslin, set fire to a department store in Frankfurt in order, they said, to show the comfortable burghers what the horrors of war in Vietnam were really like. Then they began to acquire revolvers and grenades and sub-machine-guns for the inevitable confrontation with the police. They had to buy the weapons, at first from Palestinians who were well supplied. In order to pay the Palestinians they robbed banks. And to rob banks they needed more weapons and getaway cars and so it went on. Even those who became involved for high-minded reasons found themselves gun in hand, shooting at the forces of law and order, for had not the police killed Benno Ohnesorg in Berlin without any real reason? They began to feel that they were acting in self-defence. 'They'll kill us all. They have weapons, we haven't. We must arm ourselves,' screamed Ensslin.

As had already happened in other parts of the world when terrorist groups turned to bank robbing, they soon attracted recruits drawn more by the idea of easy money than by idealism. A case in point was Karl-Heinz Ruhland, a motor mechanic, and therefore so far as the Baader crowd were concerned, a genuine member of the working class. He needed money to pay off his debts and when they asked him to doctor stolen cars for the gang, he agreed – provided that he was properly rewarded. He had not, he said, ever heard of this Marighella that they mentioned but promised to read a pamphlet and help to make the revolution. Before long he was asked to take part in a bank robbery. They gave him a sub-machine-gun and off they went to rob the bank. Nervously, Ruhland hoped that no one would give the alarm – 'All they had to do was to stay nicely away from their desks so that the police were not called too soon and I would not have to start shooting.'

After a suitable moral lecture about the propriety of taking capitalists' money, and an assurance that the 'little man' would not lose by their activities, the gang leaders shared out the loot. Ruhland was a bit disappointed with his portion,

1000 marks, but optimistically thought he would eventually be able to make a good living out of such activities. Before long the revolutionary mechanic was accompanying Ulrike Meinhof on her first successful urban guerrilla raid, the theft of identity cards and passports from municipal offices at Neustadt am Rübenberg and Lang-Göns. Soon he accepted it as entirely normal that he should go about armed, with the safety catch off his revolver.

But Ruhland lost heart with the game when it did not produce the money he hoped for, and took the opportunity of being stopped at a police roadblock to surrender and confess all. His experiences illustrate how easily men can become involved in terrorism without any burning faith in revolution.

The German groups provide numerous examples of the many different paths by which people get caught up in political violence. Some of the most ruthless members joined Baader–Meinhof through the influence of Dr Wolfgang Huber, a Heidelberg psychiatrist, who taught his group therapy patients that only revolutionary change could cure the sick capitalist society of West Germany which, he said, produced nothing but sick people. The Socialist Patients' Collective (SPK) which he set up had a 'Working Circle (Explosives)' led by Frau Huber, where the patients learned how to make bombs. Among those who attended was Siegfried Hausner who took up bombing on behalf of the Red Army Faction in order to cure his own mental disorders through therapeutic attacks on the 'sick' society. He helped to plant bombs at the Hamburg offices of Springer Publications and he eventually died after blowing himself up with his own bomb during the raid on the West German embassy in Stockholm in 1975.

Some joined for money, some for therapy, some for excitement. When the Bonnie and Clyde image of Baader–Meinhof had spread, others came into the movement attracted by the combination of excitement and the possibility of sexual pleasure. Others thought of terrorism as a kind of student happening 'with arms'. Yet the original members remained to the end self-righteous, arrogantly convinced of their own moral and intellectual superiority.

Ulrike Meinhof, the most intriguing study among the Germans, had more complicated motives for changing her life-style and becoming a terrorist. Older than most of her accomplices, she had been fashionable for some time as a radically chic journalist heroine of the New Left. As the star columnist of *Konkret*, a popular mixture of soft porn and radical politics, she had a wide following and she placed a formidable seal of respectability on the Baader–Ensslin arson attack in Frankfurt by praising it as a bold act of criminality.

She had been brought up by a gentle but firm foster mother only a little older than herself, Dr Renate Riemeck, a Christian pacifist. As a student Meinhof became a nuclear disarmer and then moved on to condemn the comfortable and prosperous society of the Federal Republic. This rather handsome woman, by then married to the playboy publisher and editor of *Konkret*, was successful and well-to-do. She seemed a thoroughly unlikely candidate for service as a terrorist leader. When a relation fired a gun during a walk in the woods she was so upset that she burst into tears. Yet not long afterwards she boasted of her skill with automatic weapons on the range at an Arab guerrilla training camp in the Middle East.

Her marriage to Klaus Rainer Rohl was not a happy one and after the Frankfurt episode she left their rather grand home in Hamburg taking her twin children with her and set up for a while in an upper-class commune in a smart section of West Berlin. Plunging into the subculture world, and the world of student politics at the Free University, she came into closer contact with Gudrun Ensslin, a daughter of the manse, brought up as a devout Protestant, who, through pacifism, had proceeded into the anti-authoritarian protest movement. Gudrun and her lover Andreas Baader had already taken to political violence. They argued that there was no longer any point in just writing and talking, it was necessary to do something, and Ulrike Meinhof agreed. When Baader was arrested and imprisoned she joined with Gudrun in plotting and then executing the raid which freed him. She literally leapt into the new life through the window of the library where Baader had been allowed to work. She drove off with him in a silver-painted Alfa Romeo. She had broken the law and was committed to a new life as a terrorist.

Jillian Becker in her excellent book *Hitler's Children* brings her own novelist's insight to bear on the real reason for Ulrike Meinhof becoming a terrorist. Writing of Baader and Meinhof making off together she had this to say:

An illusory sense of power and a certainty of victory would make them feel their own capabilities to be great. Each could seek personal relief through acts of violence and blood and terror, and always with a grandiose moral justification. They could call a lust for revenge 'a thirst for justice', and terrorism a righteous fury that 'society' had called down upon itself. In Ulrike's case 'society' was an euphemism (which she could not recognise, her insight into her own motives not having matured with her years) for her own feelings, and for Klaus Rainer Rohl. And her committing of herself to a life outside the law was a venture to overcome not governments, nor systems, but private despair.

Andreas Baader became a terrorist because he was dark, handsome, sexy and braggadocio. By the time he was twenty-five he had done nothing but fail at school and make a vague shot at being a potter. He was more interested in getting girls to bed than in getting the world put to rights, for so far as he was concerned politics was all 'shit'. Only by accident had he come to read Marcuse and the other philosophers of terror, and the accident was named Gudrun Ensslin, already a devotee of political action. They found each other highly compatible sexually and she set up with him and took him off to live in Frankfurt. It was there that they celebrated their initiation into terrorism by setting fire to the department store.

Although Andreas Baader learned to parrot the correct slogans, there is little to show that he had any real political convictions. Certainly before he took up with Gudrun his dislike for the consumer society and its horrors was based on the fact that this spoiled boy had no money to finance his expensive consumer tastes. He took naturally to the rather comfortable life of the West German terrorists. There have always been enough well-heeled sympathisers who could permit themselves the luxury of lending flats and providing money for those who want to overthrow the society in which they flourish. In Germany, students, teachers and professional people have all given help to the terrorists. 'Sheltering a Red Army man on the run is almost as good as setting up your own operation,' said one student. Providing refuge for terrorists on the run has been described as both a patriotic duty and a protest against the system. On several occasions Baader–Meinhof members, even those who are known to have murdered and maimed people, have been given protection by German clergymen and priests.

An even more remarkable fact of the situation in Germany is the number of women, most of them young and attractive, who have taken part in terrorist operations. The fact that no less than half of the twenty-eight most wanted urban guerrillas on the police list in West Germany are girls shows that they are much more than just terrorists' molls and providers of safe houses. Why this should be so is a question which has puzzled the authorities, and indeed in 1977 the German government set up a committee to try to discover the reasons.

Attention was again drawn to women terrorists during the Red Army Faction's offensive in the summer of 1977. When they raided the opulent home of Juergen Ponto, one of the country's most influential bankers, and killed him, it was his 26-year-old god-daughter who got the killers admitted to his well-defended house. 'It's me, Susanne,' cried the girl, Susanne Albrecht, and she carried with her a bunch of roses to give to her godfather. The door was opened. There was a struggle – possibly the intention was to kidnap him – and he was shot dead. Susanne, aged twenty-six, had been a student at Hamburg University before dropping out to join squatters' groups, graduating to terrorism and becoming instrumental in bringing about the murder of the man who loved her like a daughter.

Another notorious woman terrorist, who led a desperate prison breakout, is Inge Viet, a 33-year-old former children's nurse who, like Susanne, comes from Hamburg. Two other girl terrorists were in the group which broke out and escaped: Gabriele Rollnik, a sociologist and member of a well-to-do family from Dortmund, and Juliane Plambeck, a 25-year-old student of philology from Munich who is on the list of fifteen people suspected of complicity in the murder of Hans-Martin Schleyer. Miss Plambeck's other claim to fame is that she was known among her male comrades as the 'trophy for the erotic challenge cup'.

Yet another group of female terrorists is that known as the Croissant Group, because, according to the authorities, they were mainly recruited through the lawyers' office in Stuttgart run by Klaus Croissant. Before he fled to France, he ran a 'lawyers' collective' and devoted most of his energy to looking after their interests. Susanne Albrecht was one of those who worked in his office. Two other girls are known members of the same group and thought to be connected with the Ponto affair – Angelika Speitel, twenty-five, who married one of the lawyers from Croissant's practice, and Silke Maier-Witt, intelligence officer for the group. Just how these young women, most of them well brought up in decent families, came to involve themselves with terrorism remains a puzzle to the West German authorities.

The truth is that they do not simply march up and apply to join, but gradually become involved after meeting people who share their anxieties about the state of the modern world, but who have opted for violent solutions to those problems. They do not put themselves forward as candidates for membership; a terror group is like an exclusive club into which a friend invites you and once a member, you are expected to conform to the rules of that club.

One of the theories put forward by psychiatrists and criminologists to explain why so many German women are involved in urban guerrilla activities is that it provides them with a form of liberation. Armand Mergen of Mainz University believes that the girls need to emancipate themselves through violence. Because they are from good homes and have been well educated, they consider themselves superior to men and want to display that superiority in action. This may indeed be the true reason why women terrorists tend to be more brutal than their male colleagues.

A contrary theory is that the girls become sexually dependent on their male comrades. There is no doubt that sex is
powerfully connected with political violence in the elitist
groups we are examining. Certainly so far as the European
groups are concerned there is ample evidence that many who
take to the gun and the bomb start out by living in communes
where partners are easily swapped and where experimental
sex is part of the everyday life. Many of the most active
terrorists are marijuana smokers and some have taken to
heavier drugs. Excitement, sensual pleasure and comfortable living outside normal routines while still enjoying widespread approval for the high-minded ideology preached, are
all incitements to young people to involve themselves.

There is another factor to be considered when dealing with
the German groups and that is that the post-war generation
of students seems obsessed by killing and death. How far
such feelings are prompted by memories of the Hitler period
and the horrors of the Nazi system of which their parents
were a part is a question which needs much more detailed
investigation than is possible in this book. Even so it is worth
observing that there is something unnatural about the pleasure taken in German universities at news of the murders and
kidnappings of 1977. After the kidnapping of Dr Schleyer,
wall writings at Heidelberg proclaimed, 'It is impossible to
hide our joy.' The pleasure expressed in university pamphlets issued by some groups on the fringe of left-wing
politics gave the impression that these groups had a hatred of
the very concept of parliamentary democracy as well as its
'bourgeois' representatives and institutions.

Kurt Reumann, a well-known German journalist analys-
ing such pamphlets in *Encounter* (October 1977) pointed out
that after the murder of Herr Buback, the Federal public
prosecutor, the publications placed the moral guilt for his
killing not on the terrorists but 'on that sociological catch-all,
namely social conditions'. So many of the groups were
approving murder and asking 'Who will sentence to death
Herr so-and-so?' that he felt compelled to ask: 'Is the spirit of
death abroad in the land?' It is certainly true that in the
decade of West German terrorism the feelings of compassion

and humanity which stirred a whole generation into political action were soon corrupted into an avenging use of brutality in which those gentle qualities were lost. Despite the confusions in personality and upbringing of the leaders of the Red Army Faction, they founded a movement which remains among the most feared and powerful in the world of international terror. Most of those founders are now dead, but the gang and its offshoots still flourish. Those early members who survive and the new recruits who have joined them seem to be not only more bloodthirsty, but also more effective and more skilled with their weapons than those who launched the movement.

As the German groups became more violent after the end of the Stuttgart trial in 1977 at which the original leaders were sentenced to long terms of imprisonment, a similar movement on the other side of the world moved into action. The Japanese Red Army, which had been dormant for two years, carried out a most effective hijack in September 1977. By seizing a Japanese DC8 airliner in Bombay and threatening to blow it up and kill the passengers of many nationalities they forced the Tokyo government to pay a ransom of $6 million and to release six of their members imprisoned after earlier raids. It was a dramatic reactivation of the movement.

The Japanese Red Army shares many characteristics with the German Red Army Faction. Its members, though more mystical, proclaim the same general philosophy and the leader is a woman, Fusako Shigenobu. The hijack to Bangladesh marked the thirty-second birthday of this fanatic who had been called the 'Red Queen of Terror'.

Fusako Shigenobu was born into the new Japanese society of the economic miracle after the Second World War and like her political sisters in Europe she passed into the university ferment of the 1960s. Vietnam again was the cause, though in the case of the Japanese they also protested over American occupation of Okinawa. The first act of her radical career was when she smuggled oak staves hidden in golf bags to demonstrators besieged in Tokyo University.

The Red Army, composed of a small force of students, intellectuals and other middle-class supporters, did not fare well in Japan. It was because of its failure on home ground that Miss Shigenobu and her supporters turned towards the Popular Front for the Liberation of Palestine. Eventually a number of Red Army people went to the Middle East for guerrilla training in the refugee camps. Their desire, they said, was to set up 'international strongholds of the revolution' and Miss Shigenobu became the friend of Leila Khaled, the Palestinian hijacker. It was in Israel at Lod Airport that the Japanese carried out their most notorious action, slaughtering twenty-six people with grenades and machine-gun fire. Significantly, it was from the Middle East in 1977 that Fusako Shigenobu planned the Bombay hijack which restored her Japanese Red Army as a fighting force, and it was Leila Khaled who collected the ransom money for the Japanese Red Army and the PFLP.

In a letter to the PFLP newspaper, *Al Hadaf*, Shigenobu spelled out the main theme of her terrorist philosophy after an earlier hijack.

These two operations were staged to consolidate the international revolutionary alliance against the imperialists of the world. We in the Red Army declare anew our preparedness to fight hand in hand with Palestinians and wage joint onslaughts at any time to defeat the Israeli enemy. We should not be bound by international laws or by resistance within the framework of these laws . . . because only revolutionary violence would enable us to defeat imperialists throughout the world . . .

Other leaders of the Red Army have followed the same themes, adding more detail. They plan acts of terror which they hope will spark the peoples' revolution, a revolution which would destroy capitalism and imperialism. Emperor Hirohito is one of their particular targets. They believe he bears responsibility for the death of millions in the Second World War. But despite these grandiose aims the Red Army has spent most of its effort in trying to free its own members imprisoned in their earlier actions. And they are bound to the PFLP because they could not survive without the sanctuary and financial and logistic help provided by the Palestinians.

At his trial in Israel, Kozo Okamoto, the one survivor of the Lod raid, gave a frightening insight into the mentality of the Japanese terrorists. He was, he said, a soldier preparing for the Third World War – 'We believe slaughtering of human bodies is inevitable. We know it will become more severe than battles between nations.' Such bloodcurdling thoughts give some indication of the feelings of the Japanese Red Army and the fanaticism of the men and women in its ranks. Even though the group is not large in terms of manpower it has the capacity to create yet more bloodshed in the world.

The Red Brigades which have terrorised Italy for several years have strong affiliations with the other 'Red' revolutionary bands elsewhere in the world but the historic leaders of the movement are young people of extravagant personality. The life story of Renato Curcio, best known of the founders, handsome and bearded, is the stuff of which grand opera is made. Although the background from which he came was comparable with that of the West German comrades there were extra touches which can only be described as Italian.

His father, a member of the Zampa family and brother of a well-known film producer, Luigi Zampa, had a respectable position in Roman society. Married to an elderly American heiress he busily conducted other affairs, even within his own household. One of his mistresses was Yolande Curcio, a country girl placed in service with his family by the nuns. When she became pregnant she was turned out of the house. Taking her child, whom she named Renato after his father, with her she worked as a housekeeper in private houses and in hotels first in Italy, then in Switzerland and Britain. She now lives in London in a flat in Hampstead with her two poodles. She describes Renato as 'a great idealist and revolutionary. Like all great men in history before him he has been put in gaol for what he believes.' According to her, Renato had a perfectly normal upbringing and she can recall no traumatic events in his early life which might have impelled him to become a revolutionary.

After the death of Renato Zampa's wife he offered to marry Yolande. She refused though she did accept money which provided her clever young son with an excellent education at good schools in Italy. Finally he went to Trento

University in northern Italy, a place which specialises in sociology and – as might be expected – is a hotbed of revolutionary activity.

Curcio is a 37-year-old of strict Roman Catholic upbringing and we understand from conversation with Red Brigades that it was his strong and unbalanced religious temperament combined with his new found enthusiasm for sociology which pushed him into violent politics. His first venture into that field was as a supporter of an extreme right-wing organisation called New Order.

One of the star witnesses for the prosecution at the prolonged trial of Renato Curcio and his friends was Silvano Girotto, a 39-year-old Franciscan suspended from his religious duties. Known as the 'Machine-gun Friar', he suddenly appeared in Turin dressed in jeans, anorak and gym shoes 'to denounce these criminals'. But this strange personality had himself played some role in the Red Brigades, which he joined in 1974 at the suggestion of a Carabinieri, Captain Pignero, to spy on their activities. He was already known as the 'Machine-gun Friar' because he had built up a reputation as a guerrilla fighter in Bolivia and in Chile. Whether or not this was justified is not known for the friar is a fantasist who also claims that he had once joined the French Foreign Legion. Be that as it may, he was accepted by the comrades of the Red Brigades and was soon on friendly terms with Renato Curcio and familiar with their organisation. Finally he denounced them to the Carabinieri and this made possible the arrest of Curcio. At the trial he declared: 'I was convinced of the absurdity of their methods from the start'. Before disappearing once he had given the evidence at Turin, the friar denied that he had been paid by the police.

Renato Curcio's first steps into terrorism were taken in 1972 when he and his friends seized 'enemies of the people' such as Etteri Amarilo, a Siemens executive who had been personnel manager at Fiat. They also seized a man called Bruno, described as a Fascist trade union leader. In each case after a mock trial before a 'People's Court' they beat up these men and released them. After some members of the gang had been arrested they abducted a state prosecutor to try to secure their release.

In 1970 Curcio met and married a 25-year-old fellow student at Trento named Margarita Cagol. This thoughtful and gentle girl, the daughter of a rich Catholic and conservative local family was, until she took up sociology, mostly interested in music and dancing. There can be little doubt that it was the revolutionary atmosphere of Trento University which drew her into the terrorist field. In imitation of their colleagues in Berlin, the students there called it the free university and many revolutionary leaders of the time such as Dany (The Red) Cohn-Bendit and Rudi Dutschke made appearances.

For her doctorate Margarita wrote a thesis on German workers' movements. Soon she was at work with her husband and his friends trying to persuade Italian workers to occupy their premises and begin the great revolution. In this they failed to convince the workers. Many of them were staunch Communist Party members and had no wish to involve themselves with and take orders from a bunch of sociology students.

In despair Renato and his friends decided like many other such revolutionaries that they had a mission to lead, even if the others stubbornly refused to follow. They heaped scorn upon the workers for their bourgeois attitudes and attacked the Communist Party for its divisive moves towards the softer brand of Eurocommunism. More and more strongly Curcio identified himself with an uncle called Armando who had died fighting the Germans with an Italian partisan unit. He always kept a picture of his uncle near him. The mythology of the partisans has an important emotive influence on the Red Brigades.

With support from southern groups known as Armed Proletarian Cells, Curcio and his wife began raiding in the Baader–Meinhof style. They collected ransoms, kidnapped and murdered those they considered their enemies. In 1974 Renato was taken by the police but only a few months later Margarita led an armed raid on the prison at Castal Montferrato and rescued him.

That same summer of 1975 the Red Brigades kidnapped

one of the Gancias, the Italian wine and aperitif family, and held him in a 'People's Prison' – a lonely farmhouse in Piedmont. There the security forces discovered them and besieged the farm for several days before making the final assault. As the Caribinieri raced towards the farmhouse Margarita hurled a charge of plastic explosive at them like a bomb. They opened up with automatics and killed her with two bullets in the chest. Renato was luckier. He managed to break out and escape.

He survived as a terrorist leader for almost a year before he too was wounded and arrested. Threats and fresh terrorist acts continually postponed his trial and that of other squad leaders arrested with him. When the trial did finally open at Turin early in 1978 terrorists still at large shot dead one of the chiefs of the anti-terrorist group and then kidnapped and murdered Aldo Moro, one of Italy's most respected politicians.

Thus only a few months after the autumn of terror launched by the West Germans and the Japanese it was the new model Red Brigades which marched to the centre of the world terrorist stage. Although the Moro kidnapping and the murder of high officials was ostensibly planned to secure the release of the old leaders from prison, events showed that the new men of the movement were tougher and better organised than the original 'Robin Hoods'. For weeks on end they were able to throw the state into disarray. Here again there are close similarities with Baader–Meinhof where the same phenomenon was observed. In both cases the movements are still powerful and their links with the international terrorist fraternity appear to be strengthening.

Compared to the West Germans, the Japanese and the Italians, the Anglo–Saxon groups, who to some extent believed in the same causes, seem extremely mild. Nevertheless, there are those in Britain and America who set out on the same road, and similar groups may soon revive under a harder leadership to bring the same methods of terror to bear in London and Washington.

The best known of the white, as opposed to black, terror movements in the United States was the small group called the Weathermen. It came into being as a result of squabbles at a conference in June 1969 of the SDS, Students for a Democratic Society, originally a liberal and near-pacifist organisation of the New Left variety. Many supporters visited Cuba and Vietnam and, fired with enthusiasm for those places, they began learning to make Molotov cocktails ready for the onslaught on American society. They declared that unlike their models in the Third World they would make anti-national revolution, for otherwise they might fall into the trap of imperialist, national chauvinism. The familiar old clichés poured from the mouths of these student revolutionaries. They tried in vain to merge with the Black Panthers. They made arson raids, and it is claimed that the Weathermen took part in some 500 incidents of bombing and raiding in 1969. They planted a bomb at the University of Wisconsin and demanded that the Officers' Training Corps there be disbanded, and that Black Panther leaders under arrest should be released.

The Weathermen were really the creation of Mark Rudd from Columbia University who declared himself a Marxist devoted to the destruction of a 'corrupt imperialist pig society'. His aim, like that of the European comrades, was to provoke the authorities into repressive action and to make it appear that brave resistance forces were fighting against the forces of repression. But most of their acts were more like student happenings than genuine guerrilla operations. They were designed to shock the bourgeoisie and its morality by, for example, killing and eating an alley cat and expressing admiration for the murderous orgies of the Manson 'family'. On one occasion, however, they stole material from a biological warfare store and threatened to infect city water supplies.

It is doubtful if the Weathermen ever had more than a thousand supporters of whom very few were activists and it all came to an end when their store of explosives in a Greenwich Village house blew up. Most of the leaders were killed by this accident and the movement, already out of fashion, faded away. Mark Rudd, the surviving leader, went underground in 1970 and was not heard of again until he surrendered at the age of thirty to the New York police seven years later.

For a while at the height of public agitation about the war in Vietnam the Weathermen had looked dangerous but this highly personalised band of urban guerrillas was neither tough enough, nor devoted enough, to survive. The truth was that too many of its supporters were in it for kicks. They were 'guns and grass' revolutionaries who enjoyed the excitement for a while, relished the life-style more than the politics and took pleasure that they could 'épater la bourgeoisie'. When they spoke of the people, it was obvious that they had never really been in touch with them and that they were simply working off their hang-ups.

Another offshoot of the Students for a Democratic Society was the Revolutionary Union, a Maoist group with more serious political appeal and a rather more mature following. One of the founders was Professor Franklin of Stanford University and with him were Robert Avakian, a student expelled from Berkeley in 1966, and Steve Hamilton. Financed from China by way of a Hong Kong Communist-infiltrated union, the Revolutionary Union actually produced a manifesto though it created less stir than the Weathermen. From it developed yet another Maoist group called the Venceremos Organisation which had close contacts with Cuba to which a 'Brigade' was despatched in the early 1970s.

An even more extreme group, the Symbionese Liberation Army (SLA), attracted rather more attention by its violent activities in the United States. It claimed to be a 'loving' group devoted to drawing together oppressed minorities in the 'Fascist' United States. It had a number of anarchist aims and was remarkable for the number of women it drew to the cause. Because they attracted so few militants, not more than two score, the Symbionese Army turned to dramatic action to attract attention and publicity.

The SLA is best known for its kidnap of the heiress, Patricia Hearst, and her partial indoctrination. She was arrested together with two others trying to keep the organisation alive after Donald De Freeze, the organisation's black leader, and five others had been killed in a raid by FBI agents and the Los Angeles police at Compton, one of that city's all black districts.

The end of the war in Vietnam deprived the small American terrorist movements of their mainspring. None of them was able to follow the lead of the international terror groups, though there is still a danger that race problems may still provide new organisations with the necessary impetus for renewed action.

In Britain too, groups tempted by terrorism have made a thin showing apart from the Irish 'territorial' ones already discussed. But for a time the Angry Brigade, similar in some respects to the Weathermen, did cause some alarm. Between 1968 and 1971 the Angry Brigade planted twenty-seven bombs and were involved in machine-gunning public buildings in Britain. An idea of their beliefs and the kind of people attracted can be got from the words of simple faith spoken by Anna Mendelson, a young English graduate of Essex University. When defending herself at the Old Bailey trial on charges of possessing explosives and of conspiring with other people to bomb in the cause of the Angry Brigade she said: 'If you convict us, we are not going to change. We will still be who we are, and what we believe. I know that the people in this dock with me are working together for a happier and more peaceful world. That is who we are. It is your decision.'

This curious English group had many things in common with the Baader–Meinhof gang and with other international terror groups. Miss Mendelson and a number of her friends were found guilty, and she was sentenced to ten years imprisonment, though she was released in 1977 after serving only four years. Most members of the Angry Brigade were students and graduates from British universities who shared with their continental opposite numbers disappointment with the failure of the 1968 revolution in Paris. Both Anna Mendelson and John Barker, also sentenced to ten years, were veterans of the days of elation at the Sorbonne, and they returned to London determined to further the causes behind whose banners they had marched.

The backgrounds of the people concerned were not unlike those we have considered in Europe. They too attacked the consumer society which had so concerned the French students a few years before. Then, under the influence of a Spanish terrorist group called the 'First of May Group', they began to use bombs to make their point, meanwhile living in communes and financing themselves by means of stolen cheques and credit card frauds in the classical terrorist manner. When police moved in to arrest members of the group they were beginning to imitate the Red Army Faction with raids on post offices and banks.

In passing sentence Mr Justice James, who had carefully kept the trial as apolitical as possible, told those found guilty: 'I am sorry to see such educated people in your situation. Undoubtedly a warped understanding of sociology has brought you to the state in which you are.'

Whether as Miss Mendelson predicted those in prison have not changed it is impossible to know. But since the trial there have been no further manifestations of the Angry Brigade, or any successor organisation. So far as Great Britain is concerned at the moment the terrorist field is a monopoly of the Provisional Irish Republican Army.

In the summer of 1978 there were modest signs of activity from right-wing terror groups in Britain. Letter bombs were sent to the Communist newspaper *Morning Star* and to a left-wing bookshop. But these were minor incidents.

Two groups in particular attracted some attention, and both of them had a neo-Nazi flavour. Column 88, so named in memory of Hitler, whose name begins with the eighth letter in the alphabet, and the Eleventh Hour Brigade, an obscure and miniscule terrorist group, were both said to be plotting further action. Neither inspired any great fear among the public or the security forces.

However, terrorism still flourishes in other parts of the world. The same kind of people are still kidnapping, murdering, bombing and hijacking. The Palestinians went into action again to express their disapproval of President Sadat's historic pilgrimage to Jerusalem and the Basque ETA group produced a more extreme faction just as the Spanish government moved towards satisfying some of their demands. And so it continues. So long as the young extremists of 'left fascism' believe that violence is the only way in which they can achieve their political aims, so terrorism will continue on a greater or lesser level according to the success of the security forces.

By looking at some of the leaders and their troops in the worldwide terrorist movements and by observing their personalities as well as their motivations, we have tried to reveal the complexity of the human factor in terrorism. Young people are drawn into violence for many reasons, but what happens to them then? How do the innocents learn the sophisticated techniques of their trade?

Training:
4 | Indoctrination and Skills

Although terrorist groups rate political indoctrination of high importance in the formation of their recruits, Carlos Marighella, the inspirer of all urban guerrillas, was under no illusion about the importance of practical military knowledge. 'No one can become a guerrilla without undergoing a period of technical preparation,' he declared in his 'Handbook of Urban Guerrilla Warfare'. 'You can only become a good fighter by learning the art of fighting.'

For the Latin American guru of terrorism this involved everything from physical training to the learning of many kinds of jobs, especially those entailing manual skills. Writing in a fashion which would please a drill sergeant in any army, he preached that physical training was the basis of the physical resistance which every good fighter needs. After that, he wrote, the urban guerrilla should learn to fight in different ways, some involving attack and others self-defence, just like a professional soldier.

Marighella urged his pupils to go in for what might be described as boy scout activities. They were to hike, camp, spend long periods in rough country and do mountain climbing, swimming, canoeing, fishing and hunting for food. In addition he considered it important to drive, pilot aircraft and to be able to handle motor and sailing boats. Quite how many of the young ladies of Baader–Meinhof would have these accomplishments has never been discovered, but the military value of such training is undisputed.

The accomplished terrorist should know something of the

mechanics of radio, telephones and electronics; he should be able to make maps and plans, measure distance and locate his position on the ground by use of the compass. To survive in a society he is out to destroy he should also acquire a knowledge of chemistry, as well as the ability to make rubber stamps and imitate other people's handwriting in order to forge documents convincingly. And of course, it is useful for the urban guerrilla to learn basic first aid skills so as to help wounded comrades. Marighella's section on technical training concluded:

The most important element in technical training, however, remains that of handling such weapons as sub-machine-guns, revolvers, automatics, mortars, bazookas, FAL guns and other types of carbine – as well as knowledge of the various kinds of ammunition and explosives. Dynamite is one instance; it is vital to know how to use it, just as it is vital to know how to use incendiary bombs, smoke bombs, and so on. The guerrilla must also learn to make and repair weapons, to make Molotov cocktails, bombs and mines, and how to destroy bridges, dislodge or destroy railway lines and sleepers.

The urban guerrilla will complete his training in a specially organised technical centre, but only after being tested in action, having actually fought the enemy.

This is a constant theme of terrorist training, that the recruit should prove himself in action before being given complete training, and certainly there are many examples among the Germans, Palestinians and Latin Americans of this process in action. Indeed in some movements in Latin America the raw terrorist is required, as an act of good faith, to kill a policeman or soldier before he is fully accepted into the band.

The Montoneros in Argentina produced elaborate training manuals for their militants – 15,000 of them according to claims by the leadership. The cover of the most ambitious work, which shows a strong hand clutching an automatic weapon, bears the title *Regulations for Organising Political Military Activity*. Another is called the *Military Instruction Manual* and instructions are given to members on guerrilla warfare as well as urban terrorism. The manuals also deal with more technical advice on the making of bombs and how to endure torture and interrogation.

In the matter of training guerrillas for offensive action against German troops during the Second World War, a manual composed by the British Secret Operations Executive adopted a much brisker and more practical style than Marighella. In thirty-two pages it explained for beginners how to use explosives and small arms dropped to resistance groups in handy packs by the RAF. Hundreds of thousands of copies of this booklet in a plain brown cover were parachuted into occupied Europe, and it was written in five languages as well as English. The text began:

The easiest way for small parties of offensively minded men to attack the enemy is by the use of explosives. Immense damage can be caused with a small quantity of supplies.

If the instructions given in this Booklet are followed carefully, even a person with no previous knowledge of explosives will be able to hit the enemy where it will do him most damage.

Put like that it all sounds very simple. But the modern terrorist movements operating on a worldwide scale go to some pains to instruct their young devotees in up-to-date methods of destroying society, and they do not by any means concentrate on military objectives.

The most effective instructors in the strictly martial arts of terrorism are without doubt the Arabs and Palestinians. Numerous training camps in the Middle East set up to prepare young men and women for active service against Israel at first turned out guerrillas. The task of *fedayeen* soldiers was to fight a classic guerrilla war against an occupying army. But after a while the same camps switched their attention to instructing hijackers and kidnappers to carry on the war by less conventional means. This was necessary because the commandos had failed to make any greater impact on Israel than the Arab armies.

Late in 1971 the Popular Front for the Liberation of Palestine through its many international links began bringing in revolutionary-minded foreigners ready to help in their campaigns. Among them was Kozo Okamoto, a 26-year-old student from Kyoto University who was already a member of the Japanese Red Army.

Early in 1972 he arrived in Beirut, Lebanon, by way of New York on a first-class ticket provided by his recruiters. In March PFLP instructors took him and three companions to the terrorist training camp at Baalbek, the classical site of antiquity in the mountains above Beirut. He reported that training began as it would have done in any military establishment with a course of physical training to get the volunteers into shape. The Arab instructors moved them on to other subjects, starting with explosives drill and how to handle detonators and how to construct bombs. Then the small arms men took over, and they practised pistol handling and drill before progressing to the famous Kalashnikov. Finally they learnt about grenades. All this was fairly standard basic infantry training and little more, but by mid-May, that is eight weeks later, the Japanese were considered ready for a special mission and drove to the terrorists' headquarters in Beirut for a briefing. Okamoto and his friends were then given special training for the job they were to do – make an attack on Lod Airport in Tel Aviv. At this point intelligence officers briefed them about airport procedures and the layout of the arrival hall there.

A couple of days later the group flew off to Rome, where they were armed, and caught a French airliner to carry out the mindless massacre at the Israeli airport. Okamoto himself survived and under interrogation described his recruitment and training to Israeli security men.

It emerges from this example of a Japanese Red Army man who learned his deadly trade in Baalbek, one among several dozen Arab training camps in Lebanon at the time, that the training was neither long nor entirely thorough. It is typical of the kind of course offered in the Middle East.

The Japanese seem to have been apt pupils. Red Army Faction members from West Germany taking a similar crash course made a less favourable impression on their instructors. They were as keen on smoking pot and making love as on learning how to kill effectively. They behaved, according to one Arab, like a lot of tourists. Andreas Baader, the arrogant founder member of the gang, was called a coward because he refused to crawl beneath barbed wire while live bullets were fired over his head. Baader complained about this, saying that assault courses were not the right kind of training for urban guerrillas.

In this he was not entirely wrong, though the reasoning behind his argument was snobbish rather than militarily realistic. A terrorist certainly needs discipline and has to be taught the virtue of obeying orders, but after that the need is more for a grounding in intelligence work than in strictly commando-type operations. Above all what he needs is small-arms instruction, plenty of range practice and a thorough knowledge of explosives and detonators. It is clear from the study of many terrorist raids that training, whether given by the Arabs or by instructors from the operator's own movement, is not of a particularly high standard.

What the recruits lack in this respect they make up for in zeal and cruelty. And the truth is that far less formal training is needed by terrorists than that given in highly professional style to such units as the British Special Air Service and the German anti-terrorist squad (GSG9) which carried out the rescue of the passengers of the hijacked Lufthansa Boeing 737 at Mogadishu. For terrorists do not need to be so precise, nor so careful to avoid unnecessary casualties, as the forces of order operated by Western democracies.

One important subject terrorists do pay attention to is the use of disguise. In successful groups international figures who have reappeared several times look quite different on each occasion. For example Carlos was not recognised at first when he led the raid on OPEC in Vienna. He was bearded, thinner in the face and the colour of his dark hair had been altered. It is more than likely that plastic surgery had been used to remove his heavy jowls and to alter the shape of the plump face so well known to the French DST.

Western intelligence men believe that Prague has become the centre for plastic surgery to alter the appearance of known terrorists. Even without such expert specialist attention a terrorist can easily learn to change his appearance enough to fool security men who have only out-of-date identity pictures. A moustache, a bottle of dye, and a slight gain or loss of weight is usually sufficient.

Both the 'territorial' terrorist groups acting in the Palestinian cause and the 'transnational' groups of which they later became one element received a great deal of initial help from Arab countries. In the early days of the present wave of terrorism Egypt and Syria were every bit as co-operative with the guerrillas as Lebanon, Iraq and Syria. All these countries have helped to set up groups ready for action. In addition, they provided instruction in intelligence work and helped to furnish arms and false documentation. Before the Yom Kippur War in 1973, the Egyptian Army officered courses in special camps where the guerrillas learned side by side with Egyptian troops on six-month courses. Basic instruction was provided in intelligence, frogmen operations and commando work. But there were also special training lessons with heavy weapons, Katushka rockets, recoilless guns and mortars. Most of the weaponry was provided by the Soviet Union. Such courses were intended for the use of Palestinians serving as infantry with the Arab armies (there were some 8000 Palestinian regular infantry), but a number of purely terrorist Arabs also benefited from such instruction.

In this process the Yom Kippur War was the high water mark of generalised support for the guerrillas and terrorists. Since then both Egypt and Syria have shown more interest in trying to solve the Israeli–Arab conflict by diplomatic means with encouragement from the United States and to a certain extent from the Soviet Union. Their role as teachers of subversive warfare has been taken over by those who support the Rejection Front, that is to say Libya, Iraq, South Yemen and Algeria, who still believe that the Middle East problem can only be solved by force. Training colleges at Hit, Habbanya and Baghdad in Iraq hold as many as 2500 Palestinian and other volunteers. But even there the Iraqi government has shown more caution lately and now keeps the *fedayeen* under fairly tight control. The lesson of Lebanon, where the aggressiveness and arrogance of the Palestinian groups provoked a ruinous civil war, has not been lost on neighbouring Arab countries.

That is the trouble with helping terrorists – a government can never be certain that they will not become over-ambitious and turn their weapons against the host state. Even the romantic and enthusiastic Colonel Gaddafi has recently shown more circumspection in his dealings with international terrorists, though he still offers them facilities and a main PFLP training centre and base is to be found at Nahar-El-Barad near Tripoli.

According to Major Omar Mehaishi, a former friend and one of Gaddafi's ministers who defected to Egypt, the Colonel invited a number of members of Fatah and the PFLP to Libya a few years ago and put them in training camps under his personal supervision together with apprentice Libyan terrorists. The largest of these camps was at Tocra, capable of taking 5000 men, and there were smaller establishments at Tarhuna, Misurate and Sirte. Among others trained there were groups of the Libyan Special Intelligence Service and their first operation, an attempt to capture Omar Mehaishi, was so disastrous as to reflect upon the quality of the training they had received. When Egyptian security picked up the seven raiders they reported that each carried a regulation suitcase, all had bank rolls of two thousand dollars, and they all wore identical standard Libyan army-issue underpants. The Egyptian secret service gleefully spread the story of the Libyans' lack of expertise, and claimed that they had all made full confessions to having received special training with Russian-made bombs for use on Egyptian targets.

To use explosive devices of any but the simplest kind needs a good deal of training, and it is bomb work which really divides the men from the boys. To explode an infernal machine effectively demands not only technical ability, but a cool head and a steady hand. It has often been proved both by the Provisional IRA, and on at least one occasion by the Red Army Faction, that lack of experience results in what the British Army calls 'scoring an own goal'.

When the Lebanese civil war was at its height Wadi Hadad, former leader of the breakaway fanatics of the PFLP and without doubt the world's most experienced terrorist leader, set up a new training centre in the People's Republic of South Yemen, formerly the British colony of Aden. Hadad was a doctor and an Orthodox Christian by upbringing just like George Habash, leader of the mainstream PFLP. In earlier days the two men ran a clinic together in Jordan. But that was when they were concerned with healing rather than killing. Little is known of the personality of this skilled and ruthless man. At the time of his death, he was in his forties, a light-skinned Arab with a small moustache, of average height and a keen womaniser. With the approval of the South Yemen government he took over a former British Army camp at Khayat, fifteen miles from the port of Aden. Carlos joined him there to lecture and instruct as the organisation's most practised field operator.

A good deal is known about the methods of this camp because the Israelis seized a Dutch girl who arrived at Lod Airport on a reconnaissance mission in September 1976. Lidwina Anna Jansen, a handsome girl from Amsterdam, and a supporter of the leftist 'Red Aid' organisation in Holland, had drifted by way of radical student activities into terrorism. In Aden she attracted the attention of Wadi Hadad, who selected her for the mission after she attended his training course. She was to reconnoitre the Air France route from Paris to Tel Aviv and Bombay as groundwork for a hijacking.

She had first gone to Aden with a party of fifteen like-minded Dutch youngsters and was taken off to Khayat. The international nature of the training course was proved by information she gave later to Israeli security interrogators. For apart from the Dutch group, she said she had met there a party of ten West Germans who arrived in camp in July 1976 and were greeted in person by Wadi Hadad. They were put through their paces as cadet terrorists for six weeks by skilled instructors. The subjects were the familiar ones of weapon training, communications and tactics.

Miss Jansen was useful to PFLP, for after a stay in Holland at the end of her course she was able to fly into Israel, an impossibility for any of the Arab trainees. But she did not play her role with any assurance and attracted the attention of the airport's ever-alert security guards. She was arrested and promptly confessed. Another Dutchman from the same group was travelling with her, but he did not arouse suspicion and was able to slip through Tel Aviv before being arrested in New Delhi as the result of the information she gave the authorities.

While on her trip back home to Holland before the mission started Miss Jansen recognised in newspaper photographs two Arab fellow trainees from the terror school in Aden. They had been arrested at Istanbul after machine-gunning passengers waiting for an El Al flight. Four people were killed. The release of these two men was among the demands of the hijackers who forced the Lufthansa Boeing to fly to Mogadishu in 1977 and this demonstrated even more clearly the international ramifications of the Hadad training camp in Aden.

A mental hospital in Heidelberg may seem the unlikeliest of places to set up a terrorist training organisation but that is precisely what Dr Wolfgang Huber and his wife Ursula did. In their 'Heidelberg Socialist Patients' Collective' they trained their mental patients to become terrorists to fight against modern society because, argued Huber, it was that society which had made his patients sick. The 'Working Circle (Explosives)' in which the patients worked at their therapy just as if they had been weaving baskets, taught them how to make bombs. They started by mixing small quantities of explosives then took their first bomb to the Odenwald Forest, exploding it by remote control and proudly taking pictures of their success.

It was members of the Socialist Patients' Collective – SPK – who occupied the West German embassy in Stockholm in April 1975 and cold-bloodedly murdered two of the diplomats. When it became obvious that despite the killings the authorities were not going to give in to the terrorists' demands – the freeing of the Baader–Meinhof leaders – there was an explosion inside the embassy and Siegfried Hausner, who had trained in bomb making with the Working Circle, was mortally wounded. It is not known if he deliberately blew himself up along with the embassy or had 'scored an own goal'.

Another of Dr Huber's protégées was Friedericke

Krabbe, a student of psychology and sociology who in the autumn of 1977 inherited the mantle of Ulrike Meinhof and Gudrun Ensslin as the woman leader of German terrorism. Her training had been complete, for the SPK had so-called working circles on dialectics, Marxism, sexuality, education and religion. On the more practical side of things the students were also taught radio transmission, photography and judo and karate. They were shown how to jam police radios and required to take pictures of police buildings, officers and equipment. Frau Huber even managed to demonstrate her skill by placing a bug in the Senate Chamber of the university to listen in to the Senate's plans to remove her husband and close down his clinic.

No such system of higher education in terrorism was ever available to the Provos in Ireland, though they did enjoy another advantage – that some of their best recruits had already been trained during service in the British Army. One sergeant from the Parachute Regiment took his skill with mortars to the PIRA, and renegade soldiers from the Irish Guards, too, have provided expertise for compatriots. Some IRA members are encouraged by their leaders to join the British Army in order to get a first-class military training. But in general the Provos lack lavish resources whether in equipment or training. Because they need to exercise in secret in Ireland, and therefore can only practise with their weapons and explosives in small groups on the lonely banks of the Shannon or on the Northern Ireland coast near the Giant's Causeway, where they are under constant threat of detection by Irish or British security forces, the Provisionals often display signs of under-training. On numerous occasions captured Provos have admitted, 'My gun jammed and I couldn't get it going again.' That is no doubt partly because most of their weapons, old model Stens and Thompson sub-machine-guns, are no longer effective – the costly Armalites are only entrusted to the expert. But every good infantry soldier knows that jams are to be expected in field conditions, and the well trained man goes coolly through his 'IAs' (Immediate Actions), to put things right quickly.

Among the most effective training organisations for the

formation of the new generation of transnational terrorists were those set up in Cuba after Fidel Castro's success. After the Tricontinental Conference there in 1966 had proclaimed its faith in the struggle against imperialism, camps were set up under both Cuban and Russian instructors to formalise the training of young Latin Americans in guerrilla warfare and terrorism. Castro himself knew the value of good training. Before launching his successful attack on Cuba, both he and Che Guevara had been coached by Alberto Bayo, an elderly Spanish colonel who learned his trade in the Spanish Civil War. With money supplied by Castro, Bayo bought a ranch at Santa Rosa near Mexico City and equipped it as a guerrilla school. For teaching underground warfare to these two successful pupils, the colonel received a down payment of $8000.

Orlando Castro Hidalgo, a defector from Castro's DGI (Direccion General de Inteligencia) tells in his book, *Spy For Fidel*, how the training camps in Cuba were run: 'One of the first functions of DGI was the running of special schools for the training of Latin Americans in guerrilla warfare and subversive techniques. At one time, early in the sixties, as many as 1,500 men were being brought to Cuba for training . . .' Those who could not get there by air arrived clandestinely by Communist freighter or fishing boat. On arrival in Havana they were grouped by nationality, and although a squad usually consisted of between fifteen and twenty-five members, sometimes there were as few as three. For security reasons national groups were usually kept separated. In any case the different groups received specialised training; Venezuelans concentrated on guerrilla operations and sabotage techniques. Chileans, who in pre-Allende days came from a country with a strong Communist Party, were coached in using political methods to further the cause.

Guerrilla warfare courses lasted between three and six months, but sometimes continued for up to a year. And promising recruits received additional instruction to become intelligence agents back in their home countries.

A Venezuelan named Manuel Carrasquel later told a committee of the Organisation of American States about the kind of training he had received. His group was taught tactics, weapon training, bomb-making – especially how to blow up oil installations – map reading, cryptography, photography, falsification of documents and disguise.

When Carlos was at Camp Matanzas in Cuba, one of his professors was General Viktor Simenov of the Soviet KGB, who had been sent to Havana to help organise the Cuban secret service. Another instructor was Antonio Dages Bouvier, an Ecuadorian expert in guerrilla tactics, who turned up again later in London and was involved in planning the hijack at Entebbe. Carlos indeed provides a thread through the maze of international training in his own career. Like other promising candidates from Latin America he was singled out for further instruction in Moscow by way of the Patrice Lumumba University. Carlos became effective because he attended all the best terrorist schools – Havana, Moscow and finally the PFLP in the Middle East.

Lumumba University in Moscow, which gathers in students from all parts of the Third World, has many faces. It was set up by Khrushchev ostensibly to provide university education for the underprivileged, but it would be naive to suppose that it was not also used for propaganda purposes. According to one defector who taught there 90 per cent of the staff are connected to the KGB, and the Russian students who provide a quarter of the 20,000 strength of the university are carefully picked and then briefed for their task of spreading the Communist word among the outsiders. Most of the foreign students complete their courses and then return home to take up jobs as doctors, engineers and civil servants and take their place among the leaders of their country. It is only then that Russian fellow students turn up as diplomats and journalists to renew friendships and often to put friendly 'old boy' pressure upon them to perform some service to the Soviet Union.

But among the smaller percentage of foreign students who show enthusiasm and aptitude for clandestine activities on behalf of the cause, there are further courses available. The elite in this field go on to be trained by Department V, the KGB's Assassination and Sabotage Squad, where they learn the dirty tricks of the business.

A training centre for expatriate recruits was set up some years ago by Colonel Kotov, who, after serving in Israel in the guise of a diplomat, moved to Lebanon where he had contact with Palestine guerrillas. When he returned to Moscow the KGB had already formulated its own terror courses. After rigorous weapon training international intakes were schooled in surveillance methods, how to follow without being detected and how to escape when they were themselves being tailed. The final stage of the course was concerned with how to organise and then run a terrorist network. The student also received instruction in the use of disguise, fake identities and how to establish escape channels. The Russians later set up special courses in the Soviet Union and in East Germany for students to learn how to handle heavier and more modern weaponry. In particular they acquired the skills needed to operate SAM 7 hand-held missiles and how to fire anti-tank weapons. It is now known that Carlos passed through no less than four specialised training establishments run by the Russian secret police near Moscow. The specialities there after political indoctrination were sabotage, heavy weapons and unarmed combat, including karate.

This raises the question of how far the Russians and the KGB are involved in transnational terrorism. Theoretically the Soviets do not approve of terrorism, and officially condemn it as individualist and adventurist. Obviously the Soviet Union has no wish to give too much support to terrorist extremists who deviate from the classic Communist line. Yet it is tempting for them to use such people as surrogates in the cold war against the capitalist powers, and in any case by providing training and weapons for such men they can at least keep a measure of control over them and prevent them turning their attention to action within the Soviet world. Another advantage of limited participation is that it enables the KGB to keep itself informed about subversive groups. Finally the time might come when terrorism would be useful to the Kremlin as an extra weapon against their ideological enemies in Peking.

Whatever the reasons, it is certain that some help has been

given to transnational groups by the Soviet Union. In 1975 two terrorists sent to prison in Holland for plotting to hijack a train and seize Soviet Jews as hostages gave evidence that they had learned their technique at a village near Moscow.

It is through giving support to Arab groups acting against Israeli interests that the Soviet Union has been drawn into supporting some terrorist activities. On numerous occasions there has been mention of a Soviet training camp at Simferpol in the Crimea which can handle 400 trainees. There are also active training camps at Ostrova in Czechoslovakia and at Pankow in East Germany.

Such are the formal training facilities for those who seek to overthrow society by terrorist means. Instruction is provided for the most promising terrorist and for the group leaders. But there are many who go into action without courses, who simply learn by doing. We have already mentioned that Carlos Marighella in his widely circulated training manual wrote about bank robbery as a suitable entrance exam for apprentice guerrillas. 'Urban guerrilla warfare', he said, 'is a wonderful training school.'

In Latin America many a terrorist has taken this classic road into subversive activities; Lenin himself relied on 'expropriations' to finance the Bolsheviks and Ben Bella, the Algerian FLN leader, started out by trying bank robbery first. The truth is that only by taking part in a raid and by having his baptism of fire can a terrorist prove himself. The same is true of soldiers. However realistic their training they need to go into action in order to find out if they have got the 'bottle' for the job.

In several groups criminals have been welcomed into the movement for their technical skills, and sometimes because the participation of genuine working-class outlaws gives the thing a satisfactory doctrinal feel. They can provide experienced help in how best to go about specialised forms of 'fund raising'.

The growing sophistication of terrorist training in Europe, now under constant pressure from highly specialised security forces, can be judged from examination of a manual produced for the Red Brigades in Italy. Its owners had failed to comply with its last instruction which was, 'This book must not be left lying around', and police found it in a hastily abandoned terrorist hideout at 96 Via Gradoli, Rome. *Security Rules and Work Methods* – the title of this loose-leaf pamphlet – gives strict instructions about the comportment of terrorist groups. It advised them that, to avoid drawing attention to themselves, they should appear to be respectable, house-proud and in regular work, none of them easy tasks for student-type killers. Flats should be 'proletarian, modest, clean, neat and completely furnished'. From the outside everything should appear to be normal with curtains, entrance light and nameplate in place. Window boxes help to provide an extra touch of respectability. The Red Brigades' instructor warned his charges not to make a noise at night and to do everything possible to reassure the neighbours. Care was to be taken before hiring an apartment to ensure that the landlord did not live on the spot. Then the doors were to be fitted with burglar-proof locks. The pamphlet recommended great care in choosing a hideout to make certain that it was in a street where the police would find it difficult to keep watch from such traditional urban look-out places as bars, public buildings and warehouses. It warned that dirty cars attract attention and advised terrorists to spend time cleaning their cars rather than in going to neighbouring cafés and bars where they might excite curiosity. In case all these precautions failed the terrorists were ordered to retain as little compromising material as possible, keep their weapons and essential equipment in bags, and always be ready for a quick getaway.

It seems that in the case of the occupants of Via Gradoli, the strain of following the training recommendations of each choosing his role as factory worker, teacher or salesman – married or not – and then sticking to the regular work hours and arrivals and departures of such people, had proved too much for the enthusiasts who helped with the kidnap of Aldo Moro. For eventually they did attract attention during the great police search in Rome when a neighbour complained about a water leak in their apartment. They left behind a good deal of compromising evidence in the shape of false car licence plates, wigs and unused stationery stolen from Rome police headquarters.

Even more important was the fact that other documents revealed a good deal about the efficiency of their organisation, proving that the Moro kidnapping had involved the complicated co-operation of nearly sixty people, including twelve involved in the attack on the politician and his five-man escort, all of whom were killed. The group left behind banknotes linking them to ransoms collected from other kidnaps. Records found with the training manual showed that the group had spent $20,000 on the purchase of firearms. Once again it was demonstrated that terrorist operations are costly.

An interesting example of 'learn-as-you-go' terrorism is provided by Ulrike Meinhof. Until she took part in the Berlin operation to free Andreas Baader she had no experience of violent law breaking. While she was on the run, she watched with interest as another member of the gang demonstrated how to start the engine of a stolen Mercedes by short circuiting. In the stolen car they drove to a provincial town and broke into municipal offices, and there Ulrike learned how to open a locked door with a screwdriver. She entered the building and stole a quantity of passports, official stamps and one partly-completed ID card. A coded message had been sent to her with instructions on where to send them, but because she decoded badly they were despatched to the wrong address and that particular mission failed.

The next task was to acquire weapons. Ulrike and her friends went to Frankfurt and, using money already stolen, bought twenty-three 9 mm Firebird automatics from an Al Fatah man. They had to pay DM 450 each for the weapons, about three times the going rate at the time. The weapons were then issued to friends in a flat belonging to a German journalist, and they went out to practise with them. The place chosen as a range was in the woods near Frankfurt Airport so that the noise of the jets would drown the noise of the shooting. It is in such ways that expertise in subversive warfare can be built up, with the young terrorists, who are usually intelligent people, matching their skills against those of the authorities.

But in most cases the training of terrorists has become so formalised that regular courses are taught with passing-out ceremonies held to mark the end of the course. Any applicant wishing to join the Montoneros, for example, must first undergo a two-month indoctrination course, during which the romantics and ineffectuals are weeded out. The course breaks down old loyalties and replaces them with a new set of values. Family loyalty is the first to be attacked because it is the most basic of the old ties and the most difficult to eradicate.

At the end of the course the aspirant takes a written examination which emphasises the renunciation. A sample question is: 'What action would you take if your mother was in the hands of the enemy?' Required answer: 'None.' After the written examination there is a practical test in weaponry and explosives. Then comes the big moment: the passing-out examination. It is simple. The candidate must shoot a soldier or a policeman. This explains why so many Argentinian policemen are gunned down as they leave their houses; they are easy marks for passing an initiation test.

The reason for the act of killing is that it binds the would-be terrorist irrevocably to the organisation. Up to that moment he or she could back out. But once the initiates have killed, they are committed. One girl, a nurse sickened by the killing, wanted to get out. The Montoneros sent a killer squad to her home. When they burst in, her mother pleaded: 'Shoot me, not her.' The killers shot them both. Similar executions have been carried out by Baader–Meinhof and by PFLP on members who have wanted to return to normality. There is no way out except by death.

5 | Money: The Budget of Death

Money is the fuel of terrorism. The belief that the use of terror is the poor man's method of waging war is no longer valid. The Palestinian, South American and German groups that seek to destroy the bourgeois way of life are among the richest sections of the affluent society.

One or two impoverished groups remain, notably the South Moluccans who pursue their hopeless campaign in Holland and who have meagre resources. Their cause is such an impossible and unpopular one that no major power, no well-established terrorist group, can see any great advantage in supporting them and, so far, they have not learnt to hold up banks and to kidnap for ransom. Elsewhere, the picture of the ragged revolutionary living off the country, stealing his weapons and supplies from 'the forces of repression', is as outmoded as red-coated soldiers. Modern terrorists need to be rich and the transnational groups need to be very rich indeed – first-class airline tickets are expensive.

Ever more complicated arms have to be paid for, so do safe houses, radio sets, cars and hotel rooms. The terrorists themselves have to be paid and need expenses so that they can merge into the societies in which they operate. If, for example, an observation team of three were to keep watch over a businessman in order to mount a kidnap operation, they would need to be dressed in a fashion which would not excite comment in smart restaurants. As an Irish policeman put it when talking about a city-suited Provo who had just been sent to prison: 'Only the stone-throwers wear jeans. Most of the hard men are smartly dressed – they can afford to be with all the money they have coming in from bank raids.'

Harry Duggan, the leader of the Balcombe Street gang, was described as 'looking like a junior hotel manager'. Michel Moukharbel, Carlos' adjutant in Paris, was also the assassin's book-keeper and he kept detailed records of the money that he and Carlos spent on their various enterprises. Because of these details – hotel bills, train fares, car hire accounts – the authorities were able not only to trace Carlos' movements but also to build up a financial picture of the infrastructure of terror. This infrastructure closely follows the normal financial pattern of big business, even down to pension schemes for the disabled and the widows and families of men killed on 'company business'.

When Colonel Gaddafi set up his own multinational terrorist organisation he established a fund to provide this kind of social insurance. One of his men, who surrendered after hijacking a plane to Kuwait, told his interrogators that the Libyan President had promised his team before they set out that he would pay compensation of £250,000 to the families of any of them killed in the enterprise. Hans-Joachim Klein, who was wounded during the OPEC operation, had his pain assuaged by an insurance payment of £100,000 from Gaddafi. The Libyan fanatic has become to terrorism what Lloyds of London is to shipping. And in fact their worlds overlap, because Lloyds pays out on the aircraft hijacked by the men whose lives Gaddafi insures.

And so the expenses mount. Cars cannot always be stolen – the theft could attract too much attention – and so they have to be hired. Wireless equipment has to be bought, and, if the group is mixing its own explosives, the ingredients have to be purchased. The well placed 'sleepers' whose services are only called upon at crucial moments have to be funded. Officials have to be bribed and yet more money is eaten up in the mundane business of running offices. Paper and typewriters have to be bought. Telephone bills need to be paid. People, even the most dedicated of terrorists, have to eat and drink and be clothed. The air fares for a five-strong hijack team could easily amount to £3000 in addition to the money spent on the reconnaissance team which had prospected the route. When it is all added up it will be seen that the funds needed to finance a hit team are comparable to the annual expenses of a medium-sized company.

Where does the money come from? The answer to that question depends on the type of organisation involved and on the countries likely to support it. The IRA, for example, has always relied on funds collected by sympathisers in Ireland and especially upon money donated by sentimental Irish–Americans across the Atlantic, who are easy touches for the men with the collecting boxes who claim that they need the money to relieve the hardship brought about by what they term the brutality of the British Army. Some of them of course actively support the bombers and the murderers, but most turn a blind eye to the inevitable destination of their money. Even the people who run the Northern Ireland Aid Committee in New York seem genuinely to believe that the money they collect will be used for humanitarian purposes. But the British Army has traced too many Armalites captured in Belfast back to gunshops in New York for this belief to hold water.

However, after a campaign by the British government and the government of Southern Ireland to explain the true nature of Provisional IRA activities to the Irish–Americans, there was evidence by 1977 that this emotional money was drying up. The raffles and the dances and the monthly commitments raised $600,000 in 1972 but five years later this sum had fallen to $150,000. The Provos were forced to return to the classic form of terrorist fund raising – the robbing of banks. They enjoyed no small success. It was estimated that they stole £2 million in 215 attacks on banks in one year and in December 1977 Mr Lynch, the Republic of Ireland's Prime Minister, was forced to impose stringent measures to deal with the increase in armed bank raids.

In one of the classic paradoxes of terrorism, it is the Palestinians, who come from the poverty of the refugee camp shacks, who are the richest terrorists. They have never needed to mount bank raids – except of course during the Lebanese civil war, when they were able to walk into deserted banks and load the entire contents of strong rooms on to lorries. This paradox stems from the fact that their movement attracted support from the Arab world at precisely the moment when the oil states of the Middle East were beginning to savour their immense, newly acquired wealth. Because even conservative and anti-revolutionary Arabs could not resist the emotional appeals to help free Palestine of the Israelis and to recover the holy places of Islam lost to the Jews, money poured into the coffers of the Palestinian organisations. This flow of money also entailed recognition by the Arab states that none of them was strong enough to tackle Israel on the field of battle and that the only way harm could be inflicted on the Israelis was by means of terrorism – but of course that was before the Arabs realised that in control of the supply of oil they had a weapon far more powerful than even the nuclear bomb.

The fact that gives this situation a touch of Alice in Wonderland is that the oil states know that they themselves are next on the terrorists' list after the Israelis and yet, by the weird logic of Arab politics, they are forced to provide the money to keep the terrorists in being. They make an attempt at rationalisation by giving their donations not directly to the terrorists but to the Palestine Liberation Organisation, but as the terrorist groups are an integral part of the PLO, the money inevitably filters through to them and from them it is passed on to the transnational gangs, thus uniting with oil money, German nihilists, Japanese revolutionaries, Latin American romantics and Turkish nationalists. The Palestinians are indeed the plutocrats of terror.

It was estimated in 1975 that Al Fatah, the largest of the groups which make up the PLO, had an income of almost $200 million; according to the Israelis, the Popular Front for the Liberation of Palestine, the most extreme of the Arab organisations, had a similar sum at its disposal. In July 1977 *Time* magazine reported that when Yasser Arafat flew to Saudi Arabia to ask King Khalid to persuade the Syrians not to attack the Palestinians in the Lebanon the Saudi government refused. But as a kind of consolation prize Crown Prince Fahd wrote Arafat a cheque for $5 million. This gift was in addition to the annual subvention from Saudi Arabia to the PLO of $25 million.

Saudi Arabia is just one of the sources of revenue. The Kuwaitis and the Gulf Emirates also provide substantial contributions as a kind of *danegeld* to ensure that guerrillas are not tempted to get too active in their territories. In brief, the whole Arab world backs the liberation movements with money. One of the most generous backers is Colonel Gaddafi who spares no financial effort to keep the Palestine movements in action. With a production rate of 1,737,000 barrels of oil a day he amassed a balance of payments surplus in 1975 of $1,700 million. It is estimated that he paid some £20 million from his ample reserves to Black September, while similar sums went to other organisations and substantial amounts were spent on providing arms and equipment for the terrorist movement. He is well named as 'the paymaster of terror'.

In addition to his regular contributions to the funds of Palestine liberation groups, Gaddafi also offered large bonuses for successful operations against Israel. To express his appreciation to Black September for their action at the Munich Olympic Games he gave them a cash reward of £5 million. And after the seizure of the OPEC oil ministers in Vienna, Carlos received a gift of one million pounds. In addition, ransom money for the lives of the Saudi and Iranian ministers kidnapped on that occasion brought some $25 million into the Palestinian coffers. Terrorism in these circumstances can be a profitable business.

It was estimated that in 1976 organisations under the PLO umbrella received around $90 million from the Arab states. In addition there are the contributions from Palestinians who live and work in the Gulf oil states and who have a 5 per cent tax 'to sustain the cause' levied on their incomes. Colonel Gaddafi is harsher. He imposes an 8 per cent tax on Palestinians employed in his country. In addition to these sources of revenue the Palestinians receive large sums as gifts from rich individuals anxious to prove their enthusiasm for the cause – and there is no shortage of Arab millionaires.

With such a huge income the Palestine Liberation Organisation has come to resemble a multinational business corporation, with an amalgam of terrorism and diplomacy as its end product. Hardly any of its resources are used to improve conditions in the refugee camps of the Middle East where Arabs live in disgustingly squalid conditions. There is reason in this seeming inconsistency, for the camps provide the endless flow of recruits for terrorist duties. To improve conditions there, which is perfectly possible, would erode the causes of bitterness which keep good and decent Arabs ever ready to fight and destroy Israel. Even the poor in the camps are themselves forced to contribute their mite.

Most of the money is spent on military training and on terrorist operations. But a good deal also goes on financing the huge bureaucracy which now controls the movements. They have modern offices with executives, PR men, secretaries in pretty dresses and the whole paraphernalia of a modern business corporation – although the young men in the offices spoil the cut of their trousers with pistols stuck into their waistbands. In addition to its headquarters in Beirut, the PLO also runs its own diplomatic service with offices which have near-diplomatic status in no less than 100 countries and maintains an 'observer' delegation at the United Nations. The heads of these missions in the more important countries of Western Europe and the United States are paid up to $1,500 a month. Such sums are in stark contrast to the pay of a guerrilla fighting man who gets only $70 plus family allowances.

Over the last couple of years the Palestinians have none the less had some financial embarrassments, for the civil war in which they were engaged in Lebanon, their power base, cost them a great deal. One calculation puts the cost at $100 million, because the organisation had to purchase heavy weapons and also had to provide for thousands of their troops who were injured and maimed in the fighting as well as making allowances for their dependants.

During the Beirut fighting one establishment remained untouched, for it was strongly protected throughout by regular Palestinian troops. No harm came to the Arab Bank Ltd, a strong financial establishment based in Amman, Jordan, and presided over by a Jerusalem-born Arab. In the Middle East this bank, which has assets of over $4 billion, is often called the 'PLO Bank', for it is generally believed that it handles the investments made by the organisation in European and American stock exchanges. The PLO is estimated to have an investment portfolio of some $100 million. In Beirut it owns hotels and has bought land on the West Bank of the Jordan – in Israeli-held territory. Such investments give a measure of independence from the financial pressures of Arab governments.

In recent years the Palestinian organisations have increased their revenue by commercial ventures such as poultry farms, night clubs and the setting up of factories and workshops for the production of handicrafts, clothes and furniture. But not all their business enterprises are so respectable. Palestinian leaders have let it be known that they have made big money from the illegal sale of drugs in Israel. But they are less talkative about their share in the international cannabis market out of Lebanon.

In the summer of 1977 the trial and conviction in London of a British drug smuggler revealed a profitable trade in cannabis designed to bring large sums of money to the Palestinian organisations. The cannabis, grown in northern Lebanon, was taken in lorries through Turkey and Bulgaria to Yugoslavia, where the hidden cargoes were split up and smuggled across Europe to Britain in secret compartments built into private cars. The supply from Lebanon dried up during the worst period of the civil war but the Palestinians became active again as the fighting died down. Had the network not been uncovered by international anti-drug squads it is believed that the next consignment would have netted half a million pounds. And their traffic was a two-way business. The transports which delivered the cannabis through Turkey were to have returned loaded with weapons made in Eastern Europe, paid for with the drug profits. If the traffic had continued there is no doubt that pot smokers in fashionable London would unwittingly have been helping to provide terrorist weapons for Palestinians – and through them, possibly the IRA as well.

Terrorist funds, like all kinds of big money, attract corruption and criminals. Several PLO officials with ideas above their terrorist station were thrown into prison for gambling away a £250,000 chunk of organisation money in Cairo's casinos. And even the more modest funds of the Provisional IRA have proved too great a temptation for sticky-fingered comrades. One Provo who acquired £100,000 for the cause by a particularly successful bank raid transferred it to his own account in the United States. No doubt he will subscribe generously to the Northern Irish Aid Fund – if he lives to enjoy his loot.

Even terrorists who proclaim the purity of their motives are susceptible to the rustle of banknotes. Carlos, the celebrated anti-bourgeois, is no slouch when it comes to enjoying the good life in the best restaurants on his expense account and he has made a fortune from his post as chief overseas assassin for the Palestinians. It is one of the ironies of the modern world that the West, with its dependence on Arab oil, provides some of the wealth which is passed on to men dedicated to destroying the fabric of Western society.

In other parts of the world terrorists have to work harder to make their money. A good example of self-financing is provided by the ERP, the Ejército Revolucionario del Pueblo or People's Revolutionary Army of Argentina who, although formed as the armed wing of a Trotskyist revolutionary party, might well be described as the capitalists of terror. Formed in 1970, it concentrated the activity of its military cells on fund-raising by 'expropriation' or, less politely, bank robbery and kidnapping for ransom. Estimated to be 5000 strong by 1974, their ranks were increased by Tupamaros escaping from Uruguay and Mirista radicals who fled from the military *coup* in Chile which toppled the Marxist Allende government.

Their initial capital came from a bank raid in Cordoba which brought in a mere $300,000 but they rapidly increased this by kidnapping a business executive whose ransom was set, and paid, at a million dollars. Not unnaturally, this success pointed the way to a profitable line of business and they switched their activities almost entirely to kidnapping the executives of major companies, especially of the multinationals who had set up business in the Argentine and had filled many of their senior posts with their own countrymen. The kidnappings, therefore, fulfilled three functions. They brought in a great deal of money; they enabled the ERP to maintain a correct radical approach; and they pleased xenophobic Argentinians by attacking foreign concerns and foreign officials.

As a result of this branch of terrorist enterprise the ERP rapidly built up a central fund of some $30 million. They did not, however, always have things their own way. The authorities were opposed to ransom deals and tried to foil them wherever possible. In 1972 after the completion of negotiations for the million dollar ransom of Oberdan Sallustro, a Fiat executive, the police discovered and attacked the hideout where he was being held. Four of the terrorists were captured. But Sallustro paid a greater price than the ransom was worth. He was murdered when the police stormed the 'people's prison'.

The following year, after a partially successful attempt to seize a Ford Motor Company executive in Buenos Aires in the course of which he was wounded, it was reported that the company had handed over a million dollars for 'protection' against any new attempt. It is not uncommon for big firms to pay up in this way in order to avoid trouble – in the same way that some airlines make regular payments to ensure that their aircraft are not hijacked. This was one of the ERP's 'Robin Hood' actions. In accordance with their instructions the ransom was paid in the form of medical supplies and other help for the poor.

In the early 1970s the amount of money demanded by ERP continually escalated – two million dollars for Charles Lockwood, a British executive of Acrow Steel, three million for John R. Thompson, the American president of Firestone Tyres Argentinian subsidiary – until eventually it reached the then record of $14,200,000 for Victor Samuelson, an EXXON executive. After Mr Samuelson had been held for almost five months the company agreed to the terrorists' terms, but the revolutionaries then kept their man for another forty-nine days to give them time to 'launder' the money.

In June 1975 the Montoneros, the other main Argentinian terrorist group, who follow a leftist–Peronist philosophy, announced that they had pulled off the most lucrative kidnapping so far: $60 million in cash and $1.2 million in food and clothing distributed to the poor in exchange for the lives of Jorge and Juan Born, sons of Jorge Born, chairman of the Bunge y Born commercial empire. Jorge Born was held for nine months while the negotiations were conducted, but his brother Juan was so affected by his imprisonment in a 'people's prison' that the Montoneros feared for his mental health and his life and rather than jeopardise the deal, they made a realistic business decision and released him before the ransom was paid. There was no indication given about the method in which it was paid but the business is believed in the Argentine to have been transacted in several instalments with the money being taken into the country by couriers from abroad.

The government ordered an enquiry into the group's accounts after the ransom had been paid in order to ascertain whether tax or exchange control laws had been violated. Either because there had been no violations or because Bunge y Born represented too powerful a slice of the Argentinian economy for the government – beset with economic problems – to take on, nothing substantial has emerged from this enquiry at the time of writing.

The authorities have, however, pursued another enquiry with the utmost diligence. In August 1976, an executive jet with two pilots and a lone passenger crashed in the mountains south of Mexico City. The plane had been hired in the name of David Graiver, the 35-year-old scion of the Graiver family of Polish Jews who had settled in Argentina in the 1930s and had become powerful bankers in the extensive but unpopular Jewish community in Buenos Aires. Graiver was a financial whizz-kid, a flamboyant wheeler-dealer who juggled with enormous sums of money. It seemed that he had run out of luck. Although all three bodies were dreadfully mutilated, his was unhesitatingly identified by his brother Isidoro. He was cremated and his wife Lidia carried his ashes back to the Argentine in a brass urn.

When Graiver crashed, so did his empire. Banks in America, Belgium and the Argentine investigated his dealings and when the sums were done it appeared that some $50 million of other people's money was unaccounted for. It had all the hallmarks of a massive international fraud.

Then, eight months later, the affair took on a new dimension when *La Nueva Provincia*, a right-wing newspaper connected with General Iberico Saint-Jean, a hardline rightist who had been head of the secret police, accused Graiver of being the investment banker of the Montoneros. The newspaper alleged that Graiver had channelled at least $17 million of the Montoneros' money through his Banco Comercial de la Plata into investments in Argentina and abroad. This was at a time when the Montoneros' profits from their kidnappings were far in excess of their immediate needs and so they did what any major business concern would do. They invested their excess capital. The Argentinian government now estimates that the Montoneros were getting $130,000 a month from their investments and, according to his enemies – and he had many – David Graiver was providing the revolutionaries with the same 'hot money' services he had already arranged for top men in the Peronist regime.

The newspaper investigation of Graiver provided detailed information about the business cover of the terrorists. Every month two well-dressed men known as Dr Paz and Dr Penaloza took the high speed lift to the twenty-ninth floor of the Graiver bank in the centre of Buenos Aires. Because it was equipped with so many security devices this office was known as 'The Bunker'. Once there, they would collect their monthly interest in cash, stuff it into their briefcases, take a cup of coffee and leave half an hour later to put the money at the disposal of the local leaders of the terrorist campaigns then being fought both in the towns and the countryside.

The Junta led by General Jorge Videla was by now conducting a repressive but successful campaign against the terrorists, and followed up the newspaper accusation by claiming it could prove that Graiver was willingly handling Montoneros funds and had in fact become so enmeshed that his banking empire depended on the inflow of terrorist money. General Videla announced: 'This so-called Graiver group worked for the subversives. They received millions of dollars in deposits to be invested here and abroad for the benefit of subversion, and they knew where the money had come from.' Evidence against Graiver began to accumulate and the police had a windfall when they raided a Montoneros 'safe house' and found documents linking him with the organisation's finances.

The government then took action against the Graiver family and its associates, arresting some 300 people. A dramatic twist was given to the investigation when Juan Graiver, father of David, was questioned by the police and then released. The next day four young officers in sports clothes went to see him again and he asked: 'Who are you Montoneros, or what?' The police said they were guerrillas. 'Take it easy,' Juan Graiver is reported to have said. 'I'm a decent sort who pays his debts. We are going to give you your money back.' Naturally enough he was desperately worried because after the collapse of the Graiver financial empire the Montoneros had been sharing in the anxieties of ordinary investors and were demanding to know what had happened to their money. They were asking the sort of questions that did not allow Senor Graiver to sleep well at night.

In December 1977 a court martial composed of military officers sitting in secret sentenced David Graiver's father, Juan, his widow, Lidia, and his brother, Isidoro, to fifteen years' imprisonment, the maximum, for collaborating with terrorist groups. Five other relatives and associates were sentenced to lighter terms. The military communiqué announcing the sentences did not give any details of the trial but military sources said that the substance of the charge of investing illegal funds abroad had been obtained by questioning Jorge Rubenstein, a financial adviser to the Graiver banking establishments. Rubenstein will never be able to answer any more questions. He died 'while in the custody of the security forces'.

There are many questions still to be answered however. What happened to all the money? How much was the case against the Graivers part of the current wave of anti-semitism in the Argentine? And, the most tantalising of all, is David Graiver still alive? In April 1978 Robert Morgenthau, the Manhattan District Attorney, declared 'There is a basis to believe he is still alive,' and other sources reported in the *Wall Street Journal* said it seemed likely that Graiver was behind the Iron Curtain. The South American financier and five of his banking staff had just been charged by a grand jury in New York with conspiracy, misappropriating funds and falsifying bank records in an international financial scheme involving six countries. The District Attorney announced that his detectives were searching for Graiver and that they would seek the help of Interpol. This news began fresh speculation in Argentina where it is generally believed that Graiver became involved with the terrorists after the seizure of his brother Isidoro by the Montoneros early in the 1970s. After he was freed it was generally believed that the family had paid a ransom, but later there was speculation that David Graiver made a deal agreeing to manage their money in return for his family being left alone. What does seem certain is that the Montoneros lost a sizeable chunk of their ill-gotten and unwisely invested gains. It proved in fact that capitalism does not always pay.

The Baader–Meinhof group and its successors in Germany have, of course, set out to prove this point from the other direction. From the beginning of their existence they geared their organisation to theft on the precepts of Carlos Marighella, the Brazilian terrorist who taught that bank robbery was the just way of financing revolution. The fact that he was killed in pursuance of his own teaching did not deter the Germans. They mounted six bank robberies within two months in 1972 and walked away with $185,000.

Ulrike Meinhof set out her justification for robbing banks in her pamphlet *Urban Guerrillas and Class Conflict*. She wrote:

No one claims that bank robbery of itself changes anything . . . for the revolutionary organisation it means first of all a solution of financial problems. It is logistically correct, since otherwise the financial problem could not be solved at all. It is tactically correct

Weight	9.5 lb (unloaded)
	11.31 lb (loaded with full magazine)
	Later models, unloaded, weigh just over 6.5 lb
Length	34.2 in
	27.5 in, with butt folded
Magazine	Curved metal box holding 30 rounds
Cartridge	7.62 mm. Steel core gives penetrating power to short bullet
Muzzle velocity	2330 ft/sec
Rate of fire	100 rounds a minute automatic
	40 rounds a minute single shot
Maximum effective range	330 yd

Plate 1
Kalashnikov or AK 47

Weight	6.9 lb (unloaded) 8.4 lb (loaded with full magazine)
Length	33.2 in. 25 in, with butt folded
Magazine	Curved metal box holding 30 rounds
Cartridge	7.62 mm
Muzzle velocity	2330 ft/sec
Rate of fire	90 rounds a minute automatic 40 rounds a minute single shot
Maximum effective range	440 yd

Plate 2
VZ 58 V Assault Rifle

Plate 3
Skorpion VZ 61

Weight	3.5 lb (unloaded) 4.4 lb (loaded with full 20-round magazine)
Length	20.2 in 10.6 in, with steel frame butt folded over top of barrel
Magazine	Slightly curved metal box holding 10 or 20 rounds
Cartridge	.32 (7.65 mm) automatic pistol cartridge
Muzzle velocity	1040 ft/sec
Rate of fire	840 rounds a minute automatic 40 rounds a minute single shot
Maximum effective range	219 yd with butt 55 yd with butt folded

Plate 4
Heckler and Koch MP 5

Weight	5.4 lb (unloaded) 6.48 lb (loaded with full 30-round magazine)
Length	26.77 in 19.29 in, with telescopic butt retracted
Magazine	Straight metal box holding 10, 15 or 30 rounds
Cartridge	9 mm Parabellum
Muzzle velocity	1312 ft/sec
Rate of fire	100 rounds a minute automatic 40 rounds a minute single shot
Maximum effective range	220 yd

Plate 5
Armalite AR-18

Weight	7 lb (unloaded)
	7.75 lb (loaded with full magazine)
Length	36.38 in
Magazine	Straight metal box holding 20 rounds
Cartridge	5.56 mm (.223)
Muzzle velocity	3250 ft/sec
Rate of fire	80 rounds a minute automatic
	40 rounds a minute single shot
Maximum effective range	500 yd

Plate 6
Thompson Sub-machine-gun

Weight	10.5 lb (unloaded)
	12.1 lb (loaded with full 30-round magazine)
Length	32 in
Magazine	Straight metal box holding 20 or 30 rounds
Cartridge	.45 automatic pistol cartridge
Muzzle velocity	920 ft/sec
Rate of fire	120 rounds a minute automatic
	40 rounds a minute single shot
Maximum effective range	220 yd

Plate 7
Sten Sub-machine-gun

Weight	6.65 lb (unloaded) 8.05 lb (loaded with full magazine)
Length	30 in
Magazine	Straight metal box holding 32 rounds, feeding horizontally into left of gun
Cartridge	9 mm Parabellum
Muzzle velocity	1200 ft/sec
Rate of fire	128 rounds a minute automatic 40 rounds a minute single shot
Maximum effective range	200 yd

Plate 8
M1 Carbine

Weight	5.19 lb (unloaded)
	5.80 lb (loaded with full magazine)
Length	35.58 in
Magazine	Straight metal box holding 15 rounds
Cartridge	.30 short rifle
Muzzle velocity	1970 ft/sec
Rate of fire	40 rounds a minute single shot
Maximum effective range	330 yd

Weight	6.625 lb (unloaded) 8.125 lb (loaded with 30-round magazine)
Length	16.4 in
Magazine	Metal stick holding 20, 30 or 40 rounds and sliding into holder
Cartridge	9 mm Parabellum
Muzzle velocity	1250 ft/sec
Rate of fire	120 rounds a minute automatic 40 rounds a minute single shot
Maximum effective range	220 yd

Plate 9.
Beretta Model 12 Sub-machine-gun

Plate 10
Astra .357 Magnum

Weight	2 lb with 6-in barrel (unloaded)
Length	11.25 in with 6-in barrel (other barrel lengths are 3, 4 and 8.5 in)
Magazine	Six-chambered cylinder
Cartridge	.357 of various types
Muzzle velocity	1410–1550 ft/sec depending on cartridge used
Maximum effective range	55 yd depending on barrel length

Plate 11
M52 Pistol

Weight	2.11 lb (unloaded) 2.44 lb (loaded with full magazine)
Length	8.25 in
Magazine	Metal box holding 8 rounds and sliding into pistol grip
Cartridge	7.62 bottleneck cartridge with unusually powerful charge
Muzzle velocity	1600 ft/sec
Rate of fire	32 rounds a minute
Maximum effective range	70 yd

Plate 12
Browning High Power Pistol

Weight	1.94 lb (unloaded) 2.44 lb (loaded with full magazine)
Length	7.75 in
Magazine	Metal box holding 13 rounds and sliding into pistol grip
Cartridge	9 mm Parabellum
Muzzle velocity	1150 ft/sec
Rate of fire	40 rounds a minute
Maximum effective range	50 yd

Plate 13
Makarov Pistol

Weight	1.46 lb (unloaded)
Length	6.3 in
Magazine	Metal box holding 8 rounds and sliding into pistol grip
Cartridge	9 mm
Muzzle velocity	1023 ft/sec
Rate of fire	35 rounds a minute
Maximum effective range	54 yd

Plate 14
Tokarev (TT-33)

Weight	1.88 lb (unloaded)
Length	7.7 in
Magazine	Metal box holding 8 rounds and sliding into pistol grip
Cartridge	7.62 mm Tokarev 9 mm Tokagypt
Muzzle velocity	1378 ft/sec
Rate of fire	32 rounds a minute
Maximum effective range	55 yd

Plate 15
Walther P38

Weight	1.7 lb (unloaded) 2.125 lb (loaded with full magazine)
Length	8.6 in
Magazine	Metal box holding 8 rounds and sliding into pistol grip
Cartridge	9 mm Parabellum
Muzzle velocity	1135 ft/sec
Rate of fire	32 rounds a minute
Maximum effective range	54 yd

Plate 16
**Smith and Wesson
Revolver**

Weight	1.94 lb (unloaded)
Length	10.125 in
Magazine	Six-chambered cylinder
Cartridge	.38 in
Muzzle velocity	650 ft/sec
Rate of fire	24 rounds a minute
Maximum effective range	44 yd

Plate 17
**RGD-5 Anti-personnel
Hand Grenade**

Weight	0.69 lb
Length	4.5 in
Diameter	2.25 in
Colour	Apple green with RGD-5 (in Cyrillic) written on body
Explosive	110 grams of TNT
Fuse	Percussion with delay of 3.2 to 4.2 seconds

Plate 18
SAM 7 Strela (Arrow)

Weight of launcher	20.3 lb
Weight of missile	20.25 lb
Length of launcher	53 in
Length of missile	51.2 in
Rocket motor	Three-stage solid propellant
Maximum range	3792 yd
Maximum height	6560 ft
Guidance system	Infra-red

Plate 19
M26 Grenade

Weight	1 lb
Length	3.9 in
Diameter	2.25 in
Colour	Standard US Army olive with yellow lettering
Explosive	155 grams of TNT-based Composition B
Fuse	Electrical impact

Plate 20
RPG-7 Portable Rocket-launcher

Weight of launcher	15.4 lb
Weight of grenade	4.95 lb
Length of launcher	39 in
Calibre of launcher	1.5 in
Calibre of projectile	3.3 in
Range, static target	555 yd
Range, moving target	330 yd
Penetration of armour	12.6 in

Plate 21
M60 General Purpose Machine-gun

Weight	23.09 lb (unloaded)
Length	43.5 in
Feed	Disintegrating link belt
Cartridge	7.62 mm
Muzzle velocity	2800 ft/sec
Rate of fire	550 rounds a minute cyclic
	200 rounds a minute automatic
Maximum effective range	2000 yd with tripod
	1000 yd with bipod

because it is a proletarian action. It is strategically correct because it serves the financing of the guerrilla.

But the German terrorists also had financial help, as did the Japanese Red Army, from Arab funds made available to help them in return for services rendered, such as attacks on Israeli offices and factories working for the Israelis. The Red Army Faction did not need such large funds on its own account as some terrorist movements, for a great deal of its support was provided by well-to-do German sympathisers. There was never any shortage of comfortable flats in which they could hide; and cars and equipment were easy to acquire in an affluent Western country. Even though Andreas Baader liked his comforts and Ulrike Meinhof complained when she had to live in an unheated building, money was never a problem for these middle-class terrorists. Miss Meinhof had money of her own, and many of the girl terrorists were able to get it from their prosperous parents.

Klaus Rohl, husband of Ulrike, revealed in his biography that both of them had been secret members of the Communist Party from 1956 until 1961. He further stated that his magazine *Konkret* had been subsidised from Soviet funds. On clandestine visits to East Europe he and Ulrike had collected upwards of a million marks by way of Prague.

Whenever the Baader–Meinhof crowd did run short of money they simply organised more bank raids. Even in 1977 that same process was still continuing. So common was it for West German banks to be held up at pistol point that they became known as 'terrorist treasuries'. Robbers were making off with up to two and a half million pounds a year, most of which went into terrorist fighting funds.

The early bank raids did not always produce as much as the Baader–Meinhof gang would have liked. In one case Baader managed to steal only DM 8000 having failed to notice a carton of notes worth more than ten times as much. The comrades mocked him for his failure, saying: 'You could earn that much doing dirty work for *Konkret* magazine.' Other members of the gang went in for small-scale fraud. One of the travelling terrorists declared that he had lost his travellers' cheques and claimed the insurance on them in the Middle East. After he had collected the money he flew back to Europe and cashed the original travellers' cheques. A cheap little trick but then, all things are permissible as long as they serve the cause.

Perhaps the most revealing words on the financial philosophy of terrorism may be taken from Horst Mahler, who, on entering a bank, declared: 'This is a stick-up! Hands up and keep quiet and nothing will happen to you. After all, it's not your money.'

But while bank raids and small-time chicanery kept the money flowing, the really big profits came from hijackings and kidnaps. As a result of the kidnapping of the politician Peter Lorenz in West Berlin, five imprisoned terrorists were released and flown to South Yemen with DM 20,000 apiece as pocket money. While this did not equal the *coup* of Wadi Hadad, the old master – who in 1972 forced Lufthansa to pay $5 million into his PFLP fund at a time when it was cut off from the main stream of Arab money in return for the release of a hijacked Jumbo – it did help.

Hadad, incidentally, smarted for years over this hijack because the South Yemenis charged him a million dollars as a 'landing fee' and also, his hit team failed to discover that one of the passengers was Joseph P. Kennedy III, the son of the late Robert Kennedy and obviously worth more in ransom money than all the other passengers put together.

In Italy the Red Brigades took a leaf out of the Mafia's book and began operating their terrorist network as a money-making organisation. When anti-terror investigators made a breakthrough in the mid-1970s and succeeded in arresting the original leadership and breaking their networks they discovered detailed accounts. By that time ransom money and protection payments had come in in such quantities that the Red Brigades had a budget of a milliard Lira. The terrorists' finance managers had prudently invested large sums. It was estimated that 300 million Lira had been placed in property and real estate and the income from this was used to purchase weapons, cars and equipment. Some of the property bought by Red Brigades was used to provide safe houses and 'people's prisons', but usually their real estate was used simply to provide a solid income. Like the Palestinians the accountants of the Red Brigades put aside large sums to pay their terrorist operators and they also operated a social security system to look after the dependants of those killed or imprisoned in the course of their terrorist activities. Despite the healthy income enjoyed by the Red Brigades they still had money worries. While in prison awaiting trial, Renato Curcio complained about the high and increasing cost of keeping underground units operational.

The Japanese Red Army has always had the reputation of being as much a mercenary force as an ideological one. Because the Japanese police cracked down on them after their first small operations at home, this group was forced to flee and re-form abroad with no visible means of support. They went to work for the Palestinians in return for subsidies to keep their movement in being but also turned to hijacking to maintain a semblance of independence. However, they were not particularly successful and so the Red Army's woman leader, Fusako Shigenobu, planned a series of kidnappings of Japanese businessmen in Europe to restore the financial situation. In order to do this the entire Red Army treasury – $10,000 – was sent by courier from the Middle East to Paris to finance the operations. But the courier was arrested at Orly airport and when the dollars were examined they were found to be poor forgeries.

The Red Army had to turn again to the PFLP to bail them out. It was not until the summer of 1977 that the Red Army made a startling comeback by seizing a Japanese Airlines plane just after it had taken off from Bombay and forcing it to fly to Bangladesh and then to Algiers. The Japanese government abjectly surrendered to their demands and agreed to release a mixed bag of six imprisoned terrorists and criminals. They thus provided the Red Army with a renewed fighting force. And, by handing over a ransom of $6 million in used $100 bills, they provided the capital to re-establish the Red Army as a powerful force in international terrorism, part of the new group which in late 1977 was being set up by Wadi Hadad and Carlos in Baghdad, an enterprise which was halted by Hadad's death.

We said at the beginning of this chapter that money is the fuel of terrorism – without it nothing runs. But at the same time it is probably the easiest of essentials for terrorists to obtain. For, once they have abandoned normal morality and convinced themselves that anything is justified in pursuance of their cause, then bank robbery, kidnapping and hijackings become not only justified but actual acts of virtue. When this philosophy is joined with the sophisticated investment of its rewards and is backed by the flow of Arab petrodollars to organisations judged to be of assistance to the Palestinian cause, there are fortunes to be made. But these are not fortunes to be frittered away by playboys or to be invested wisely for the benefit of mankind. They are fortunes to be used in destroying the democratic civilisation which has evolved in the Western world, the fruit of 3000 years of struggle. Remember that Stalin started his revolutionary life as a bank robber.

6 | The Weapons of Terror – Guns

The weapons of terror have become industrialised since the Old Man of the Mountains sent his Assassins armed with their long knives to persuade his enemies of the justness of his cause and Jael, one of the first of the 'freedom fighters', carried out the political assassination of Sisera by hammering a tent peg through his skull. But the three essential requirements of such weapons remain the same: availability, simplicity and efficiency. Other requirements have been added over the years. It is now necessary for terrorists to be able to kill a number of people from a distance, so firepower has become important. This entails the use of automatic weapons but not those with too rapid a rate of fire, for the limited amount of ammunition that can normally be carried on a mission of terror precludes its waste. The guns and ammunition must have stopping power for it is dangerous to allow a man to remain capable of firing back; one lucky bullet could wreck the whole operation. To conduct urban terrorism, weapons need to be concealed, so miniaturisation is also essential. When these characteristics are added to easy access to guns, the bullets to fit them and the simplicity which precludes weapons jamming at a vital moment, the perfect weapon of terror emerges.

The following weapons possess these requirements to a greater or lesser degree; some are more efficient than others but they all carry the same guarantee of usage. These are the chosen weapons of terrorism.

Kalashnikov or AK 47 (Plate 1)

This Russian assault rifle is the true weapon of revolution.

The brilliant invention of a Siberian peasant boy who became a soldier and designed weapons while he was convalescing after being wounded in the tank battle for Bryansk in the Second World War, hundreds of thousands of various versions of this rifle have been made in the Communist countries and supplied to Russia's clients and revolutionary movements around the world. It is the standard weapon of the Iron Curtain countries, the Arab armies, the Palestinian movements, Cuba and the armies of black Africa. Its success stems largely from its reliability. It functioned in Vietnam under conditions which jammed the American M16. It can be smothered in mud and sand and will still work impeccably. Solid and dependable, it is the weapon for ill-educated peasant armies. Used by Black September at Munich, Palestinian raiding parties across the Israeli border, and by ZANU terrorists in Rhodesia. There have been reports that the IRA also has a small number. Two hundred and fifty of them were seized when the IRA arms ship *Claudia* was captured in 1973.

Assessment   This excellent weapon is reliable and, despite its short barrel, not noticeably less accurate than Western rifles. It has good stopping power. Captured Kalashnikovs were preferred by American troops in Vietnam and by Israeli soldiers to their own weapons.

VZ 58 V Assault Rifle (Plate 2)

This Czech designed and made weapon was used by the three Japanese Red Army terrorists when they carried out the massacre at Lod Airport in 1972, using buttless VZ 58s and grenades which they had hidden in their luggage. Following this exploit a unit of the Japanese Red Army gave itself the name: VZ 58. It is sold commercially by Omnipol, the Czech arms-selling organisation.

Assessment   This effective weapon at first sight resembles the AK 47 but differs quite dramatically in design and manufacture. It is not as foolproof as the AK 47 in that it can

be assembled and fired without the locking piece thus causing an explosion in the breech. It can fire the same rounds as
the AK 47 but the magazines are not interchangeable.

Skorpion VZ 61 (Plate 3)

This tiny, Czech-made machine pistol is one of the most
popular weapons of terrorism. It was used by the Red
Brigades to kill Signor Aldo Moro, and ballistics showed that
it was the same gun which had been used previously to kill
Signor Francesco Coco, the chief prosecutor of Genoa. It has
also been supplied to a number of African countries and
forms an important part of the arsenal of urban guerrillas in
Southern Africa. It has been used particularly by assassination gangs in Johannesburg. It also figured in the cache of
weapons left behind by Carlos in one of his Paris hideouts,
and it was used in the attempted assassination of Princess
Ashraf of Iran in Juan les Pins, September 1977. It is a
standard weapon of the Czech security forces. The cartridge
is unique for weapons made in Communist countries in that
it is of American design.

Assessment This has all the qualities for a weapon of terrorism. It is light and so small it can be easily concealed. It has
an effective rate of fire and is deadly at close range. It can also
be fitted with a highly efficient silencer. The silencer reduces
the effective range to about a hundred yards but as terrorist
operations are rarely carried out at a range of more than ten
yards this is of no consequence. The silencer, apart from
deadening the sound of shooting, has the additional quality
of spreading the shot around, giving the weapon something
of a shotgun characteristic, making a hit more probable. It is
no longer being made; existing stocks are being sold off by
Omnipol.

Heckler and Koch MP 5 (Plate 4)

This sub-machine-gun was developed from the G 3 rifle
which is a standard arm of Germany and thirty-four other

countries. Made at the Heckler and Koch factory outside Stuttgart from designs being developed by the German Army towards the end of the Second World War, the G 3 is also produced in Britain and France. The sub-machine-gun version has become almost as widely used by terrorists. It is particularly favoured by the Baader–Meinhof gang's successors and was used in the kidnapping of Herr Hans-Martin Schleyer in Cologne in September 1977. The MP 5 has been issued to the various police forces of Germany and has also been bought by the security forces of several other nations. Those used in the Schleyer kidnapping, in which three bodyguards and a driver were killed, were among a batch stolen in Switzerland. A drawing of the MP 5 set against the background of a five-pointed star forms the insignia of the Red Army Faction which carried out the kidnapping.

Assessment This conforms to the highest standards of German automatic weapon production. It is probably the most efficient terrorist weapon now in production. It fulfils all the requirements and is particularly suitable for German terrorists because it can be stolen from police armouries, and the ammunition is available in quantity.

Armalite AR–18 (Plate 5)

This American designed rifle is the weapon of the IRA terrorists who lay up in ruined buildings or take over flats with a commanding view and then pump a burst of small, high-velocity rounds into an army vehicle or patrol. Originally produced as the successor to the AR–16, America's standard infantry weapon in Vietnam, it was not adopted by the US Army because so many AR–16s had been produced. It has however been produced commercially in Japan, California and, under licence, by the Sterling Armament Co. in England. One version, the AR–180, which has only a single shot capacity, is on sale as a sporting rifle in both London and New York. The IRA has acquired some of these weapons from Japan but most of them come from the gunshops of New York state where they are bought legitimately and then smuggled in small batches on board ships sailing to Ireland. Some of these AR–180s have been modified by IRA gunsmiths to fire bursts but most remain single-shot guns and are only issued to expert shots who are able to get off three or four aimed rounds very quickly. It is the weapon which has killed more British soldiers than any other in Ulster.

Assessment This weapon's accuracy and the penetrating power of its small bullet make it a deadly weapon. The bullet can penetrate body armour, medium steel plate and steel helmets at 500 yards and inflict a devastating wound. The shock of even a minor wound inflicted by these high velocity rounds can kill. It is, however, too large a weapon to be used in a normal terrorist operation. It must be broken down and smuggled into and out of a firing position by 'gun carriers' and therefore can only be used in Ulster-type situations.

Thompson Sub-machine-gun (Plate 6)

This weapon, which achieved such notoriety as the gangsters' 'Chicago Piano', was originally designed by General John Thompson as a means of breaking the stalemate on the Western Front in the First World War by giving Allied troops portable fire power for their attacks on the well-defended German trenches. His prototype, produced in 1917, was called the 'Trench Broom' but it had not been accepted by the authorities by the time the war ended. Then, despite its gangster phase, it languished until the start of the Second World War when it was put into mass production and used in quantity by the Allies. By then, however, it had become the favourite weapon of the old-style Irish Republican Army gunmen in the trench coat and Tommy Gun era. The IRA has retained its affection for the gun and although it has been replaced by more modern weapons there are still a number of well-oiled Thompsons hidden in rabbit holes and barns throughout Ireland – and some of them are occasionally taken out and used. It is estimated that nearly a million and a half of various types of these guns were made. Also used in London by the Angry Brigade, so far England's only native terrorist movement of the Baader–Meinhof type. It collapsed in 1972, when most of its members were arrested and sent to prison for long terms the following year.

Assessment   A first-class Second World War field weapon which proved extremely effective for house-clearing, it is too big and cumbersome to appeal to modern terrorists. It would seem that only the romanticism of the IRA and the fact that they are available keeps them in use in Ireland. The old-fashioned drum magazines which held either 50 or 100 rounds are still available but these gangster models tended to jam under field conditions and were replaced by straight boxes in the military version.

Sten Sub-machine-gun (Plate 7)

Mass-produced for the British Army and the European resistance movements during the Second World War, over two million Sten guns were produced and its development, the Sterling, is still in service with the British Army. With this great number of weapons spread around the world – thousands were parachuted into occupied Europe – many drifted into the hands of terrorist organisations. They are, however, too large for most urban terrorist work and have largely been replaced by smaller, more efficient automatic weapons in the European and Middle Eastern terrorist groups. The IRA, however, still retains its affection for the Sten. One of them was found among the armoury of the Balcombe Street gang and, like the Tommy Gun, it is brought out of its caches during times of trouble in Ireland. Also used in London by the now defunct Angry Brigade. Models of the Sten range from the mass-produced, crude Mark II, to the rather elegant, wood-stocked and silenced Mark VI. The Mark II is the most common terrorist weapon and the figures on Plate 7 relate to this gun.

Assessment   This excellent mass-produced weapon provides automatic fire at close range but, because it was mass-produced, has several quirks which are still dangerous to its users today. It tends to jam so that it will not fire or, even more disconcerting, jams on full automatic. This was principally because the lips of the stamped metal magazine could easily be damaged. The fault was largely rectified on later models. Another dangerous quirk was that a sharp blow on the butt could jar the bolt out of its safety catch and cause the gun to fire. A number of British soldiers jumping from the backs of lorries and hitting their Sten butts on the road shot the men behind them. Nevertheless, an efficient weapon when used as the Balcombe Street gang did, to spray a crowded restaurant from a passing car.

M1 Carbine (Plate 8)

This Second World War weapon, like the Tommy Gun and the Sten gun, has virtually disappeared from the armouries of terrorism except that of the IRA where it still figures quite prominently. Two of them were among the weapons captured from the Balcombe Street raiders who were the most successful of the Provisional IRA's Active Service Units operating in England. It was developed by the Winchester arms company in a very short time, the design being accepted in October 1941 only one year after the United States Ordnance Department had issued a specification for a light rifle. Production began almost immediately and the huge total of 3,527,827 of various marks of this carbine were made by nine companies.

Assessment This carbine was particularly suited to jungle warfare, being light and handy, and for that reason is also suitable for street fighting. Reliable and safe with no vices, it is a useful weapon for training recruits and is used in that role by the IRA.

Beretta Model 12 Sub-machine-gun (Plate 9)

This compact, accurate weapon is the latest of the Beretta series of sub-machine-guns and is issued to commando units of the Italian Army. It has also been sold to countries in Africa, South America and the Middle East. Two of these were among the equipment used by the Carlos gang to mount the raid on OPEC headquarters in Vienna. Carlos carried one of them and the other was used by Hans-Joachim Klein who was seriously wounded when a bullet from one of the guards hit the magazine of his Beretta, fragmented, and riddled his stomach.

Assessment This weapon ranks with the Czech Skorpion as one of the most efficient automatic weapons. It is simple, elegant, has two safety systems and with a 40-round magazine gives terrorists a heavy concentration of fire power in an urban guerrilla role. With its metal stock unfolded it can also be used effectively at longer ranges.

Astra .357 Magnum (Plate 10)

This is the Big Bertha of assassination weapons. Made in Spain, it is on sale commercially in Britain and has been advertised in the *Police Review*, but it can only be bought legally with the proper firearms certificates. The size of its bullet and its tremendous power makes death almost an inevitability if it is used at close range. The Balcombe Street gang used it to kill the right-wing propagandist Ross Mc-Whirter in 1975 – because he had offered a reward of £50,000 for the capture of the 'Active Service Unit' which was terrorising London. This particular gun was found in the Balcombe Street arsenal and was matched by ballistics experts. A similar gun was used to murder businessman Alan Quartermaine while he was being driven home in Chelsea in 1974. Ballistics tests show that the gun that killed Quartermaine was used to cover the retreat of an IRA squad after a bomb attack on the Naval and Military Club in Piccadilly in December 1974.

Assessment This brutally efficient weapon's only drawback is its size. It is the most powerful handgun in the terrorist armoury.

M52 Pistol (Plate 11)

Another well-made, reliable weapon designed and made by the Czechs who seem determined to remain independent of the Soviet's armouries. Has been phased out of front-line service in Czechoslovakia and passed on to various 'liberation groups'. Carlos had a number of these weapons in his various caches in London and Paris. He used one of them to kill Michel Moukharbel, the friend he thought had betrayed him, and two French police inspectors, and seriously wound Commissaire Jean Herranz in the shooting in the Rue Toullier when he was being arrested in a girl friend's flat.

Assessment   At the close ranges at which terrorists are taught to use pistols, any reliable weapon is just as effective as another when it comes to killing. Where the M52 differs, however, is in its extremely powerful cartridge which gives it a muzzle velocity of more than twice that of an old-fashioned British service revolver. One of the shots which killed Moukharbel as he was lying on the floor passed through his body, the floorboards, the ceiling of the flat below, a moulded plastic table and then buried itself so deeply in another set of floorboards that it was impossible to dig out. It is an assassin's weapon.

Browning High Power Pistol (Plate 12)

This is probably the best known of all the automatic pistols. Designed in 1925 by the gun genius John Moses Browning it was used in various versions throughout the Second World War by the Western Allies and was also made in Belgium for the special use of the SS. Many thousands have been produced and it has drifted into general use throughout the world. It was a gun of this type which Carlos fired at Teddy Sieff, President of Marks & Spencer, in December 1973. Mr Sieff was lucky that Carlos did not use the Czech M52, the other pistol in his armoury, for although the Browning is high powered, Sieff's strong front teeth absorbed the impact of the bullet and it came to rest a fraction of an inch away from his jugular vein. If Carlos had used the M52 its even higher powered cartridge would probably have taken the Zionist leader's head off. Ballistic tests showed that the Browning found in Carlos's London cache was the gun which had been used in the Sieff operation. Gudrun Ensslin of Baader–Meinhof was carrying one of these guns when she was arrested in a boutique in Hamburg.

Assessment   This reliable, effective weapon for close-range work is easily available and there is no difficulty in acquiring suitable ammunition. One of its advantages is the large capacity of its magazine which holds thirteen rounds.

Makarov Pistol (Plate 13)

This is the Communist equivalent of the Browning pistol and is in general service with the Russian-supplied armies of Eastern Europe and Soviet client nations. It is also made by China. Like the Browning, many thousands have been made and it is now in general use throughout the world. It has come into terrorist hands particularly through the Arab terrorist organisations which have been supplied from the Soviet arsenals. The most spectacular operation in which it has been used was the Carlos-led assault on OPEC headquarters in Vienna on 21 December 1975. Each of the six-strong kidnap team carried a Makarov as a personal weapon along with a mixed bag of sub-machine-guns, grenades and explosives. Gabrielle Krocher-Tiedemann, one of the German Baader–Meinhoff gang who took part in this operation, carried two. With them she murdered two men, an Austrian policeman and the bodyguard of the Iraqi oil minister. Carlos used his Makarov to kill a senior member of the Libyan delegation who grappled with him and almost succeeded in wresting his sub-machine-gun from him. Carlos, at the time of writing, is still alive. Gabrielle was arrested gun in hand by Swiss police on the French frontier in 1977.

Assessment   This is a solid reliable piece of work. Simple to use, it proved its worth as a close-range weapon of terrorism in Vienna.

Tokarev (TT-33) (Plate 14)

This Soviet pistol has now been replaced by the Makarov in the Eastern European countries but is still effective and is used by many Asian Communist countries with numerous examples filtering through to Arab terror groups. One variant, the 9 mm Parabellum Tokagypt, has a curious history. It was made in Hungary and supplied in large quantities to President Nasser when he was seeking the arms refused him by Secretary of State Dulles. The Egyptians were, however, not too keen on it and deliveries were halted. But it was a powerful weapon, accurate at long range, and as there was no comparable 9 mm Parabellum being made in the United States, American arms dealers contracted to buy the surplus stocks. The guns were then stamped with the name 'Firebird'. But once again the sale went wrong when the US government rescinded the import licences. The Firebirds were then put on the commercial market in Europe and a large consignment found its way to the Arabs. It was these pistols on which Ulrike Meinhof and Andreas Baader were taught to shoot at an Arab training camp in Jordan and which eventually became the standard weapon in the Baader-Meinhof armoury. A number of Firebirds were bought by gang member Rolf Pohle from German gunshops. He used forged papers and licences but was eventually caught when an arms dealer in Ulm became suspicious of his papers.

Assessment This is an old-fashioned pistol in the classical style, but despite its military obsolescence it is still an effective weapon of terrorism – as the Baader-Meinhof gang has proved.

Walther P38 (Plate 15)

This pistol is so popular with the Italian Red Brigade group of terrorists that they have become known as the 'P Thirtyeighters'. In 1975 they started a clandestine journal entitled *Mai più Senza Fusile* ('Never without a gun') and the P38 was that gun. It has been used in kidnappings and particularly in the crippling shootings in which the Red Brigade specialises in which victims – right-wing journalists, lawyers, policemen, etc. – are ambushed and shot in the legs.

Assessment This is a modern weapon, in service with the German armed forces, and is available in a commercial version. It is simple to operate and works effectively under most operational conditions. It is a good all-round weapon.

Smith and Wesson Revolver (Plate 16)

Nearly a million of these revolvers were produced from 1940 to 1945 and they became a standard weapon of the British Forces. It was also issued to police forces in England and Ireland. A large number of them have come into the possession of the IRA and they have been used in many assassinations. Two of them were found among the armoury of the Balcombe Street gang. One of the gang, Edward Butler, who was later sent to prison for life, always carried a .38. 'I would not go shopping without it. I carried it everywhere.' It is a favourite weapon of the 'kneecappers', for with its low muzzle velocity it cripples without destroying.

Assessment It used to be said by cynical weapons instructors in the British Army that the best way of bring down an enemy with one of these revolvers was to throw it at him. Certainly it takes an expert shot to hit a man at anything over ten yards. Nevertheless, at short range this is a reliable and effective weapon and there have been many funerals in Ireland to prove it.

RGD–5 Anti-personnel Hand Grenade (Plate 17)

This modern Russian grenade was used by the FLOSY terrorists in Aden in their attacks on the British Army and the sight of one of these smooth-skinned apple-green bombs rolling towards a patrol along an alley in the Crater was always unpleasant. It was used by the Viet Cong and also by Carlos and his gang during the raid on the OPEC headquarters in Vienna. Hans-Joachim Klein threw one of them at the policemen on guard at OPEC shortly before he was wounded in the stomach by a ricochet off the butt of his sub-machine-gun. Those used in Aden were made in China and supplied to FLOSY by Peking.

Assessment Light, this grenade can be thrown for some 35 to 40 yards and with its killing radius of 18 to 22 yards is an effective weapon. Its egg-shaped steel body has a serrated liner which bursts into a pattern of killing fragments. Deadly in a confined space.

SAM 7 Strela (Arrow) (Plate 18)

The SAM 7, translated, is the seventh type of surface-to-air missile produced by the Soviet Union. It is also known by the NATO code-name of Grail but achieved its fame as SAM 7 along with the SAM 2 and SAM 6 in shooting down Israeli aircraft during the Yom Kippur War in October 1973. Its use by terrorists was first revealed earlier that year when Italian police raided a top floor flat at Ostia just three miles along the main flight path from Rome's airport and there found two SAM 7s hidden in a wardrobe.

Assessment This hand-held anti-aircraft weapon is similar to Western missiles such as the American Redeye and the British Blowpipe and like them was developed for battlefield use by individual soldiers to protect units against low-level strafing. Its infra-red guidance control automatically homes in on the heat given off by the attacking aircraft's engine. It can be confused by electronic counter-measures and evasive action by high-speed fighters but would be deadly against big jet liners approaching slowly along a flight path. Its drawback is that its high explosive warhead is not particularly powerful and a well-built aircraft could, if not hit in a vital area, survive its explosion. Its advantage as a terrorist anti-aircraft weapon is that it can be carried around in the back seat of a car and fired whenever a target comes within range. All airports must now take note of the possibility of its use. At Heathrow regular Army exercises are held on the assumption that terrorists armed with SAM 7s are mounting an attack.

M26 Grenade (Plate 19)

This is a standard American Army weapon, known as a fragmentation grenade because of its coiled inner liner which is notched to fragment when the grenade explodes and so cause the maximum number of casualties. This has given rise to its own language; American troops in Vietnam who thought that their officers were becoming too keen in their search for a fight with the Viet Cong were apt to throw an M26 into the officer's fox hole. This became known as 'fragging'. This grenade became notorious as a terrorist weapon after a large number were stolen by the Baader–Meinhof gang in 1971 from the US Army base at Miesau in Germany. They were then distributed to various terrorist organisations throughout Europe. They were used by the Japanese Red Army in their occupation of the French embassy in the Hague in September 1974; by Carlos when he killed two and wounded thirty-four uninvolved customers in his attack on Le Drugstore in Paris designed to coincide with the Japanese occupation of the embassy; and were carried by his gang during the OPEC raid in December 1975. The use of this stolen batch of grenades, traceable by their serial numbers, enabled the security forces of Europe to connect the links between terrorist groups as the grenades were passed on from one to another.

Assessment The notched inner lining of this grenade, coiled under tension, makes it a deadly anti-personnel weapon, ideal for terrorist use in crowded places where the maximum number of casualties can be inflicted and the maximum amount of terror caused. It is provided with secure safety devices and its weight of 16 oz gives it the right balance for throwing.

RPG – 7 Portable Rocket-launcher (Plate 20)

This Russian weapon is the artillery of terrorism. It was used extensively by the Viet Cong and became feared by the American Army both in its role as an anti-personnel fragmentation weapon and as an anti-tank rocket which could blow the turret off a modern tank. It has been supplied to the Rhodesian rebel organisations and to the various Palestinian groups. In purely terrorist terms it was used on two occasions by Carlos' gang in Paris when they attempted to destroy Israeli passenger jets on the runway at Orly. It is possible that this was the weapon which a mixed German and Palestinian 'commando' attempted to use against an El Al plane at Nairobi Airport in 1976, another raid which was foiled by an Israeli secret service tip-off. They have also been used against British Army posts in Ulster by the Provisional IRA, a small batch being supplied by Colonel Gaddafi. A much larger consignment was seized when the arms ship *Claudia* was captured off the Irish coast on the last stage of its run from Libya.

Assessment   This is not a particularly accurate weapon, especially at long range and in high winds. Nevertheless it can do a fearsome amount of damage. It is simple to make – Al Fatah has its own RPG factory – and easy to fire, but care must be taken to make sure no one is standing behind the weapon when it is fired, as the burning gases from the rocket motor can do almost as much damage as the grenade itself. It gives an individual the ability to deliver an explosive charge the equivalent of a medium gun shell and then pick up the launcher and walk away with another half a dozen projectiles slung in a bandolier across his shoulders. In urban guerrilla terms it gives the terrorist an artillery capacity denied the security forces in the early stages of a confrontation.

M60 General Purpose Machine-gun (Plate 21)

A great fuss was made early in 1978 when the IRA paraded one of its newly acquired M60s, standard equipment in the

American Army. Between three and six of these machine-guns were believed to have been smuggled into Ulster from the Middle East via Cyprus and Antwerp concealed aboard a tanker. They were displayed during a parade marking the sixth anniversary of 'Bloody Sunday' (when the British Army opened fire during a riot in Londonderry and killed thirteen). One M60 had already been used in January in an ambush of three Royal Ulster constables in Londonderry. The feeling about this blatant display was that it was done to demonstrate that the Provisional IRA was not yet finished – a view which had been increasingly expressed by the government. Certainly the appearance of the M60 gave force to the Provos claim that they were receiving shipments of sophisticated weapons, and were by no means at the end of their tether. By the middle of 1978 two of these weapons had been captured by the security forces, one in Eire and one in Ulster.

Assessment   This is an excellent infantry weapon but it has serious drawbacks as a weapon of terror. Most terrorist weapons are used in ambush and in urban surroundings. The M60 has too fast a rate of fire, is too heavy and too long to be a successful weapon of urban warfare. It could be used by the IRA in open country firefights but even there it has its drawbacks, for in order to change a hot barrel the Number Two on the gun is issued with a 'Mitten Asbestos MI942', which he uses to pull the barrel out while the Number One presses down on the stock with his right hand while lifting the fore-end with his left. Such complications do not accord well with the tactics of terror operations. An essential of this type of warfare is that a weapon should be light, simple and not need more than one man to handle it. One is left with the feeling that anything an M60 can do in this role, an Armalite can do better. It is in fact a weapon of propaganda rather than terror.

The Japanese security forces, clearing up after the latest student attempts to block the opening of the new Tokyo airport, discovered several examples of a new weapon of terror, a sophisticated 'cattle prod', a two-pronged electrical staff about three feet long connected to a current-producing belt pack. This weapon can deliver a charge of some 500 volts and is capable of knocking a man out and, in some cases, of killing. This could be an effective weapon in the type of mass street battles in which the Japanese specialise.

An even more extraordinary weapon was used to kill the Bulgarian defector Georgi Markov in London in September 1978. Markov, who broadcast details of Bulgarian leaders' sexual habits, fell ill and died after complaining of being jabbed in the thigh while waiting for a bus on Waterloo Bridge. At first it was thought that he had been killed by a poisoned umbrella but an autopsy showed that he had been shot by a surgical 'gun' normally used to inject radioactive pellets into cancer victims. In Markov's case the gun was used to fire a tiny, poison-packed pellet into the back of his leg. A similar pellet was extracted from the back of another Bulgarian defector–broadcaster, Vladimir Kostov, who was attacked in Paris but recovered. The authorities know the identity of the man who carried out the attacks and know that he was ordered to do so by the Bulgarian secret service.

7 | The Weapons of Terror – Bombs

The modern terrorist's bomb still fulfils the same function as the crude device of 'the Professor': it is used to kill, or threaten to kill, and thereby destroy the economic and social life of a country, to instil fear; in fact, to terrorise. But the bombs themselves, their mechanisms and their explosives have become far more efficient. They are easier to make, safer to handle, can be made much smaller, and can be triggered by a variety of ingenious methods, thus enabling them to be used in circumstances which were out of reach of nineteenth-century terrorists. Terrorists of that period could derail a train but they did not have at their mercy Jumbo jets carrying 400 people at 600 miles an hour 35,000 feet above the ground. The derailing of a train could kill a number of people but when an airliner is blown out of the sky everybody dies. So not only are today's bombs more efficient, they are also capable, because of the development of mass air travel, of causing far greater losses in human and material terms and of instilling a maximum of fear. It is this potential which makes the aerial hijacker's slab of plastic explosive such a powerful weapon.

In this chapter we propose to show how the modern bombers go about their business. If the information is not as detailed as some of our readers might wish it is because we have set out to report how things are done and not to provide a textbook on how to make bombs. Almost every schoolboy knows how to mix gunpowder and pack it into a cardboard tube to make a firework, quite a number know how to make explosives out of fertiliser, and most men who have served in the army know how to handle plastic, gun cotton, fuses and grenades. There is a great deal of expert knowledge freely available. We do not wish to make it any easier for people to construct bombs but intend to demonstrate how the bombers use their explosive expertise to attack society.

One of the difficult tasks of the security forces is to cut the terrorists' supply of explosives. When the terrorists are supported by countries with diplomatic representation this becomes almost impossible, because those countries which actively encourage terrorism have no compunction about using the diplomatic bag to smuggle weapons and explosives to their surrogate warriors. Libya has been particularly to blame in this respect. Colonel Gaddafi has often used his diplomatic missions abroad to supply Soviet-made arms and explosives to 'anti-imperialist' terror groups in many different countries. The embassy in Rome on various occasions has been very busy indeed in this field.

The advantage of such a supply route is that once the supporting country has decided to send arms, the terrorists do not need to go through any risky process to obtain them, the lines of communication are secured by diplomatic usage. The explosives supplied are of a military type, usually plastic, which is stable and can be moulded to any required shape. A circle of it can be used to cut down a tree, or it can be wrapped in a destructive embrace round the exhaust pipe of a car.

Palestinian terrorist groups are also heavily involved in the supply of arms and explosives to groups which support their cause. The favourite explosive is again military plastic. The stability of this explosive makes it easy for it to be smuggled – sometimes moulded into innocent shapes like children's putty – by boat, car, even the rucksacks of travelling students. This last method was the one used by the Scottish anarchist Stuart Christie. He was arrested in Madrid in August 1967 carrying five packets of plastic (French in origin, not Arab), seven detonators and chemicals for making explosives. They were to be used by Spanish anarchists in an attempt to blow up General Franco at a football match. It was a military type of plastic, RDX, which was used in the bomb planted on the London Post Office Tower's observation platform in October 1971. Responsibility for this bombing was claimed by the 'Kilburn Battalion of the IRA' and experts who examined the remnants of the bomb and its timing device saw no reason to disagree with this claim. It was a typical IRA-type delayed-action bomb.

The second main source of supply is the theft of commercial explosives from mines and quarries. It is a simple matter to raid the magazines of isolated workings and such raids, often with the connivance of sympathisers on the workforce, have provided much of the explosive used by the IRA and the South American movements. The Angry Brigade used French commercial explosives in their bombs. These explosives, Nitrotex, Nitromite and Gomme L, were handed over to women couriers by French sympathisers and smuggled into Britain on the cross-Channel ferries. At that time there was no means of tracing bomb-fillings except back to its manufacturers. But since then, security forces have met with some success, especially in Britain and Ireland, in making the source of commercial explosives identifiable by the insertion into each batch of either a combination of coloured threads or certain chemical compounds which can be identified after an explosion and so traced back to the point where it was switched from legal to illegal use. This device helps to make things more difficult for terrorists.

The third main source of supply is that most peaceful of pursuits, gardening. It is here that we come into an area where it is best not to publish too many details, but it is commonly known that the IRA makes a large proportion of its bomb-filling from a mixture of certain types of chemical fertiliser and diesel fuel. In an agricultural society such as Ireland it is impossible to control the sale of large quantities of both fertiliser and of diesel fuel for tractors. And this type of mixture will always be available to the bombers although the manufacturers are being urged to cut the explosive ingredients to as low a proportion as possible. The disadvantage of this type of explosive is that it is quite difficult to urge into detonation and needs a priming charge of gun cotton or a couple of sticks of gelignite. The advantage is that it can be obtained and transported in bulk and is therefore ideal for the 100 lb and 200 lb car bombs which have caused such damage in Northern Ireland.

Another way of obtaining explosives is by raiding military establishments. But any terrorist who does this must be prepared for a pitched battle if things go wrong with his plans. It is a tactic pursued more in South America than anywhere else. An even more desperate method, usually only attempted by guerrilla movements in the initial stages of their development, is to remove the filling from unexploded shells and bombs. This is a most hazardous method and those who practise it are more likely to meet a sticky end than their enemies.

Having obtained the explosive, the terrorists need to build it into an 'infernal device' and provide the fuse to set it off. Fuses come under four main headings: flame; chemical; electric; and mechanical.

Flame fuses are probably the least used because their comparatively fast burning time allows the bomber little time to get clear of the explosion and because the burning fuse provides visible evidence that something nasty is going on. Military or commercial fuse of various types provides a fixed burning rate per foot, so that the time between ignition and explosion can be judged by cutting the fuse to a certain length. It is fitted into a detonator, normally a metal tube about two inches long filled with a sensitive explosive, usually fulminate of mercury. The detonator is fitted into a priming charge of explosive which is buried in the main body of the explosive. When the flame reaches the detonator it explodes, setting off the priming charge which in turn sets off the main charge. Such detonators can also be exploded by firing a cap similar to that used in the base of a bullet cartridge, or by passing an electric current from a battery through a fuse wire or a wire filament such as that used in a light bulb.

Chemical fuses are basically similar to the fuse used by 'the Professor', but modern methods call for a phial of acid to be crushed inside something which provides a time lag. The most popular is a rubber contraceptive. The acid gradually burns through the rubber before it comes in contact with the chemical and produces the spark which sets off the explosive. Metal containers can also be used. A rough guess can be made about the time which the acid will take to do its work, but this is an inexact form of time fuse because it is almost impossible to judge precisely the strength of the acid, the strength of the container and therefore the length of time the process will take. And if the contraceptive is faulty, the result could be even more embarrassing than if it were used for its proper purpose. In their early bombs the Angry Brigade used a combined chemical-mechanical fuse in which sulphuric acid dropped slowly on to a retaining tape. This burned through and released a striker.

Electric devices are the most common form of time fuse. They involve the use of clocks and watches wired so that when the hands reach a certain position on the clock face they touch terminals connected to a battery which then, with the circuit completed, sends a charge of electricity through the detonator and explodes the bomb. Baader–Meinhof used clockwork egg-timers to provide the spark for some of their bombs, and in Belfast the IRA bought up a supply of the clockwork buzzers which tell you when your time is up at the parking meter. Both these devices have their limitations because of the lack of flexibility in their timing sequence, but they work efficiently enough as long as a delay of no more than an hour is needed.

Another method is that familiar to moviegoers of wires strung from an explosive charge and connected to a plunger which when depressed produces a current and sets off the bomb. This type is commonly used to set off heavy charges placed under roads, in culverts and hedges or in buildings. A plunger is not always necessary. The charge can be exploded by completing the circuit on a battery. But a disadvantage of this system is that it requires wires to be trailed through a building or across fields and they can be detected by security patrols. Also, the bombers need to be within visual distance of the bomb so as to set it off at the correct time and there they are liable to capture by pursuers.

A more remote and therefore safer form of electric fuse is the radio fuse. By using the same system as that used for controlling model planes and boats, the bomber can send a signal which will explode his bomb instantaneously. Depending on the strength of the signal the operator could be miles away, receiving the order to fire by telephone or by some form of visual signal.

Another form of electric signal was used by the Israelis when they killed Mahmoud Hamshari, the PLO representative in Paris, after the Munich massacre in 1972. They staked out his apartment, noting the time when his French wife, Marie-Claude, took their daughter, Amina, to nursery school. One Israeli, posing as an Italian journalist, made contact with Hamshari on the pretext of interviewing him. While they were meeting at a cafe another member of the execution squad took an impression of the lock on the door of the apartment. The 'Italian' arranged a further meeting with Hamshari and this time, using a key made from the impression, the second Israeli walked into the apartment and fitted an electronically controlled bomb into the base of Hamshari's telephone. The next day the phone rang just after Mrs Hamshari and Amina had left. Hamshari answered it. A voice at the other end said: 'This is the Italian journalist who has a rendezvous with you today. That's really you, Mr Hamshari?' The Palestinian replied 'Yes, this is Mahmoud Hamshari.' As soon as he said that the telephone blew up in his face. He lived long enough to tell the police what had happened and they were able to piece together the electronic device which had killed him. The trigger mechanism was based on the same sort of mechanism as that fitted to scrambler telephones.

Mechanical fuses at their simplest are activated by pulling out a safety pin which releases a spring which in turn either causes a firing pin to strike a detonator as in a hand grenade, or closes an electrical circuit or, by friction, produces a spark. These fuses can be set off by opening a door, lifting the lid of a box of chocolates, or opening a car boot, an action in fact which involves the movement of some component.

Pressure fuses are another simple form of mechanical detonation. A bomb may be set under a car seat or a floor board or a mattress so that the pressure of the victim's body will release a plunger and so explode the bomb. A more sophisticated pressure bomb is that used in aircraft. These bombs work on the barometric principle and are so delicate that the change in pressure exerted on the bomb as the aircraft rises through the atmosphere sets it off.

The decision on what type of fuse to use is dictated by several factors: what fuses are available, the level of expertise of the bomb-maker, and what type of bomb he wants to make. There is no point in making time-bombs if there are no delayed-action fuses available. Similarly it is futile to make a bomb to throw into a crowded restaurant if it cannot be fitted with an instantaneous fuse. It is the marriage of the explosive, the case, the fuse and the timing that makes the perfect bomb.

At its simplest, the modern bomb is still crude. The IRA uses several sticks of gelignite or dynamite bound together and set off by a short length of combustible fuse. These bombs are often wrapped with six inch nails or coach bolts which form a lethal burst of shrapnel when the bombs explode. Other simple bombs are constructed of lengths of pipe filled with pieces of metal junk, which with a certain grim humour the IRA calls 'shipyard confetti'. The Baader–Meinhof gang used army water bottles as outer cases for their early bombs, and they too made pipe-bombs, 7½-inch sections of steel pipe 6½ inches in diameter. As Jillian Becker describes them in *Hitler's Children*, her excellent account of the gang, 'each of these had a bottom plate welded on to it and a top plate with a narrower pipe sticking out into which a screwing thread was cut'. Pipe terminating nuts were then screwed into the narrower pipe and 'the detonators were fitted into these nuts and connected on a circuit to a 50 volt dry-cell battery via an egg-timer giving a maximum delay of sixty minutes'. Baader–Meinhof also used a larger version, converting gas cylinders into bombs.

The problem for terrorists in making these crude devices is that they are so simple that every raw recruit thinks he is a professional, and before they learn the errors of their ways it is too late, they have 'scored an own goal' and blown themselves to pieces.

The use of commercial explosive which has started to degrade, to sweat, is one cause of accidents. And so, astonishingly enough, is the practice of smoking while making bombs. One theory is that it was a carelessly handled cigarette which caused the Weathermen to blow themselves out of existence when they were making bombs in their Greenwich Village headquarters in 1970. Three of them died and although a reconstituted Weather Underground has carried out some bombings since then, they no longer pose a serious threat.

But the greatest cause of 'own goals' is clumsiness when setting the electrical systems on time-bombs. It is only too easy to bring the terminals into contact with each other. It was because of this that IRA experts instituted a safety device so that the young people they sent to plant bombs could not blow themselves up. This device was a simple pin which had to be withdrawn before the clock started to tick. But many of the youngsters were in so much of a hurry to get away or were so frightened of the bomb itself that they neglected to take out the pin. The expert instructors then attached tags to the pins ordering the bombers to return the pins in order to prove that they had set the bomb properly. This had unfortunate results for at least one of the experts when a young bomber still forgot to take out the pins: when the army found his unexploded bombs the pins very conveniently gave them the address to call on.

In their campaign designed to wreck the economy of Ulster the IRA have learnt that fire is their best friend. With explosives, and especially detonators, becoming more difficult to obtain, they have turned away from big, destructive bombs to easily concealed small ones which they surround with tins of petrol. One of their favourite devices is an incendiary bomb made out of a tape recorder cassette. Such machines are comparatively easy to smuggle past the Army and police searchers, and to conceal in piles of inflammable merchandise in shops, timed to go off after the store has closed. One rather special incendiary bomb was defused by the army after the IRA had tried to plant it at Fortwilliam Golf Club. It consisted of a golf bag filled with five pounds of commercial explosive, a timing unit, incendiary mix, three petrol containers and one pound of firelighters. Another of the tricks the IRA have developed is to make use of the safety mesh which encloses most business premises in Ulster. They build a hook into the bomb and then hang the bomb from the safety mesh.

The car bomb, filled with explosives and made dangerous to handle by booby traps, is very much an IRA weapon. A car stuffed with 200 lb of explosives can cause absolute devastation in town centres. Sometimes the IRA bombers have their little jokes. In 1977 they hijacked a whole fleet of bakery vans. They filled several with explosives which, when they went off, showered Belfast with loaves of bread, but they left the others, locked but harmless, on street corners. Each one had to be dealt with – usually by the army blowing off their doors with a controlled explosion – and the resulting cost and disruption was considerable. The army in Belfast has developed a number of techniques for dealing with such incidents. They have dogs trained to smell out explosives and chemical devices, 'Sniffers', which perform the same function. They also developed the 'Goliath' which looks like a large toy tank and is remotely controlled. This invention is used to inspect a suspect vehicle and, if necessary, blow open doors or destroy what could be a bomb by firing a shotgun at it.

The other common form of car bomb is the device concealed inside a car designed to kill the driver. There are a number of types, the simplest being the 'Mafia' type which is a bundle of explosive wired to the starting system so that when the ignition is switched on car and driver are destroyed. This was used so often that most people at risk prudently inspected their engines before switching on. This precaution was circumvented by attaching plastic to exhaust pipes which exploded when the pipes grew hot enough, or, as in the case of Mohammed Boudia, who was PFLP's chief operative in Europe, putting a pressure bomb under his seat. He was killed by an Israeli hit team and his death had the unforeseen result of bringing Carlos on to the terrorist scene, for Carlos, 'sleeping' in London, was called upon to replace Boudia.

Professor Gordon Hamilton-Fairley, the cancer specialist, was killed in October 1975 when he bent down to
examine a suspicious package under his neighbour's car. It
was designed not for him, but to kill his neighbour, Tory MP
Hugh Fraser, a forthright opponent of the IRA, when he
drove off.

Another way of killing a man in a car is the 'big bang',
designed to destroy a vehicle as it passes a certain spot. The
British Army has become only too familiar with mines buried
in the roadside. This is an account of one such mine as
reported in *Visor*, the army newspaper in Ulster:

A two-day clearance operation, involving an overnight 'stake-out'
of a suspected explosive device within fifteen hundred metres of
the border resulted in the successful neutralisation of a one
hundred and fifty pound terrorist landmine.

The device, dug into a roadside verge, consisted of home-made
explosive packed into three beer kegs. Each keg, apart from
containing fifty to eighty pounds of explosive, had a five to ten
pound booster charge attached and all three kegs were linked to
explode simultaneously. The mine was to have been electrically
detonated and a command wire was discovered, partially buried
along a hedgerow, which led to the firing point concealed in a
nearby derelict building.

The authors of this book, on one of their visits to Ulster,
landed by helicopter close to the South Armagh border soon
after a similar device, made out of a milk churn, had been
destroyed by the army. It had made an impressive hole in the
bank and the road and shattered windows over a wide area.

Often the army is not lucky enough to discover these
ambushes before they are sprung, and the resulting explosions have been known to somersault ten-ton Saracen armoured personnel carriers.

The IRA have a special liking for culvert bombs, packing
explosives into the drains which run under so many Irish
roads. The army has become very suspicious of these culverts and always checks them before driving across. The
Israelis used to do exactly the same in the early 1970s when
Palestinians would cross the border and lay culvert mines.
But the Israelis had a special device for doing it – a girder
sticking out of the front of an armoured car with a steel plated

seat welded to the girder's end. The crew members of the armoured car would then take it in turns to perch out there and study the road surface for mines and wires. It was truly a hot seat.

It was a matter of shame and stupidity that similar expertise was not used to guard Christopher Ewart-Biggs, the British Ambassador to Dublin who was assassinated by a culvert bomb 180 yards from his official residence in July 1976. There were only two ways for the ambassador to travel before he reached main roads. There is no doubt that a routine inspection before he left the house would have found the mine, which consisted of at least 100 lb of explosives and was detonated by wire from a wooded hill some 300 yards from the road.

Another man killed by a version of the culvert bomb was the Premier of Spain, Admiral Carrero Blanco in December 1973. He made the mistake of travelling by the same route every day. His killers took a basement room on that route and dug a tunnel twenty feet under the road. They planted three charges of nearly 40 lb each under the street, timed to explode at intervals of a tenth of a second to match the speed of his car. Red sighting marks were painted on a wall facing the terrorists' house so that they would know when to fire. One of the assassins sat in a window with a walkie-talkie watching the marks. When he gave the command another pressed the plunger and Carrero Blanco was blown, literally, over a church.

A less sure way of killing a man, but one that when widely practised causes much alarm, is the letter or parcel bomb. Richard Clutterbuck, in *Living With Terror*, tells how to recognise a letter bomb.

It is likely to be at least a quarter, and more probably, half an inch thick – so it will feel like a paper-back book or perhaps a folded report or pamphlet, rather than a simple letter. It will, however, probably feel heavier than if it contained the same thickness of paper. The explosive may 'sweat' causing greasy marks and there may be a smell of marzipan. The package will also bend in a different way, either giving a suspicious feeling of rigidity or an equally suspicious feeling of lack of elasticity – in other words, it may have the 'dead' feeling of putty or clay, rather than the springy feeling of a pamphlet or a sheaf of papers.

Such a device, containing only three or four ounces of explosive, can kill if it is opened close to the body. Dr Ami Shachori, the Israeli Agricultural Attaché in London was killed by one in September 1972. It was a thick buff-covered envelope measuring six inches by three. It exploded as he opened it. Most of the blast funnelled downwards towards his desk so that he escaped the initial explosion, but by the worst possible piece of luck he was killed by a splinter from his shattered desk.

That bomb and most of the others that were sent at that time to Israelis and Zionist sympathisers all round the world, was set off by a mousetrap-style mechanism. A spring attached to the detonator is folded back when it is put into the envelope and is held in position by the pressure of the closed envelope. When the envelope is opened, the pressure is released and the spring strikes the detonator head. Another method of fusing a letter bomb is to use an incendiary adhesive which sparks when the envelope is opened. Parcel bombs, because they contain more explosive and give less evidence of their contents are more efficient. A batch of gaily wrapped Christmas parcels looking like boxes of chocolates were sent to Israelis in 1972 and were found to contain eight ounces of explosive – more than enough to kill.

The Israelis are themselves experts in the use of letter and parcel bombs. Bassam Abu Sherif, spokesman for PFLP, is hideously scarred – the result of opening a similar box of chocolates – and a number of other Palestinian officials have been killed and wounded by letter bombs.

A most bizarre form of letter bomb came to light in October 1972 when a Dutchman of Jewish origin received a letter posted in Karlsruhe, West Germany. He was suspicious and passed the letter to the police, who found it was not a letter bomb but a poison gas bomb. It contained 40 grams of cyanide in powder form. In chemical reaction with the oxygen in the air it would have produced cyanide gas.

Another terrifying development in bomb-making was perfected by the International Spanish Communist Party, a Maoist group, who in January 1976 taped a bomb to the chest of Dr Joaquin Viola Sauret, a former mayor of Barcelona. The bomb was booby trapped so that it could only be safely removed when instructions were sent by the terrorists. These instructions were not to be given until certain demands had been met. But the bomb went off prematurely, killing Dr Sauret and his wife and injuring one of the terrorists. It was similar to one which had killed Señor Jose Harques, a rich Catalan industrialist in May 1977. He refused to believe that it would explode, tore it off his chest and died.

Perhaps the most cynical form of terror device is the barometric bomb. This appalling weapon is designed to destroy an aircraft in flight and therefore everybody on board, innocent men, women and children, even sympathisers to the terrorists' cause, all die. In August 1972, two Palestinians in Rome, Adnam Ali Hashan and Ahmed Zaid, picked up two English girls on holiday. The girls fell for the handsome Palestinians who suggested they should all go to Israel. The girls agreed and the Arabs bought them tickets to Lod Airport and gave them a tape recorder. At the last moment the two men, who were posing as Iranians, said they had to fly to Tehran to collect money. They arranged to meet in Jerusalem. The girls, fortunately, did not carry the tape recorder on to the plane as hand luggage but had it put in the hold with their other luggage. It was filled with explosive and its barometric firing device was set to explode when the plane reached a certain height. It exploded precisely as it was designed to do, but the force of the explosion was contained by the armoured hold, built into all El Al planes following tests with explosions in mid-air over the desert. The damaged plane landed safely, and when the two girls told their story, Hashan and Zaid were arrested in Italy. But like all captured terrorists they were an embarrassment to the authorities and were soon given 'provisional liberty' on the curious grounds that the explosive charge they used 'was not adequate to destroy the airliner'. They disappeared from Italy as soon as the prison gates opened.

Radio-fired bombs are the latest to come from the bombers' bag of tricks, and at first sight they seem to have the advantage over all other bombs of being absolutely under the control of the bomber. There is no need for him to set light to a fuse or to start a mechanism which will inevitably fire at a fixed time – unless it is stopped manually – or even to trust the uncertain effect of acid on a contraceptive. He can decide when the explosion is going to take place. He can make adjustments for unforeseen circumstances. He can advance or retard the timing of the explosion. And he can do all this from safety with nothing apparently connecting him with the bomb. He might even be out with his son, playing with his radio controlled aircraft. All he has to do is to send a certain signal and the bomb blows up. There is a drawback, however, for if the security forces are sufficiently adept at signals intelligence, there are ways and means for them to send signals which would ensure that the terrorists were blown up with their own bomb.

And that brings us to booby traps. Almost anything can be booby-trapped. A man's pipe can be booby-trapped so that it blows his head off when he lights it. A dead soldier can have his backside stuffed with explosive so that he blows up the men sent to carry him in. Likely souvenirs, weapons and field glasses, can be booby-trapped so that they explode when picked up. A favourite ploy in Belfast is for a caller to report suspicious activity in an abandoned house. The Army cannot ignore such reports, they must investigate, and booby traps could be anywhere, a trip wire across the door, a mine under a loose floor board, it is as easy as the schoolboy joke of balancing a bucket of water on top of a door. With a sufficiently wild imagination allied to a sober expertise, anything can be booby-trapped. And dealing with the traps involves a tedious, dangerous battle of wits between the bomber and the bomb disposal squads. Occasionally the two sides get to know each other's work very well, even to appreciate the finer points of a good technical piece of work carried out by the opposition.

This war within a war becomes personal when anti-handling devices are included in a bomb's mechanism. They include fuses which are sensitive to x-rays and are designed to explode when suspicious parcels are x-rayed. Another anti-handling device is a photo-electric cell which explodes the bomb when it is exposed to light, either by the opening of a suitcase bomb or when a torch is shone on a bomb hidden in a dark place. Then there are 'trembler' devices which are activated after a bomb has been carried to the place where it is to explode. When it has been set any movement will cause a steel ball to roll or a pendulum to swing, either action completing an electrical circuit and so exploding the bomb. And there are fuses connected to secondary fuses which explode when the first is made harmless and withdrawn. The simplest-looking bomb of a type which the bomb disposal expert has defused many times can be adjusted to contain one or other of these devices. It was in this fashion that the Balcombe Street gang killed bomb disposal expert Captain Roger Goad in August 1975. It is fortunate that there are not many bombers with the expertise to fit these booby traps, but truly, the bomb disposal men earn their pay.

One other type of bomb remains to be discussed, the ultimate: the nuclear bomb. In essence the terrorists' task in constructing a nuclear weapon is the same as that in making a conventional bomb. First he has to acquire the material and then he has to build the bomb.

Of the two tasks the acquisition of the material is the harder. For the fact is that with the information contained in a good university library any reasonably bright student of physics can do the theoretical work. And that is precisely what a 20-year-old student at Massachusetts Institute of Technology did in just five weeks in 1975 using published technical works. He did it in answer to a challenge by an American television programme and the producer of the programme said in stunned disbelief: 'We found it was frightfully easy to design such a bomb. Basically it is simply a matter of bringing two shaped pieces of plutonium together with sufficient force for them to "go critical".' According to evidence given in 1977 at the public enquiry into building a nuclear fuel reprocessing plant at Windscale, Cumbria, only 8 kilogrammes of plutonium is required to produce a bomb big enough to wipe out a city centre. Scientist Dr Kit Pedler, creator of the television *Doomwatch* series, explained in an article in the *Daily Express* of 18 May 1977 that 'if a solution of plutonium nitrate was dried, packed as crystals into two stainless steel mixing bowls and surrounded by ordinary blocks of TNT, a nuclear explosion would probably occur if the critical mass of the nitrate when imploded had been calculated properly'.

The Royal Commission on Environmental Pollution, headed by Sir Brian Flowers, put the technical side of building a 'nuke' into perspective in a report in September 1976 when it said: 'The equipment required would not be significantly more elaborate than that already used by criminal groups engaged in the illicit manufacture of heroin.' In fact the technical know-how is well within the compass of one of the IRA's bomb experts, a point made by the French magazine *L'Express* (27 January–2 February 1975), which presented a scenario of a group of terrorists stealing containers of nitrate of potassium from a factory. 'It is not necessary', the magazine said, 'to be a Nobel prize-winner to extract plutonium from this solution.' And then, in a series of children's-book 'How to do it' panels, it showed how a bomb could be made.

How easy is it then to fulfil the other task, to acquire the explosive material? In 1972 Professor Theodore Taylor undertook a study for the Ford Foundation of the security at six nuclear installations in the United States and he found that plutonium was being carried across the country in ordinary lorries with only two men on board, without an escort and without radio contact. Since he made his report security has been considerably tightened in the United States. But, he insists, it is still not strong enough to stop a determined band of terrorists.

In 1976 a report by the Royal Commission on Environmental Pollution stated that terrorists could make a crude but effective nuclear weapon using stolen plutonium and argued that the government had not appreciated the full implications of this possibility. It also reported that members of the commission who visited nuclear installations in Britain got the impression that not enough attention was given to some aspects of security. We understand that their criticisms centred on the lack of security on shipments of radio-active material. As in America, security arrangements have now been strengthened and the Ministry of Defence is playing a large part in guarding shipments. The greatest danger, according to Sir Brian Flowers, Rector of Imperial College, London, comes from an 'inside job' with the persistent theft of small quantities by someone working in the reprocessing and fabrication plants.

Ralph Lapp, the American nuclear scientist, estimates that a worker taking out twenty pellets of atomic fuel a day for 160 days would accumulate enough plutonium to make a bomb equivalent in power to the one that destroyed Nagasaki.

The blackmail potential of such a weapon is enormous. A leaflet called *Towards a People's Bomb*, which was published in London in 1972 by a London group called Undercurrents, told its readers how to extract plutonium and even published a diagram of a crude bomb. It might have worked, but the implications of its threat were that if it was detonated in the left luggage office in Charing Cross station, it would destroy among other things 'Buckingham Palace, the Houses of Parliament, Scotland Yard and the Elephant and Castle – not to mention vaporising a fair chunk of the River Thames'. What government could resist the demands of a terrorist group if proof was given that a nuclear weapon had been placed in just such a spot? The whole world could be held to ransom.

There are other ways in which nations can be held to ransom or even dealt crippling blows by terrorists and individual madmen. Water supplies could be poisoned, the theft of nerve gases – one minuscule drop of which can kill a man – could create panic, and as we saw at the beginning of 1978, agricultural terrorism could be employed to wreck a nation's economy. The discovery of a few Jaffa oranges injected with mercury had a serious effect on Israel's citrus fruit sales. An organisation which called itself the Arab Revolutionary Army claimed that it was 'poisoning thousands of export-selected oranges before plucking' and 'poisoning thousands of oranges during export preparation'. 'Our aim', it said, 'is not indiscriminately to kill your population, but to sabotage the Israeli economy.' In fact, the oranges were not poisoned in Israel but a few were jabbed with hypodermic syringes filled with the contents of broken thermometers by Palestinian sympathisers in a number of northern European countries.

The fact remains that the people who jabbed the oranges with mercury-filled syringes were able to induce fear. And that is what terrorism is all about. That fear would be multiplied a million times if all the dangers of a nuclear explosion – explosive destruction, fire, radio-active poisoning, the genetic effect on future generations – were used in the cause of terrorism. The 'Big Nuke' is the ultimate weapon of terror.

Tactics and Strategy:
8 | And How Democracy
Fights Back

Although the Euro-Arab terrorist offensive of 1977 proved again that a good deal of the urban terrorist's time is devoted to fund raising, it also demonstrated that the tactics are geared to ensure that the transnational groups should become self-perpetuating. Tactically, the terror club needed to secure the release of Germans, Japanese and Arabs who had been captured in earlier raids. The Japanese Red Army in particular was short of trained operators and the hijacking of one airliner was all that they needed to put them back in business after a two-year respite in their activities. And it was with the co-operation of one powerful Arab group, and with support from the Germans, that they were able to carry it out successfully.

A gang of five experienced terrorists took over a Japanese Airlines DC8 carrying 156 passengers soon after it had taken off from Bombay. They obtained from the Tokyo government the release of six imprisoned terrorists and were paid a ransom of $6 million for the lives of their hostages. It was a classic, successful terrorist operation.

Just to complete the ritual picture, the Japanese and their released comrades made their way to one of the traditional havens for hijackers – Algiers. From there the eleven men and women terrorists were able to make their way back to their base in the Middle East, ready for further action – and with the money to finance it. Part of their wealth was paid into the funds of their backers, the PFLP.

While that operation was taking place, the Red Army

Faction in West Germany, which had already killed a prominent banker and the public prosecutor responsible for the trial of the Baader–Meinhof leaders, kidnapped Hans-Martin Schleyer, an industrialist and leader of the employers' federation. The kidnappers then entered into weeks of negotiations, bargaining his life against the release of their own leaders incarcerated in the fortress prison at Stammheim.

Chancellor Schmidt's government refused to give in and played the long, hard bargaining game, demanding proof that the terrorists did indeed hold their prisoner alive, while encouraging the terrorists by asking a number of Third World countries whether they would agree to the prisoners being delivered to their countries.

Then a dramatic development took place, which demonstrated how the international terrorists have improved their co-ordination and become more sophisticated in their tactics. They increased their pressure on the German government by mounting a new hijack from an entirely different quarter. Four Palestinians, two men and two women of Wadi Hadad's PFLP–Special Operations, operating from Baghdad, seized a Lufthansa Boeing 737 homeward bound from Majorca packed with German tourists and a party of six beauty queens. Demanding the release of the same Baader–Meinhof leaders as the kidnappers of Herr Schleyer, together with two Palestinians held in Turkey (the same pair that the Dutch girl Lidwina Jansen recognised at the Aden training school), they forced the aircraft to fly around the Middle East until finally it landed at Mogadishu in Somalia. There, while the bargaining still continued, the German government ordered a counter-raid, Entebbe style.

This was conducted with great skill and dash by twenty-eight men of the GSG9, the 180-strong anti-terrorist force which had been created and trained for just such an operation. This time it was the terrorists who died. But what was even more important in the long term was the fact that a British Major and an NCO from the Special Air Services Regiment also went to Mogadishu taking with them cardboard-bodied grenades which stun and blind their victims for some six seconds but do no permanent damage. These grenades were developed by the SAS specifically for dealing with hijacks. Here at last was a fine example of co-operation between Western powers in fighting the common enemy. For the SAS men, goggled to protect themselves from the grenades' effect, put the hijackers out of action long enough for the German commandos to have at them and shoot them without harming the passengers. For once the terrorists were literally blinded by science.

It was a famous victory which heartened the anti-terrorist forces who had had little success since Entebbe. Yet it was only one battle won, and much remained to be done. Although the forces of terror had been beaten, they were still able to strike back by murdering the unfortunate Dr Schleyer, whose body was dumped in an abandoned car in Alsace. The hunted kidnap squad took refuge in the Middle East. The fact that the imprisoned Baader–Meinhof leaders, Andreas Baader, Gudrun Ensslin and Jan-Carl Raspe, were able to commit suicide in their maximum security prison after learning that the attempt to free them had failed, produced an immediate counter-effect. Those sympathetic to the radical cause demonstrated and some German establishments in other European countries were bombed because the radicals believed that Baader and his comrades had been murdered in prison. Others who were not at all sympathetic to terrorism found it difficult to eradicate the suspicion that even if the authorities had not murdered their prisoners they had remembered the axiom – 'Thou shalt not kill but needst not strive officiously to keep alive.' As we have seen in earlier chapters describing the rise of the terrorist movements, it is an event of this kind which can influence the young and eventually provide more recruits for the infantry of terror.

While the long drama of the 1977 autumn offensive played itself out, it seemed that political life in Germany was at a standstill, paralysed by governmental concentration on this one problem. Chancellor Helmut Schmidt was unable to receive James Callaghan, the British Prime Minister, and he had to postpone his own official visit to Poland. It began to look as though the maxim of Ulrike Meinhof – 'A few dozen fighters, who go into action without endless talk, can fundamentally change the political scene' – had been proved correct. Popular clamour for the death penalty and ever more security measures stimulated by the wave of terror played into the hands of the Red Army Faction and their international friends. For shooting in the streets and police revenge is what terrorism feeds upon.

The perverted yet naive intention of Baader–Meinhof was to bring about 'fascisification' of West Germany in order to provoke 'a revolutionary reaction from the masses'. In face of this the West German government stood fast and remained reasonable, and finally it was bold and exasperated enough to refuse the terrorists' demands, and then to strike back and use legitimate force against violence. In this it finally received strong public support from its partners in the European community, Britain and France. Before the nations of Europe finally joined themselves into a Common Market, there was a plan to achieve unity through the creation of a European Army. This plan came to nothing, so it is one of the ironies of history that the terrorists, by their revolutionary activity, have helped to persuade European leaders to unite their armies in the nucleus of a Common Market anti-terrorist force. If the process continues this may eventually result in a strengthening of European unity in an alliance against the very forces which seek to destroy its way of life.

A further heartening sign that the industrial democracies were strengthening their combined resolve to contain international terrorism was provided by the summit conference of leaders of Britain, West Germany, France, Italy, the United States, Canada and Japan in July 1978. Meeting in Bonn they unanimously agreed to take stern measures against countries which refused to extradite or prosecute terrorists and hijackers, or which refused to return hostages and aircraft. The matter was raised by Takeo Fukuda, Prime Minister of Japan, and the powers agreed to punish such offending nations by suspending their air traffic connections with the Seven. Suggestions that an economic boycott might be organised was rejected on the grounds that it would be unworkable.

This plan is the strongest collective effort against terrorism so far made. It seems likely that countries such as Libya, Algeria and Southern Yemen may be discouraged from offering safe havens to terrorists by this threat to refuse landing rights in all signatory nations to their national carriers. The statesmen of the West certainly hope that their stand against air piracy will discourage terrorists and hostage-takers in general.

Faced with a common international enemy, the nations of Western Europe consulted and secured general approval for a counter-action. The tragedy is that it had taken no less than five years for the powers of this sophisticated continent to combine against a multinational terrorist force, not strong in numbers – there are probably less than 1000 activist men and women – but which by its tactics had spread death and fear throughout the world.

The truth is that when the hijackers, assassins and kidnappers first began to strike in Europe their tactics took the West by surprise. Their acts were unexpected in liberal countries where freedom of expression exists, in democracies whose one over-riding advantage is that governments can be changed by the simple process of voting, without men having to go out in the streets and kill in order to bring down an unpopular administration. It was known that in Latin American tyrannies guerrilla tactics might be justified to overthrow brutal regimes; it was accepted that the Palestinians, and even the Irish, might take up arms in the cause of national aspiration. But why should innocent men and women be slaughtered by gunmen in peaceful societies? The first response was that the terrorists must have some reasonable demands and that therefore their aims should be studied, and attempts made to deal with their grievances. It is in the nature of Western societies to listen to argument and to try to discover what has gone wrong. Added to that, in Germany and in Japan there remained feelings of guilt about earlier regimes whose brutalities had plunged the world into war.

If the young, and especially the university intellectuals, were worried enough to take up arms in the cause of changing and improving society they should be heeded. That was the attitude, and during the time it took for us to realise that the terrorism was in fact a destructive force, an abberration of reformist thought, rather than a worthy expression of disquiet, governments chose to give in to their tactical demands and to hope thereby to satisfy them.

By the time realisation of the true nature of terrorism set in, and the West was prepared to recognise their strategic demands for the fraud they were, the tactics had hardened into a formal pattern, and their surprise value had been lost.

There is no mystery about the tactics. They shocked only by their unexpectedness and novelty, and by the fact that television coverage of violent events brought them into every home. The main terrorist activities consist of:

1. Murder by gunning down people in the streets.
2. Assassination of political leaders and other well-known people.
3. Bombing of public places or the homes of private individuals.
4. Kidnapping of prominent people for ransom or the release of prisoners.
5. Hijacking aircraft and using the safety of the crew and passengers as a bargaining counter to secure the same aims.
6. Armed bank robbery and raids to get money, weapons, documents, etc.

If there is no mystery about the methods it is equally true that there is no magic formula or secret weapon which will easily counter them. It is obvious that in each case straightforward security measures involving more efficient police work, security checks and personal precautions need to be taken for protection against terror. But even more important is better intelligence work, and more effort to discover who the terrorists are and how they operate. The routines of security need to be improved, while freedom of movement and action for individuals is preserved. There is the rub. For the best defence against terrorism is undoubtedly to set up a police state such as that which exists in the Soviet Union, where

anybody can be declared an enemy of the state and incarcerated without any process of law. And any dissident can, and
often is, sent to a mental home for 'treatment'. Surely, the
argument runs, anybody who protests about life under
Communism must be mad. Such dire precautions of course
involve the setting up of a gigantic apparatus of state security.

Such procedures are unthinkable in the West, and what
has to be contrived is a system of increased security which
does not impose too much restriction on freedom. That said,
it must be obvious that some freedom must be sacrificed in
order to protect citizens from death and intimidation by
terror and the very fabric of the state from disintegration.
For example, it may be tiresome and even humiliating to be
body-searched, and have security men examine one's most
personal possessions in a suitcase, but it is greatly preferable
to being blown up in mid-air, or threatened with revolvers by
demented terrorists to whom you must cringe for permission
to go to the toilet in a hijacked aircraft. The real battle of wits
which calls for skill and nerve takes place in terrorist acts
involving the kidnap of individuals or the holding hostage of
groups of people. In such events a body of violent case law
has built up over the last ten years and to a large extent the
moves on both sides have become as ritualistic as a folk
dance.

Let us take the early aircraft mass hijacks carried out by
Arab terrorists. Two or three pirates boarded an aircraft with
concealed arms and grenades; one moved forward to
threaten the aircrew while the others held the passengers at
bay. Then the leader announced over the aircraft radio that
he was captain of the martyr squad now in command in the
aircraft. His tactic was to fly it to an airfield in a safe country,
or one sympathetic to his cause, and there to utter increasingly terrible threats until the government of the place from
which the aircraft came agreed to his demands.

In the case of the mass hijack to Dawson's Field in Jordan
in September 1970, when outside governments were unused
to such high drama, it was not long before they gave in. Even
the British government with its long tradition of respect for

the rules of law, speedily and thankfully released Leila Khaled, the Palestinian girl terrorist, who had unsuccessfully tried to seize an El Al flight which landed at London Airport. Although she ought to have been held, charged and tried, the government was only too pleased to be rid of her in exchange for the safety of passengers on a BOAC flight held at the desert airport.

Large sums of money were paid out, airliners and new crews were provided, solemn communiqués were read out and convicted killers were released from prison. Then, as one raid followed another, the attitudes of governments began to stiffen. The Israelis, accustomed to living with violence, showed the way. They placed armed guards on El Al flights, armoured the vital parts, locked the door to the flight deck and refused to be blackmailed. That at once reduced the number of attacks on their flights. But it was not until after the sensational hijacking to Entebbe of the Air France flight from Athens with more than 300 passengers on board that a new game developed. The story of the Israeli commando raid upon the terrorists who had separated the Jewish passengers from the rest and were holding them hostage at Entebbe is well known, and its successful after-effects gave new courage to governments throughout the world.

As the international terrorists increased the number of their raids, Western governments began to make the necessary preparations for firmer action. Slowly the means of communication between different police forces were improved – though the flow of information between countries is still not fast enough and there remains a tendency demonstrated again by the French in the Abu Daoud affair early in 1977 simply to shuffle off responsibility by getting rid of a wanted terrorist by immediate expulsion. Even so there are hopeful signs.

In London there already existed a bomb squad accustomed to dealing with Provisional IRA outrages. It was expanded and its methods improved as it was transformed in 1976 into an anti-terrorist squad which was kept busy by Provo activity, and was therefore sensitive to the possibility of international terrorism as well. Because the British Army has long experience of subversive warfare in the colonial wars – it has been engaged worldwide since the end of the Second World War – a specialised military unit was already in being to cope with the new techniques of terror. The Special Air Service, with 1000 carefully selected officers and men highly trained for delicate operations, was ideally suited for use in so-called Phase II operations, that is to say when a situation has developed with which the police are no longer able to cope. At this point they must call in superior firepower and essential military skills.

The 22nd SAS Regiment provides just such an elite anti-terrorist unit which is held on a three-minute standby. It can also call on army bomb disposal teams and conventional infantry and even armour if necessary. The process is officially known as MACP – Military Aid to the Civil Power.

Since the Second World War the SAS has fought in Malaya, Kenya, Oman and is in action day after day in Northern Ireland. Its units have served in small groups, the equivalent of terrorist cells, in many parts of the world both in uniform and plain clothes. Recruitment tests for this volunteer unit are very strict and only 19 of every 100 are accepted for SAS service. Selection procedures include personality tests planned for the selection of men who have above-average intelligence, are assertive and self-sufficient without being too extrovert or introvert.

At their regimental headquarters in Hereford the SAS added a new speciality by training on mock aircraft and developing new methods of storming such an aircraft taken over by hijackers. In consultation with the weapons research department of the Ministry of Defence, they experimented with a whole new range of 'dirty tricks' weapons, including the non-lethal flash and bang grenade used at Mogadishu. They guard London Airport in moments of crisis and are ready to go anywhere in the world terrorist-hunting. A team went to Rome to advise on tactics after the kidnap of Aldo Moro.

After the massacre of the Israeli athletes at Munich in 1972 and the disastrous police counter-attack the West German government set up its own specialised para-military unit known as GSG9 (Border Protection Group 9) under the command of a tough professional officer named Ulrich Wegener. The recruits are all intelligent, exceptionally fit and highly trained in everything from swimming to karate and knife-fighting. In fact, their training more than lives up to the rigorous super-boy-scout instruction to which Marighella thought his terrorists ought to aspire. Their small arms instruction covers everything from a Smith and Wesson .38, by way of machine pistols and machine-guns to the Mauser 66 sniper rifle. Ulrich Wegener has a large budget and uses it to purchase the very latest anti-terror weapons. After five years of careful preparation, their first big operation at Mogadishu lasted seven minutes and was totally successful.

The German force had received advice and training from Israel's General Intelligence and Reconnaissance Unit 269. This group descends from an anti-terror unit developed by General Arik Sharon, who led Israeli forces into Egypt in the Yom Kippur War. Among its battle honours are Entebbe, and the freeing of ninety hostages aboard a Sabena aircraft which had been seized by Palestinians and forced to land at Lod Airport in 1972.

The United States was slow to respond to the international terrorist threat but in March 1978 President Carter finally gave orders for the establishment and training of a specialised force 200 strong. This was a delayed response to the clear demonstration of the efficacy of GSG9 and the SAS. The new force, to be called Blue Light – which recalls the flash and bang grenades used at Mogadishu – will have special weapons and equipment. The specially selected recruits at once began training under the command of Colonel Charles Beckwith, a 49-year-old Green Beret with great experience of clandestine operations in Vietnam. Some of his recruits on the course at Fort Bragg, North Carolina, were veterans of the 1970 raid into North Vietnam upon the Son Tay prison camp.

It was the lesson of the Mogadishu raid which belatedly convinced the President that new steps were urgently needed to remedy America's lack of means to cope with such incidents. Until then only small groups of US troops had received sporadic training in anti-terrorist operations. The new unit will take several months to complete its course and the Pentagon estimates that not for two or three years will it reach the proficiency of German and British units. Meanwhile an emergency force of sixty Blue Light men will plug the gap.

The French have a 40-strong special squad composed of men of the Gendarmerie National (which is the oldest regiment in the French army), known as Gigene. This unit has already proved its value in action abroad, for it rescued the children of French servicemen hijacked on their school bus by terrorists operating in Djibouti in 1976. In addition there are special anti-terrorist brigades of police set up after the Munich massacre. Some of these men were on standby duty in Holland during the capture of the French embassy in the Hague by Japanese terrorists. For assault operations the Italians rely on the 50-strong Squad R Anti-commando, which was called to Rome Airport when the hijacked Lufthansa DC9 from Majorca landed there in November 1977. But huge forces of police and troops were called in for the anti-terror sweeps and searches after the Moro kidnap.

In Holland a special squad of marines assaulted the train captured by South Moluccans. They too received help and advice from a detachment of the Special Air Service from Britain although they turned down the offer of the 'stun grenades' preferring to use their own method of throwing the terrorists off balance – low-level flights by fighters whose pilots suddenly cut in their after-burners.

Not until such forces as these were in being and the political climate had been created for them to intervene in a crisis did governments feel able to take a tougher stand in the negotiation phase which precedes any assault on terrorists who have seized hostages.

After Mogadishu West Germany began a counter-offensive, despatching three-man *Zielfahndung* (target squads) to snatch terrorists in foreign countries. This, of course, could only be done with the co-operation of authorities in the countries concerned. A notable success was scored through this new form of international co-operation when one such squad grabbed 28-year-old Angelika Loder, 27-year-old Gudrun Sturmer, and 28-year-old Gabriele Rollnik, at Bourgas, a Bulgarian Black Sea resort. They were all involved in the raid on the Moabit prison in Berlin which released Till Meyer, a June 2nd man on trial for numerous offences. He too was arrested in Bulgaria and flown back to West Germany. This was the first recorded case of co-operation being given by a Communist East European state in the war against terrorism.

The obvious success of the Israeli assault at Entebbe and the West German one at Mogadishu created a rather smug feeling that so long as Western states took a strong line against terrorists, and provided they had at their disposal a specially trained commando force all would be well. This is a dangerous supposition, for as many things can go wrong in a counter-terror raid as in any form of warfare. Thorough training of the assault troops is important but even the best trained troops in the world are not always victorious unless they are lucky. The good guys do not always win and in some future operation it is only too likely that some action on a foreign airfield will end in carnage among innocent passengers as well as the troops involved.

As if to point up this message there is the example of the Egyptian commandos at Larnaca Airport, Cyprus. They were good troops from the Egyptian army, an army which succeeded only a few years ago in making a crossing of the Suez canal against the opposition of the Israeli Army, also one of the best in the world – yet their anti-terrorist raid ended in farce and disaster. In February 1978 two Palestinian gunmen made their way into the Hilton Hotel, Nicosia, and shot and killed Yusuf Sebai, an Egyptian editor and a personal friend of President Sadat. They then took hostages and eventually forced the Cypriots to provide them with an Air Cyprus plane. Finding every airport in the Middle East closed to them, they eventually returned twenty-one hours later to Larnaca.

Furious at the murder of his friend and having received

intelligence reports that Palestinian terrorists were moving into Cyprus to rescue their brethren, President Sadat determined to take bold action, Mogadishu style. He despatched a force of commandos, which had already liberated one hijacked aircraft in Egypt, across the Mediterranean to Cyprus.

General Nabil Shukri personally commanded the 72-strong force aboard an Egyptian airforce Hercules and he had orders to get the two terrorists and free the airliner they were holding. Insufficient diplomatic preparation had been made for this raid. Although President Sadat and President Kyprianou of Cyprus later gave quarrelsomely different accounts of the affair, it seems clear that the Egyptians did not have clear authorisation for their mission. The result was that when the Egyptian commandos assaulted the plane, they were attacked by strong forces of the Cypriot National Guard, lost fifteen dead, and were unable to get into the aircraft. The terrorists, terrified by the battle going on around the plane, eventually surrendered to the Cypriots, were tried and found guilty of murder.

But the confused battle of Larnaca demonstrates how easily things can go wrong if anti-terrorist assault forces are not highly trained and are not given proper back-up from their own government. It may serve as a warning to any government planning such action.

While in Western countries the police and the military developed their assault techniques, which are very much more delicate than those of the terrorist who does not care whether or not innocent people are killed, other methods were put forward. Academics analysed terrorists' actions and habits. Psychiatrists started to probe the terrorist mind, and to suggest ways in which trained negotiators might exploit their weaknesses in the bargaining phase of a terror action.

The first instinct in dealing with men who hold hostages, and are besieged, is to attack them. But that may simply result in the death of those held prisoner rather than that of the 'bad men'. There is no place for cowboys in a terrorist scenario.

One of the pioneers of the victory-through-talk technique of dealing with such situations is Dr Harvey Schlossberg,

director of Psychological Services for the New York Police
Department. It was he who devised the methods of talking
out the hostage-holders which were put into practice by
Lieutenant Frank Bolz, of the New York Negotiating
Squad, whom we quoted in our first chapter as saying: 'We
aim to bore them to death.' His method of operation is
two-edged. He sets out to calm the hostage-taker while at the
same time increasing the pressure upon him, until he can be
convinced that the only way out for him is to free the people
he holds. In practice it has been proved that the best person
to conduct the negotiations is a police officer or some similarly recognisable representative of authority with a psychiatrist
giving advice but remaining in the background. Negotiators
are now being trained by the Federal Bureau of Investigation
in refinements of Dr Schlossberg's techniques and are employed by police forces throughout the United States.

What has been demonstrated by the use of such methods is
that the advantage does not always lie with the terrorist. A
display of firmness which breaks down the willpower of the
terrorist can compel him to surrender his hostages without
bloodshed. In 1975 the Irish security authorities tried out
this technique in the eighteen-day seige of the Provos Eddie
Gallagher and Marian Coyle, who had kidnapped the Dutch
businessman, Dr Tiede Herrema, and were demanding the
release of several comrades – especially Gallagher's mistress,
Rose Dugdale – in return for his life.

Troops and police surrounded the house in County Kil-
dare where Dr Herrema was being held and made use of
modern surveillance gadgets, cameras and listening devices
in order to discover every move and word of the kidnappers.
Psychiatrists then advised the negotiator to choose times
when the terrorists were relaxed but in low spirits to press
them to surrender. At moments of tension they were soothed
with offers of food and comforts. The authorities were
particularly fortunate in this case in that the calm and strong
personality of Dr Herrema himself made it possible for him
to bring his own strength to bear in the developing relationship with his captors. Eventually it was Eddie Gallagher and
Marian Coyle, renowned for their wildness even among the

Provos, who broke and surrendered. None of this would have been possible had not the Irish government made it clear that they would not capitulate under any circumstances and that they refused to make any deals or concessions. Such tactics demand a strong will and a realistic appreciation of what can happen.

During the Herrema incident the Irish authorities called upon the resources of the Scotland Yard Technical Support Branch to take advantage of the latest surveillance and monitoring technology and for help with communications. This branch in Britain works closely with the anti-terrorist squad which we have already discussed. Both units played a notable part in employing the 'wait-them-out' technique against the IRA in the now famous siege of Balcombe Street in London in December 1975. Four of the Provo's Active Service Unit were chased into an apartment in Balcombe Street where they held the occupants, Mr and Mrs Matthews, prisoners in their own flat. The Commissioner of Police made it clear from the start that he would make no concessions and surrounded the apartment with men of the Metropolitan Police Special Patrol Group. This SPG squad consists of uniformed men trained to use Smith and Wesson .38 revolvers and can be given more powerful support by men from D 11, marksmen of the specialist firearms squad. The SAS were alerted in this case and prepared a number of plans of attack but once again the terrorists, faced with the inevitability of death or prison, surrendered and released their hostages unharmed.

It must not be forgotten that the first step in such operations is to discover the place where the terrorists are holding their victims. Until they can be pinned down and surrounded no action can be taken at all. The kidnap in Rome early in 1978 of Aldo Moro showed the power of the Red Brigades and the impotence of security and police forces, who for weeks on end were unable to track down the terrorist hideout where Signor Moro was being held. The talk-out technique depends entirely on good detective work and it cannot be stressed too strongly how important it is for the police either to infiltrate terror movements or to get infor-

mers among their members. Without detection nothing can
be done. Hijackers, always in search of publicity, perform
part of the security task themselves by announcing where
they are, but kidnapping, where the lair remains secret, is a
stronger form of terrorist war.

In order to succeed it is essential that the talk-out special-
ists know that a well-armed force of police is in position to
take action if it becomes necessary. Even in Britain where
police and public alike have long opposed the idea of an
armed police force, it is now recognised that in present-day
conditions the forces of order must have specialist weapons
available. It is better from every point of view to employ
policemen trained with the right weapons than to use soldiers. For the police are trained in a different fashion and a
soldier is in the nature of things disposed to be more aggres-
sive than his civilian colleague in uniform. There are perhaps
some advantages here in the continental system of policing,
where it is customary to have a third force of gendarmes who
are neither simply police nor entirely soldiers.

This means that along with the psychological method of
dealing with terrorists, attention must be paid to providing
the forces of order with the best possible weapons for the job.
Revolvers and pistols have the advantage of being light and
easy to conceal in delicate situations but they are not always
accurate. One of the newer weapons now recommended for
such work is the L39A1 sniper's rifle with the Rank image-
intensifier night sight, particularly when it is remembered
that most police actions requiring weapons take place by
night. But the disadvantage of such a weapon is its penetrating power. Like many modern weapons it is too powerful to
be used by any but the most accurate and most disciplined of
marksmen, for its bullets can penetrate concrete and ricochet
over 100 yards and are therefore highly dangerous in built-up
areas.

British police units now tend to favour the Parker–Hale
.222, a high velocity rifle without the fault of over penetration. A new American sub-machine-gun, the 180, is now
coming into use fitted with a laser sight. The advantage of
this weapon is that the laser beam itself terrifies the terrorist

as it seeks him out, and can of itself bring about a peaceful surrender, for there can be few things more frightening than to see a red spot centred on your heart and to know that if the man behind the beam pulls the trigger, you are dead. The laser sight also makes the weapon easier to aim so that less training in marksmanship is needed.

At the Balcombe Street siege a police officer conducted the negotiations with a psychiatrist advising him. But when South Moluccan terrorists captured a train holding many hostages in Holland in the summer of 1977, it was the psychiatrist himself who negotiated with the terrorists. The siege ended only when Dutch marines stormed the coaches after terrorists had been alarmed by Starfighter jets buzzing the train. Although the psychiatrist in question, Dr Dick Mulder, is a specialist in the talk-out technique, and has the authority of a colonel in the reserve, having dealt with previous sieges by Palestinians, Japanese Red Army and other South Moluccans in Holland, criticisms were afterwards voiced of the way the negotiations were conducted. Anti-terrorist experts and other psychiatrists claimed that he had not been sufficiently authoritative and had failed to put enough pressure on the Moluccans.

He later explained his technique in detail. He believes that the first step is to build up a psychological picture of the terrorists, a difficult thing to do during phase one, which is the most dangerous period during which the terrorists are acting wildly, making extravagant threats and often shooting. After making it clear that there is no quick solution and that he and the government are ready to wait, he even favours allowing the terrorists to speak to the press and television on the grounds that this satisfies their inflated egos.

At this time Dr Mulder also prepares for phase two by arranging to have one direct telephone line to the terrorists for his own use. He begins to assert his own will by cutting off all other communication, then controlling what the terrorists shall eat and at what time. Eventually he claims that he can tell them when to sleep by bidding them goodnight. In this way it is possible for the psychiatrist controller to know what the terrorists are doing throughout the day.

In the view of the Dutch expert this leads ineluctably to phase three which starts when the terrorists begin to feel that they are losing their campaign and their natural reaction is to want to go back to the shooting and adrenalin pumping time of phase one. At this point threats are made all over again and great care must be exercised by the control.

The situation was particularly delicate in this particular case because the Moluccans in the train were holding 56 hostages while another group held 105 children in a school not far away. Both groups demanded the release of imprisoned comrades and recognition of a non-existent independent state of South Molucca which it was not in the power of the Dutch government to grant. It is significant also that the Moluccans were to some extent prepared for Dr Mulder's technique, for he had already employed it against their friends in an earlier siege. This is the first known case of terrorists themselves having undergone psychological training as a result of earlier experience. At first they neither made contact with the outside world, nor asked for contact to be made with them and until there was some means of talking it was impossible for the negotiator to begin his work.

The terrorist leader was called Max and he told Dr Mulder that he did not want any psychological talk. So the Dutch Colonel had to find another basis for conversation, chatting and suggesting things that could be done like starting to clean the train. Max again did not respond but began to talk mystically about the sadistic side of Moluccans and declared that he was willing to stick out the siege for a year if necessary. It was at this point that the psychiatrist began to worry about the state of mind of the hostages and to wonder whether or not they had the inner resources to survive for a long period. There were also doubts about the ability of Max to sustain his leadership in increasingly difficult circumstances.

As discipline on the train broke down after twenty days, Dr Mulder had to admit that the talking-out technique was unlikely to succeed and he advised the government that the time had come for military action. Here again the psychiatrist thought fit to suggest the tactics to be adopted. The attack should be made at dawn when the terrorists were least alert and he was able to tell the military commander that most of the Moluccans slept in the front coach. It was Dr Mulder also who hit upon the idea of getting airforce Star-fighters to dive low over the train with after-burners blasting in order to throw the terrorists off-balance. Finally the marines went in to the assault, killing Max and five other Moluccans. Unfortunately two hostages were also killed, largely because they stood up although they had been told to lie down when the assault started. When Dr Mulder was interviewed at length on BBC television he said that he felt he could now speak freely about the tactics he had employed because he knew that the terrorists were by now perfectly familiar with them and for this reason he would have to devise a fresh approach for the next situation.

As in true warfare it is sometimes the defence and some-times the attack which has the advantage. It would be foolish to forget that terrorists are intelligent and crafty people perfectly capable of learning operational lessons from experi-ence. There is evidence that Provos in Ireland have been trained to resist the modern interrogation techniques of the British Army. Their men are taught, for example, to avoid looking into the eyes of the questioner and how to evade his trickeries. At Mogadishu the new grenades caught the raid-ers by surprise and the fact that the GSG9 group wore new lightweight bulletproof vests made them less vulnerable. Although these facts are unlikely to find their way into terror training manuals for some time there can be little doubt but that in some Middle East camp terror controllers are trying to buy the right kind of goggles and bulletproof vests for their teams next time.

Events in Rome early in 1978 showed that members of the Red Brigades had learned tactical lessons about the psychological warfare aspects of their campaign. The Red Army Faction and other groups had always insisted, once their victim was incarcerated in a 'people's prison', on the broadcast of communiqués laying down the political aims of their group. The Red Brigades employed different tactics. Instead of boring the public with their policy statements they announced that Aldo Moro was himself on trial before their 'people's court'. What is more they issued a series of letters written by Moro which sowed doubt and confusion among fellow members of his Christian Democratic party, whom he accused of betraying him and failing to accept Red Brigades demands in order to save his life. The accusatory and self-pitying tone of his letters themselves created a political effect to the advantage of the terrorists.

There were plenty of Italians who took the letters at face value as though they had been written by a statesman in normal circumstances. But terror watchers and psychiatrists who have specialised in this field know that after a man has been held even for a few days by threatening terrorists it is unlikely that any but the strongest willed is capable of writing letters anything like those he would normally compose. It is not torture, not even simply the fear of death, which brings aberrations of the mind. Just the circumstances of loss of freedom and loss of hope can transform a person's way of thinking. The exploitation of such circumstances is a dangerous new development in terror techniques. It is ironic that if such methods were used in liberal societies against captured terrorists there would be cries of 'torture' and strong liberal protests and demonstrations.

Although anti-terror squads have greater resources for invention and improving their equipment, the terrorists too take advantage of published material to improve their tactics and weapons. It is suspected, for example, that they have been buying a Swiss Army handbook detailing easy sabotage methods originally issued to army NCOs but then put on semi-public sale. Entitled *Handbook on Guerrilla Warfare*, it was written for the guidance of Swiss soldiers should their country ever be occupied by enemy forces. In autumn 1977 the Swiss were asked to take steps to prevent it falling into the wrong hands.

The security forces of Western nations must remain constantly on the alert if they are not only to counter terrorist raids but also to stay ahead of the game. Whenever a particularly dramatic terrorist raid takes place the public at large begins suggesting what should be done. The tactics of public opinion, unlike the hard-headed ones of both terrorists and counter-terrorists, are always full of the formulae of wishful thinking and belief in magic weapons. During the autumn offensive of 1977 the old suggestion was again put forward that gas should be pumped into hijacked airliners to put the pirates, and indeed the passengers to sleep. How simple that sounds.

Such hopes were effectively dashed by Professor D. R. Lawrence of the Pharmacology and Therapeutics Department of the University College Hospital Medical School in a letter to *The Times* in late 1977. 'When I consider the technology and skill required of my specialist colleagues in anaesthesia, caring for one unconscious person at a time, I tremble for the likely loss of life if a plane-load were simultaneously anaesthetized. Utopia might possibly develop such a gas, but Utopia would presumably have no need of it . . .'

The second panacea of public opinion is the death sentence for terrorists. For would not that deprive the terrorists of further targets as they are always demanding the release of imprisoned colleagues? This too is a false argument. Death penalties would do no such thing, for it would be the negation of democracy for them to be shot on the spot after drumhead courts martial and would provide the terrorists with the support they so desperately need; if the sentences were not carried out immediately, the lengthy processes of appeal before sentence could reasonably be carried out would provide ample time for their comrades to launch raids to try to secure their release.

And so the war goes on, just like any other war, with both sides seeking for advantages, changing their tactics and strategy, introducing new weapons and methods. There is no easy road to victory.

9 | The Who's Who of Terror

Terrorist organisations emerge for a variety of reasons; they flourish like laboratory cultures of radical chic and international publicity, but each needs its own special cause to initiate its life-cycle. For some, like the Palestinians and the South Moluccans, it is nationalistic – they use terror as one of their weapons in trying to establish national right to an area of territory. For others, like the Baader–Meinhof gang and the Japanese Red Army, the cause is world revolution. Some, like the Spanish and Italian groups, have internal political reasons for turning to terror and there are others still, such as the Moslem insurgents in the Philippines and the Warriors of Christ the King in Spain, who owe their existence to religion as much as to politics.

In each case the origin seems simple. The combination of a grievance and a vision can make a man throw a bomb. But after the first clear burst of enthusiasm, rationalisation tends to blur. Some of the Palestinian groups, for example, have developed a commitment to world revolution almost as total as their devotion to the recovery of their homeland. The failure of the German and Japanese groups to plan a viable alternative society to the one they want to destroy points to anarchy. And the cynical support of the Soviet Union for almost any group which could embarrass the West, whatever that group's political alignment, blurs the picture even more.

Nowhere could there be more confusion than in the welter of reasons the Provisional IRA gives for its campaign of terror. National, political, social and religious causes mixed together with a generous dollop of historical mysticism provide the Provos with their rationalisation. The Provos are, of course, unique. But they do demonstrate the great range of justification that exists for blowing up cinemas, hijacking airliners and assassinating 'bourgeois pigs'. And even the Provos are bound by two basic laws of the terrorist experiment:

1. The use of violence is obligatory in order to induce fear and chaos.
2. It must be aimed at the people and the institutions of the established order.

This may seem a statement of the obvious. But these laws are the foundation of terrorism, for they provide the cement which surrounds each terrorist brick and binds together into a unity of purpose even those who are violently opposed to one another.

This unity is often disguised. Groups change their names – sometimes they split and amoeba-like spawn other groups – or they may undergo a change in ideology, and discard their old identities, while others give themselves new names in order to disguise their affiliations. Splinter groups with exotic names are sometimes set up in order to carry out specific operations. For example, the combined PFLP and Baader–Meinhof group led by the Venezuelan Carlos which carried out the raid on the OPEC headquarters in Vienna, called itself 'The Arm of the Arab Revolution'. On a more permanent basis, Black September was formed as the terrorist arm of Al Fatah. Its origins were kept secret in order to prevent political embarrassment of Fatah's leader, Yasser Arafat, and through him the whole of the Palestine Liberation Organisation. Those of us who traced this killer group to Fatah, and showed that it was led by Arafat's deputy, Abu Iyad, were bitterly attacked for denigrating the good name of Fatah.

We have prepared the following 'who's who' of the most active of the terrorist groups in an attempt to clarify and codify. This section is planned to show how the groups came into being, who runs them, what their aims are. It also demonstrates their inter-group and international links, as well as their transpolitical and transnational capacity which is possibly the most dangerous weapon of modern terrorism.

GERMANY

Baader – Meinhof Gang (Red Army Faction)

Origins This group grew out of the Berlin student demonstrations of 1967–8. Given a cause by the shooting of Benno Ohnesorg and a reason by the failure of the demonstrations, various left-wing cells were brought together on the initiative of Horst Mahler, a young lawyer, to form the Red Army Faction, a name adopted from the Japanese Red Army. It came to be known as the Baader–Meinhof gang after two of its leaders, Andreas Baader and Ulrike Meinhof. It would have been more appropriate to name the movement after Gudrun Ensslin, Baader's mistress, for she was the operational commander of the gang, but the honour went to Meinhof because her ability with words enabled her to propagandise the gang's ideology among Germany's left-wing bourgeoisie.

Ideology and aims Anarchist, anti-bourgeois, anti-American, revolutionary. Its confused philosophy was set in order by Meinhof. She described its objective as being 'to hit the Establishment in the face, to mobilise the masses, and to maintain international solidarity'. Though not overtly Communist there is evidence that through Meinhof – whose husband's leftist, soft-porn magazine, *Konkret*, was partly financed by the Russians – it received some loose support from Moscow via East Germany.

Activities The original group pursued a campaign of terror and bank robbery until 1972, when most of the early leaders were arrested. They carried out bombings, attacks on US Army installations, assassinations and arson. They stole arms and grenades from gun shops and armouries, and passports and identity documents from town halls. They lived off the proceeds of their bank robberies, grants from the PFLP and money provided for them by their left-wing 'respectable' friends. After the arrest of the leaders their campaign was carried on by successor groups, among them the June 2nd Movement and the Holger Meins Commando, which recruited its members from a psychiatric institute at Heidelberg. Their greatest publicity triumph was achieved with the kidnapping of Hans-Martin Schleyer and the back-up hijacking of a Lufthansa plane to Mogadishu by a PFLP team. These outrages virtually brought governmental and political life in Germany to a standstill. But they suffered disaster at this moment of notoriety. Meinhof had already committed suicide in her cell. Now, following the failure of the kidnapping and the hijacking to get them out of jail, Andreas Baader, Gudrun Ensslin and Jan-Carl Raspe took their own lives.

International links   Strong connections with the Popular Front for the Liberation of Palestine, and Al Fatah's terror branch, Black September. Baader–Meinhof members have undergone training in terrorist tactics in the Middle East, mainly in Syria and Lebanon. The group also has links with the Italian Red Brigades, the Armed Proletarian Cells (NAP), and Armata Rossa. Its closest link in Western Europe is with the Dutch 'Red Help' group which is so intimately involved with the German terrorists that it can be described as the Dutch branch of Baader–Meinhof. It has also worked closely with Carlos. Baader–Meinhof members were part of his group in Paris, where they took part in the attempt to destroy an El Al plane by rocket; at Vienna where they formed part of his team for the assault on the OPEC headquarters; and Entebbe – which he planned – where two of the hijack team were Baader–Meinhof members and both, Wilfried Böse and Brigitte Kohlmann, were killed by Israeli commandos.

Achievements   Red Army Faction activity forced the West German government to pass harsh laws in order to wage war against terrorism, something that the Germans, with their recent Nazi history, were most reluctant to do. Has forced senior businessmen, politicians and government officials to live tightly guarded lives in homes turned into fortresses.

Strength   Some 50–60 hard-core members, many of them

young women from middle-class homes, and about 2000 sympathisers, mainly in Berlin (East and West), Munich, Hamburg and Frankfurt. Important members: Verena Becker, Gabriele Krocher-Tiedemann, Jorg Lang, Juliane Plambeck, Ingrid Siepmann, Inge Viett, Susanne Albrecht, Knut Folkerts, Siegfried Haag, Wolfgang Huber, Hanna-Elise Krabbe, Friedericke Krabbe.

Future prospects Not great. The gang still has the capacity to murder but most of the second-generation leaders have now been arrested along with the lawyers who, while not involved in actual acts of terrorism, acted as liaison officers and planners. Others, now known to the police forces of Europe, are being harried from country to country.

JAPAN

The Red Army (Sekigun)

Origins Formed in 1969 in the general upheaval of students and turmoil caused by opposition to the war in Vietnam. In 1972 nine of its members joined forces with the twenty-member Keihin Ampo Kyoto to form Rengo Sekigun. There have been a number of regroupings, especially following the brutal murder of fourteen offenders against Sekigun discipline – the crime of one was to become pregnant. She was tied naked to a tree and left to freeze to death. Three groups are still active in a support role in Japan but the group which has carried out acts of international terrorism is the 'Arab Committee' led by a woman, Fusako Shigenobu, who left Japan for Beirut in early 1971.

Ideology and aims Revolutionary socialistic with strong nihilistic and mystical tendencies. Anti-American, pro-Palestinian.

Activities Following a series of robberies and kidnappings and one hijack in Japan, the Red Army went international when three JRA members working for the PFLP murdered twenty-six people at Lod Airport, Israel. It has since been involved in hijackings and seizures of embassies, mainly in efforts to secure the release of imprisoned members and to raise money through ransom.

International links   The JRA outside Japan is completely dependent on the PFLP. These two groups first made contact in 1970, when Sekigun members were lectured by PFLP propagandists and later travelled to the Middle East to discuss co-operation and to get training. In co-operation they set up a Japanese medical team to work in Palestinian refugee camps. The JRA has also been helped by Carlos in his role as the PFLP operational commander in Europe.

Achievements   Entirely because of the Japanese government's refusal to risk innocent lives threatened by JRA hijackers who had proved that they would kill without compunction, the JRA has been able to rebuild its organisation with members and criminals released from prison. It has also acquired some $6 million as ransom for a hijacked aircraft, though this money was probably handed over to Wadi Hadad of the PFLP for the central treasury.

Strength   In Japan, about seventy. The international 'Arab Committee', about thirty. Important members: Fusako Shigenobu, Osamu Maruoka, Jun Nishikawa, Junzo Ukudaira, Haruo Wako, Kazuo Tohira, Kunio Bando.

Future prospects   In Japan, apart from sporadic bombings, the JRA is not active, and does not promise to become so. The police appear to have a firm grip on the situation. The prospects of the 'Arab Committee' depend entirely on what happens politically in the Middle East and how long Wadi Hadad's successors can retain his safe bases in Iraq and the Yemen. Without the PFLP and these bases the Japanese would find it extremely difficult to operate.

PALESTINE

Black September

Origins Formed by Yasser Arafat's Fatah organisation as a weapon of terror. It was based on Fatah's intelligence branch, Jihaz al-Razd, and took its name from the September of 1970, when King Hussein destroyed the power of the Palestinian guerrilla movement in Jordan. Fatah has always denied its connection with Black September in order to keep Arafat clear of charges of being involved in terrorism, thus enabling him to continue his political role, but evidence of the connection is now so damning that even Fatah tends not to protest too much. Abu Daoud, one of Fatah's leaders, provided confirmation of the link when he was arrested while on a Black September mission to attack government ministries in Amman.

Ideology and aims Nationalistic. The overthrow of Israel and its replacement by a Palestinian state governed by Fatah and led by Arafat.

Activities Black September started its operations with bombing attacks on commercial installations in Europe which were connected with Israel. When these proved successful the name of Black September was announced to the world, and this was done in the most horrific fashion on 28 November 1971 with the murder of the Jordanian Prime Minister Wasfi Tell on the steps of the Sheraton Hotel in Cairo. The Palestinians blamed Tell for their defeat in Jordan and, apart from King Hussein, he was their number-one target. There followed a series of outrages: the Munich Massacre, the killing of the diplomats at Khartoum, the letter-bomb campaign of 1972, the hijacking of a Lufthansa jet to secure the release of the survivors of the Munich gang. Black September also engaged in the war of kill and counter-kill which raged throughout Europe in the early 1970s. It ceased operations in 1974 when it became obvious that its terrorist outrages were harming the political image of Fatah and the PLO. At a time when Arafat was appearing before the United Nations, and presenting himself as the potential leader of a sovereign state, he could not afford to be linked with terrorism. However, there is an element within Fatah, led by the Black September leader, Abu Iyad, who is Arafat's second-in-command, which still believes in the use of terror and this group sometimes breaks out. It was, for example, Abu Iyad and his Black Septembrists who tried to kill King Hussein at the Arab summit meeting at Rabat in October 1974. There are also other renegade Black September groups, particularly that led by Abu Nidal, which still persevere with terrorism as a weapon of Palestinian nationalism.

International links   Because of its intimate but clandestine involvement with Fatah, Black September is able to use all of Fatah's associations with the Communist world. Arms, training and military support are provided by the Soviet Union, Czechoslovakia and East Germany and they can legitimately claim that this help was given to Fatah and not to Black September. Funds are channelled from the oil-rich Arab states through Fatah to the terrorists. There are links with the major European terrorist groups and with supporters in France. Black September also used sympathisers among the many Arab students and workers in West Germany. This connection was important to them in setting up the Munich Olympic Games operation.

Achievements   Its activities have ensured that the whole world knows about the Palestinian cause. With the massive TV coverage of the Games, the Munich operation was transmitted into millions of homes around the world. In the will they left behind, the terrorists wrote: 'Why should the whole world be having fun and entertainment while we suffer with all ears deaf to us?' What the rest of the world saw as a terrible act of murder was considered a great triumph by the Arabs. However, Black September's later operations, especially the killing of the three diplomats at Khartoum – which may have been carried out by a splinter group –

proved counterproductive. Khartoum was the last operation officially claimed by Black September.

Strength This is impossible to assess, for Black September never existed as a separate entity. It had no organisation, no office and no paperwork. When the various leaders of Fatah who were concerned with terrorism decided to mount an operation they selected men for the job from Fatah, from other Palestinian groups and from foreign groups to form the strike force just for that particular operation. The men named by Abu Daoud as the warlords of Black September with authority to mount operations are: Sallah Khalef, the man code-named Abu Iyad, who is Arafat's deputy; Ali Hassan Salameh, thought to have master-minded Munich; Fakhri al-Umari, accused of planning the killing of Wasfi Tell; and Khalil al Wazir, code-named Abu Jihad.

Future prospects This concept – it was never an organisation – is dormant, but it could be reactivated at any time. At the time of writing the indications are that Abu Iyad, engaged in an attempt to seize power from Yasser Arafat, is prepared to move back into terrorism in an alliance with the Rejection Front hard-core of Abu Nidal in opposition to any attempt to make peace with Israel. Black September could start operating again at any time, possibly under a different name and this time in direct opposition to Arafat.

PALESTINE

Popular Front for the Liberation of Palestine (PFLP)

Origins Formed in December 1967 following the disaster of the Six Day War by the merger of several small guerrilla groups associated with the Arab nationalist movement. It is led by the founder of the ANM, Dr George Habash, and the operational commander until his death early in 1978 was Dr Wadi Hadad.

Ideology and aims Nationalist and Marxist. Is opposed to any settlement with Israel, leads the 'Rejection Front' and insists on the complete liberation of Palestine. This, however, is only the first of its objectives. It aims to bring about the Arab revolution in all the Arab states and then move on to join with other revolutionary groups in establishing world revolution. Its targets are Israel, imperialism and capitalism.

Activities   Terrorism of the most ruthless nature. It fought the Israelis on the West Bank and especially in the Gaza Strip after the 1967 war but the Israelis wiped out the PFLP fighting cells and the group was forced to operate first from Jordan, then from Beirut and now from Aden and Baghdad. Since their defeat by the Israelis they have concentrated on international terrorism. Many acts of hijacking and murder stemmed from Wadi Hadad: the multiple hijacking to Dawson's Field; the Lod massacre by Japanese Red Army kamikaze killers; the raid on the OPEC headquarters in Vienna; the Entebbe hijack; the Mogadishu hijack. In 1975 it was announced that George Habash had expelled his friend Wadi Hadad because he opposed Hadad's obsession with terrorism, but there is evidence which shows that the expulsion was for propaganda reasons and that Hadad's 'Foreign Operations Group' enjoyed a relationship with PFLP similar to that of Black September with Fatah. Hadad concentrated on building up links with foreign terrorists and his operations almost invariably involved terrorists from other countries. He established training camps for transnational terrorists and built up a truly international gang. After Hadad's death his organisation was taken over by his old friend Dr George Habash, who by that time was moving into a more extreme position. With the help of the Iraqi government it began preparing for further action though there were signs from Baghdad that the new management had come to the conclusion that hijack operations were no longer the most satisfactory ones.

International links   The PFLP is supported by all the 'Rejectionist' countries, Libya, Iraq, Algeria and the South Yemen, with offices in all these countries. In addition, Habash established close ties with North Korea. He also maintained a love–hate relationship with both China and the Soviet Union. It was Hadad however who established close operational links with European, Japanese and South American terrorists. The links become obvious when studying his operations. Entebbe was undertaken by Germans and Palestinians, OPEC by Germans, Palestinians and Carlos, Mogadishu by Palestinians in support of the German kidnappers of Herr Schleyer, Lod by Japanese. Carlos was Hadad's number-one hit man. There are connections with groups in Italy, Holland, France, Turkey, Iran and even the IRA. The PFLP can truly be described as the framework without which international terrorism could not work.

Achievements PFLP, apart from keeping Palestinian claims to the forefront among the turmoil of world affairs, has done little to advance the Palestinian cause. Its actions have been so extreme and so cruel they have occasioned nothing but disgust. The PFLP is truly terrorist, it influences by fear and not by reason.

Strength Active membership is now thought to have declined to about 500. The organisation commands an international gang of about fifty but can call on the services of a number of sympathisers throughout Europe.

Future prospects As the world's security services become more efficient in fighting terrorism so this group is becoming less effective. Both its last major operations, Entebbe and Mogadishu were disasters. Before his death Hadad replenished his core of killers with Japanese released from jail by hijack and by Baader–Meinhof members fleeing from Germany, but the world is closing in on his organisation. Much depends on the political situation in the Middle East. PFLP can only exist in a state of war. If peace comes it is finished. It remains to be seen what effect the death of Wadi Hadad will have on this group. It may be that Carlos, who worked closely with him in many operations, may become even more important. On the other hand, the fact that he is a foreigner may weigh against him, and there were indications in the spring of 1978 that Abu Nidal was improving his position within a new organisation known as The Corrective Movement for Al Fatah, and that from the Baghdad base he shared with PFLP he was getting closer to Abu Iyad as both felt that more violent action was needed to upset any new moves for Egyptian–Israeli rapprochement.

PALESTINE

As-Sa'iqa (Thunderbolt)

Origins   Came into being in October 1968 as the military wing of the 'Vanguards of the Popular War for the Liberation of Palestine' which was formed before the Six Day War in 1967 from the Palestinian branch of the Syrian Ba'ath Party and the Palestine battalion of the Syrian Army. Is a Syrian creation and dependent on Syria.

Ideology and aims   Nationalist, but subservient to Syria.

Activities   Has been involved in small-scale guerrilla warfare in Israel and in the internecine fighting in the Lebanon. Its leaders declare themselves opposed to international terrorism but it was members of this organisation, calling themselves 'Eagles of the Palestine Revolution', who attacked a train in Austria carrying Soviet Jews on their way to Israel in September 1973. By holding hostages they forced Chancellor Kreisky of Austria to promise to close Schonau transit camp for Jewish emigrants from Russia. In a similar exercise in September 1975 four Sa'iqa members were arrested in Amsterdam. They had planned to take train passengers hostage to force Holland to stop helping Jewish emigrants.

International links   Delegates visit the Soviet Union for talks on political co-operation but there is no evidence of terrorist links. It is suspected however that in the Schonau attack the terrorists were allowed to cross the border fully armed with the knowledge of the Czech authorities.

Achievements The pressure they put on Chancellor Kreisky and his capitulation produced an unforeseen result. The Israeli government, and in particular the then Prime Minister, Golda Meir, were so enraged that their attention was diverted from the build-up by Egypt and Syria for the launching of the Yom Kippur War.

Strength Believed to have a fighting strength of some 2000 but very few of these are engaged in terrorism. Leader is Zuheir Muhsin, a former Syrian Army officer who is also head of the Palestine Liberation Organisation's Department of Military Affairs.

Future prospects Will do whatever the Syrian government requires. Has no future without Syrian support.

PALESTINE

Democratic Front for the Liberation of Palestine (DFLP)

Origins Formed in 1969 by the breakaway of extreme left wingers from the PFLP. This secession led to bitter fighting in the streets of Beirut by adherents to both groups. A number were killed before Fatah intervened to stop the fighting.

Ideology and aims Marxist–Leninist. The only Palestinian guerrilla group which subordinates armed struggle to political struggle. It was among the first to support the principle of Jewish national rights inside a liberated Palestine and has called on all 'progressive Israelis and Jews' to merge with it in one popular Palestinian front.

Activities Opposed to the PFLP policy of international terrorism and has not been involved in any major operation outside Israel. It qualifies as a terrorist organisation by its attacks on a school in the Israeli village of Ma'alot in May 1974 in which twenty-two children were killed and on an apartment house in Beth Shean in November 1974.

International links Has no international terrorist connections but has political links with left-wing students in Europe and America. Is supported by the Soviet Union and has good relations with China where some of its members have been trained.

Achievements Political rather than military. Attempts to woo Israeli leftists have had more positive results than the raids on Ma'alot and Beth Shean which caused only outrage.

Strength About 300. Led by Naif Hawatmeh, a Greek Orthodox Christian who graduated from the University of Beirut with a degree in philosophy and the social sciences.

Future prospects Interesting. Although without military muscle, its policy of appealing to left-wing Israelis could pay off with influence in any political settlement.

PALESTINE

Popular Front for the Liberation of Palestine – General Command (PFLP–GC)

Origins Stemmed from a small commando group called the Palestine Liberation Front formed in 1959 by the ex-Syrian Army captain, Ahmed Jibril. Its aim was to wage a guerrilla war inside Israel. After 1967 it joined with other groups, some associated with the Arab Nationalist Movement to form a branch of the PFLP. But a year later the Jibril faction broke away again, protesting that there was too much emphasis on ideological squabbling in the PFLP and too little fighting.

Ideology and aims A purely military organisation which, as a member of the Rejection Front, opposes a Middle East peace settlement except on Arab terms.

Activities In keeping with its aim for fighting a guerrilla war this group has made a number of forays across the border into Israel with fighting patrols of three to five men. In May

1970 an ambush party fired a rocket at a schoolbus on a road running along the Lebanese border, killing eight children and four other passengers. In April 1974 a three-man team attacked the Israeli village of Qiryat Shemona, mainly populated by refugees from North Africa, and killed eighteen people before it was wiped out. Ahmed Jibril said that this attack was aimed at bringing into existence a 'new school of struggle based on the highest degree of revolutionary violence'. However there is no record of his group carrying out any attacks since that time. Between 1970 and 1972 the PFLP–GC also became involved in international terrorism. It specialised in letter bombs and the blowing up of aircraft. Its aircraft technique became familiar. Agents persuaded naive girls to carry apparently harmless parcels on board aircraft heading to Israel. The packages contained bombs which exploded when the aircraft reached a certain height. On 21 February 1970, one of the group's bombs destroyed a Swissair plane en route from Zurich to Tel Aviv. Forty-seven people were killed.

International links Supported by President Gaddafi of Libya and by Syria.

Achievements None, apart from slaughter.

Strength About 500 active members. Commanded by Ahmed Jibril. His second-in-command is believed to be Talal Naji (Abu Jihad Talal) who is the group's representative on the PLO's Executive Committee.

Future prospects Negligible, but as a member of the Rejection Front could cause trouble for the peace-makers.

PALESTINE

National Arab Youth for the Liberation of Palestine (NAYLP)

Origins President Gaddafi formed this group in 1972 from a mixed bag of Black September and PFLP militants who wanted to carry out acts of terrorism so extreme that even their own organisations turned them down. Gaddafi chose as its leader Ahmed al-Ghaffour, a Lebanese who had been one of Arafat's closest colleagues. Arafat had sent him to Libya to act as his ambassador to Gaddafi. But al-Ghaffour, disappointed by Arafat's adoption of political rather than military methods, deserted to Gaddafi and extremism.

Ideology and aims The use of terror to bring about a total Arab victory and the destruction of Israel.

Activities Some of the most vicious acts of terrorism were the work of this group. One hit team carried out the Rome massacre, throwing two thermite bombs into a Pan American plane, killing thirty-two people and wounding eighteen. When the killers eventually surrendered after hijacking a plane to Kuwait, they told their interrogators that it was Gaddafi himself who had ordered them to carry out the attack. Even so, they said, it was only a secondary target: Gaddafi had originally wanted them to assassinate the then US Secretary of State, Henry Kissinger, to wreck any prospect of a negotiated peace settlement. This group is also believed to have been responsible for the machine-gun attack on passengers waiting to board a TWA flight at Athens Airport. Three passengers were killed and fifty-five wounded. This group concentrated its activities on aircraft and airports.

International links Libya.

Achievements Blackmail-release of several members arrested for acts of terrorism.

Strength No longer believed to exist as a terrorist group. It split up and its members drifted to other groups, especially that of Abu Nidal, after al-Ghaffour had been arrested and executed by Fatah as a traitor. Fatah had tried him *in absentia*, but confident in his role as a terrorist leader, and certain that Gaddafi would protect him, he took no notice of this sentence. He went back to Beirut, where he was captured by Fatah's own internal security force – run by the fearsome Abu Iyad, leader of Black September. The Libyans remembered him in a later operation by naming a hijack team 'The martyr Ahmed al-Ghaffour group'. But that was the last that was heard of him.

Future prospects   Nil.

PALESTINE

Black June (The Corrective Movement for Al Fatah)

Origins   Formed by Sabri al-Banna, code-named Abu Nidal, as a renegade Black September group to carry on the fight against Israel by means of terror. Abu Nidal took a number of al-Ghaffour's men into his group and he has been sentenced to death *in absentia* by Fatah just as al-Ghaffour was. His crime was to attempt to assassinate moderate Fatah leaders. He has been described as the 'outstanding practitioner of pure unbridled terrorism'.

Ideology and aims   In late 1976 Abu Nidal told an interviewer that in his view inter-Arab terrorism, however regrettable, was the price that had to be paid for precipitating the all-embracing Arab revolution that alone could lead to the liberation of Palestine.

Activities   Almost completely confined to inter-Arab terrorism. Black June was responsible for the murder of the moderate Said Hammami, Fatah's representative in London in January 1978. He was killed because he had established a dialogue with equally moderate Israelis. The group is totally dependent on the Iraqis, it has its headquarters in Baghdad and a training camp outside the city by the Euphrates. It undertakes terrorist missions on behalf of the Iraqi government, particularly against the Syrians. Three members of the group were publicly hanged in Damascus in 1977 after attacking a hotel and seizing hostages.

International links   Has a considerable following among radical Arab students, especially in London.

Achievements   Has terrified those Arabs who are seeking to bring about a peaceful settlement in the Middle East. He has made good men frightened of being involved in peace talks and can so claim a measure of success in his aim of preventing any settlement which does not involve the destruction of Israel.

Future prospects   Bleak. If he is abandoned by the Iraqis he will almost certainly be killed by Fatah or the Syrians. However, he is not completely without allies. The polarisation forced on the Arabs by Sadat's mission to Jerusalem brought him closer to Wadi Hadad, who also had headquarters in Baghdad, and to Abu Iyad who, early in 1978, was once again showing signs of rebelling against Arafat's political line.

IRELAND

Provisional Irish Republican Army (PIRA)

Origins   The 'Provos' came into being in 1969 as the military wing of the Provisional Sinn Fein, when they split away from the main body of the IRA, the 'Officials'. In a reverse procedure to most such schisms, this was a breakaway of traditional, religious nationalists from a movement which was becoming more and more Marxist in outlook. The Officials had also 'gone soft', they were looking for a political victory rather than a military one. The Provos then embarked on one more round of 'the troubles' which have bedevilled Ireland for the last 400 years.

Ideology and aims   According to the Provo leader, David O'Connell, their primary objective is to 'destroy British rule in Ireland'. This is to be achieved by following a formula used in Algeria: 'Armed action plus political action equals revolutionary action.' There is, however, more than a hint of fascism in their pronouncements and actions.

Activities They have attempted to force the Protestants who form the majority in Ulster to abandon their claim that Ulster is a country in union with the United Kingdom. In order to do this they have taken on the British Army and have attempted to bring normal life to a standstill in Ulster. They have murdered, blackmailed, bombed, firebombed and engaged in skirmishes with the army both in the cities and the countryside. They murdered the British Ambassador to Dublin, and have carried their fight to England using 'Active Service Units' composed of small groups of men and women to bomb and murder. In the nine years that this present round of fighting has lasted nearly 1900 people have met violent deaths in Ulster.

International links Contacts with the Breton and Basque movements and some links with the Palestinians, particularly the PFLP. Some members trained with the Arabs and Colonel Gaddafi has given them financial support and a small amount of arms. However, even the Arabs are wary of too close an association with the Provos, who have achieved a reputation for wildness which makes the Palestinians seem tame. Most of the Provos' overseas links are with the large Irish immigrant population in the United States, although in 1977 there was a noticeable cutting back in this support.

Achievements In a strictly military sense the small core of Provo guerrillas have fought with skill and no small measure of success against a British Army which for political reasons has not been able to use its full power. At the height of its success, the Provos held part of Londonderry as a 'liberated area' and reduced the Irish police force to impotence. There were also areas of the border country, especially Armagh which was classed a 'bandit country' and where the army itself was at risk. In London, when the Balcombe Street gang was bombing seemingly at will in Mayfair, normal police activity was brought to a halt and the West End of London was swamped with policemen. They succeeded in bringing about a state of anarchy in Ulster, and for a short while held

London in fear. But those days are now past – London is so big it can swallow terrorism. The Royal Ulster Constabulary is back on the streets and even making arrests for crimes committed five and six years ago. Many of the Provos' best men are dead or in jail. The Special Air Service has cleared up Armagh. The Provos are on the defensive throughout the province. They can still mount attacks, they can still destroy businesses. But their strength is ebbing away. Politically, they may have achieved more than they yet realise. Certainly the Roman Catholic population of Ulster will benefit both politically and socially once this round of the troubles is over. There can be no going back to a status of second-class citizens for them. What the Provos have failed to achieve is their main objective, the incorporation of Ulster into the Republic of Ireland in a federation of the country's historic provinces. Although the British people are heartily sick of the Irish problem, the British government has no wish to face another bout of fighting in a few years' time, and the British Army has no liking for fighting with one hand tied behind its back, it is extremely unlikely that after nine years of war and the expenditure of millions of pounds that the British government could throw the Irish Protestants to the wolves – although they may be sheep in wolves clothing.

Strength The hard-core membership is estimated at 300–400. But the 'Godfathers', the leaders who never appear on the streets, can summon stone-throwing gangs of youths at a moment's notice and a demonstration of women and children can be organised in an instant. They would however be useless if it were not for the twenty or thirty real professionals who can organise a 'snipe' or build a sophisticated bomb with built-in booby traps. Leading members are: David O'Connell, Seamus Twomey, Martin McGuinness, Joseph Cahill, Gerry Adams, Billy McKee, J. B. O'Hagan, Eamon Doherty.

Future prospects As the army gradually gets on top of the Provos and curtails their activities, it is likely that more and more of the militants will fall away, give up the fight for the time being or turn to political work. But the history of Ireland shows that even if one violent branch of the nationalist movement is defeated, there is always another ready to take its place in a few years' time.

ARGENTINE

Ejército Revolucionario del Pueblo (ERP)

Origins Founded in 1969 by Roberto Santucho as the armed branch of the Revolutionary Workers' Party. It started operations in 1970, three years after the death of Che Guevara who had rejected the Argentine as the most suitable place to set up a revolutionary *foco* and had chosen Bolivia instead, a choice which was to lead to his death.

Ideology and aims Marxist–Leninist, with a strong vein of Trotskyism. Dedicated to the overthrow of the capitalist system in the Argentine and other South American countries.

Activities Has carried out a unique combined programme of urban terrorism and rural guerrilla warfare. In the towns it has concentrated on the raising of money through the kidnapping of foreign businessmen, the use of hostage-blackmail through the kidnapping of diplomats, murder of officials and of members of right-wing assassination teams, and a general assault on the structure of society. In the countryside large forces of combined ERP and Montoneros fighters, sometimes in battalion strength, have taken on the army in pitched battles. The bloodiest of these actions took place on 22 December 1975 when an estimated 500 ERP guerrillas tried to storm the barracks at Monte Chingolo, only a few miles south of Buenos Aires. The garrison seems to have been forewarned and was ready for the storming party. The fighting went on all night and at the end of it, six civilians, nine soldiers and eighty-five guerrillas lay dead. It was a devastating blow and it followed a series of defeats in the guerrillas' attempts to occupy a 'liberated area' in the wild mountains and jungle of Tucuman. It is estimated that they lost some 600 men in this campaign, including Santucho's brother, Asdrubal. These losses forced a change in tactics. Fewer large-scale operations were mounted and none of them involved more than fifty men and women. The group turned increasingly to urban warfare and selective assassination. In July 1976, however, the ERP was dealt a blow which may prove fatal. Roberto Santucho, his second-in-command, Jose Urteaga, and several other leaders were killed when the police raided their hideout in a Buenos Aires apartment. Since then the scale of activity has dropped dramatically.

International links   ERP co-operates with most of the other South American groups through an organisation called the Junta de Co-ordinacion Revolucionaria (JCR). Established in 1974 to facilitate joint planning, funding and support, the JCR was dependent financially on the ERP. Since the authorities in South America began to inflict heavy casualties on the revolutionaries in the mid-seventies the JCR's overseas headquarters in Paris has become increasingly important. Assassinations of South American ambassadors in Europe have been carried out under the auspices of the JCR, terrorist cells have been set up in a number of countries and links have been established with European and Palestinian groups. Other members of the JCR are Bolivia's National Liberation Army (ELN), Chile's Movement of the Revolutionary Left (MIR), Paraguay's National Liberation Front (Frepalina) and Uruguay's Tupamaros (MLN).

Achievements   The ERP has become rich and has caused the death of many people. But it has failed in its aim of bringing about revolution in the Argentine. It is one of the beliefs of terrorists that if they succeed in provoking a right-wing *coup* or the enforcement of extreme repressive measures, then there must inevitably be a counter-movement which will destroy the government and bring about the revolution. But in both Uruguay and the Argentine exactly the opposite has happened. The right-wing governments brought to power because of revolutionary terrorism have crippled the terrorist movements in both countries. ERP activities also caused the formation of right-wing terrorist groups, notably the Alianza Anticomunista Argentina, better known as the Triple A. This organisation, which operated with some official support and included policemen and soldiers in its ranks, killed anyone suspected of supporting the ERP or the Montoneros. They tortured, then shot their victims and left them lying literally in heaps around Buenos Aires. They fought a war of kill and counterkill even more ruthless than that fought between the Arabs and the Israelis after Munich. However, with the decrease in the ERP's activities and the strong line taken by the military government of General Videla, this organisation, too, has become less active.

Strength Despite the losses among the fighters there is still considerable support for the aims of the ERP, especially among intellectuals, radical priests of the Roman Catholic Church and left-wing trade unionists.

Future prospects As its strength is being whittled away it is likely to turn more and more to classic urban terrorism, operating in small units. It remains in being but is hard pressed and could only return to its days of glory if there was a political upheaval in the Argentine.

ARGENTINE

Montoneros

Origins Formed by left-wing supporters of Peron, it has strong affiliations with the trade union movement. Disappointed with Peron's performance and that of his widow who succeeded him, the Montoneros emerged in 1975 as the guerrilla wing of the Authentic Peronist Party.

Ideology and aims It was reported in the *Guardian* in February 1976 that this group saw itself engaged in a 'war of liberation' involving a socialist revolution and the defeat of

the 'imperialism' of foreign capital. Its aims in fact hark back
to the original ideals of Peronism with their glorification of
the 'Descamisados' (the shirtless ones).

Activities Has carried out assassinations, bombings and
kidnappings, and has made an attempt to seize control of the
trade unions through an underground amalgamation of
unions called the Confederacion General de Trabajo en
Resistencia (The General Confederation of Workers for
Resistance). Also took part in the rural guerrilla campaign
with the ERP and armed itself by setting up weapons
factories – with expert help from the trade unions – to
produce its own arms.

International links None known, the Montoneros is essentially an Argentinian group.

Achievements Has had considerable success in its trade
union activities, provoking strikes and engaging in industrial
sabotage. But is under increasing pressure from the security
forces.

Strength At one stage it was estimated to have a well-
organised military force of some 7500 – this has now been
whittled down to less than 2000. Roberto Quieto, one of its
founder-leaders, was captured in December 1975 and control now rests with Mario Firmenich. It still has extensive
support in the factories and, like the ERP, among radical
priests, though less so among the intellectuals.

Future prospects In the latter part of 1976 and 1977 the
Montoneros became less effective due to the pressure of the
military government, but through working-class support it
could still pose a threat to Argentina's stability, although this
would stem more from industrial action than terrorism.

URUGUAY

Tupamaros – Movimiento de Liberación Nacional (MLN)

Origins This group takes its name from the Inca chief Túpac Amaru, who rebelled against the Spaniards and was burnt at the stake. It is a Marxist group which began operations in the early 1960s as a rural guerrilla force but soon changed to urban operations in the capital, Montevideo.

Ideology and aims Marxist and revolutionary.

Activities Has virtually ceased to exist since 1972 but we include it because it was the prototype for the other urban guerrilla movements in South America. It specialised in the kidnapping of diplomats and it was this group which held the British Ambassador Sir Geoffrey Jackson prisoner in a 'people's prison' for eight months in 1971 and had previously murdered the American diplomat Daniel Mitrione. It also carried out a series of attacks on foreign establishments in Uruguay.

International links Some connection with the PFLP but its strongest links are with the Argentinian ERP and the consortium of South American movements, JCR, in Paris. Also has links with the Basques.

Achievements Provided the other South American movements with a blueprint for organisation and action. It was also the first of the modern movements to be destroyed by repressive measures forced on a traditionally democratic country. Most of the Tupamaros are dead or in prison, but the repressive measures that the military government took are so harsh that ordinary democratic life has ceased in Uruguay. Freedom of the press and all political trade union rights have been suspended. Perhaps the Tupamaros may have a posthumous success, the one that terrorists always argue should be achieved: a revolution provoked by the repressive measures taken to contain terrorism. But there is no sign of this at present.

Strength Those members who are not dead or in prison have fled abroad. Some are fighting with the ERP in the Argentine while others are carrying on their struggle in Europe.

Future prospects Nil. If any future organisation becomes powerful in Uruguay it is likely to be on pure Communist lines with the backing of the Soviet Union.

FRANCE

Front de Libération de la Bretagne – Armée Révolutionnaire Bretonne (FLB–ARB)

Origins Emerged from a number of Breton nationalist and cultural groups, undertaking its first violent action in June 1966. It is a member of the Comité National de la Bretagne Libre whose Secretary-General is Yann Goulet, a veteran Breton activist convicted of wartime collaboration with the Germans, who lives in the Irish republic.

Ideology and aims Liberation of Brittany from French rule. It demands 'a free Brittany, the Bretons their own masters, a Breton Assembly and Government'. Another group, the Front de Libération de la Bretagne – Pour la Libération Nationale et le Socialisme (FLB–LNS) accuses it of representing the 'Breton right-wing' and having 'Fascist overtones'.

Activities Responsible for a wave of bomb attacks in the late 1960s which were ended when sixty members were arrested in 1969. However, they were amnestied and the bombings resumed in 1971–2. They were stopped for a time when eleven members were arrested in 1972 but started again the following year and have continued sporadically. The group has not so far carried out any hijackings or assassinations.

International links In October 1972, Saor Eire (Free Ireland) said that sixteen FLB members had received arms training in secret camps in Ireland, and there were reports in the same year of contacts between the Basque Euzkadi Ta Azkatasuna, the IRA and the FLB, resulting in agreement on political aims and co-operation, including supplies of arms. The group appears to be outside the mainstream of transnational terrorism and does not have much in common with radical left-wing groups.

Achievements Apart from drawing attention to its claims for Breton autonomy, it has achieved nothing.

Strength No more than 150–200 activists.

Future prospects Negligible. The Free Breton movement is fragmented, thoroughly penetrated by the French police and while many Bretons would like to achieve autonomy, the group's terrorist activities command little support or respect.

FRANCE (CORSICA)

Action pour la Renaissance de la Corse (ARC)

Origins Founded in 1967 to promote the regional identity of Corsica. In particular, it protests against the concentration of the island's economic resources (essentially vineyards and tourism) in the hands of non-Corsicans – especially 'pieds noirs' French settlers forced to leave Algeria – while many native islanders have to emigrate to mainland France to earn a living. Set out to be non-violent but has become increasingly radical and militant. The largest of half a dozen Corsican groups of varying political allegiances.

Ideology and aims   Nationalistic. Wants an autonomous Assembly and Executive within the framework of the French Republic.

Activities   Mainly bomb attacks. Its most spectacular exploit was the occupation in August 1975 of wine vaults owned by a French repatriate from Algeria. Some fifty armed farmers led by Dr Edmond Siméoni carried out the occupation and killed two policemen before they surrendered. Siméoni was sentenced to five years imprisonment, two years being suspended. Bomb attacks have been mainly directed against targets on the island but some have been exploded on the mainland.

International links   None, though it has been claimed that Colonel Gadaffi of Libya offered money.

Achievements   Has forced the replacement of some high officials by men of Corsican origin and the removal of the 3000 French Legionnaires who traditionally train on the island.

Strength   Has large following on the island which draws on its tradition of banditry to provide bombers whenever needed. A crowd of 10,000 demonstrated for Dr Siméoni's release. Important members: Dr Siméoni and his brother, Max, who is secretary of the group.

Future prospects   Could well win the measure of autonomy that it demands. It would then cease to exist as a terrorist group because it seems to have come to terror by default rather than design, and is not involved in transnational terrorism.

HOLLAND

Republik Malaku Selatan – Independent Republic of the South Moluccas

Origins   Sprang from the desire of South Moluccan exiles

living in Holland to return to an independent state of South Molucca. These exiles, former soldiers of the Dutch East Indies colonial army in Indonesia, came to Holland after Indonesia won its independence in 1949 and the South Moluccan nationalist movement was crushed by the Indonesian Army. Some 12,500 left for Holland. Their numbers have grown to 40,000. The movement was political among the original exiles but has turned to terrorism among the young – who have spent all their lives in Holland and have never seen the islands in the cause of which they now conduct terrorist operations.

Ideology and aims Independence from Indonesia and the right to set up their own nation on islands which have been internationally recognised as part of Indonesia since 1949.

Activities Campaign of bombings and occupation of Indonesian offices in Holland started in 1970. It was disclosed in April 1975 that the Dutch police had discovered a plot to kidnap Queen Juliana by an extreme faction, the Tamaela group. On 2 December 1975, seven South Moluccans belonging to the radical Free Young South Moluccans Movement hijacked a train near Beilen and held it for twelve days. They murdered three of its twenty-three occupants. Two days later seven more terrorists stormed the Indonesian Consulate-General in Amsterdam and took forty-three hostages. They surrendered after fifteen days. Both groups were tried and imprisoned. This led to the hijacking of another train at Assen and the occupation of a nearby school in May 1977. After twenty days Dutch commandos stormed the train and killed six of the terrorists. Two of the eighty-five hostages also died. The terrorists in the school surrendered.

International links Some of the South Moluccans have established a link with Arab groups and have received training at Palestinian guerrilla camps. A few have been to Moscow but both these links are tenuous and there is little real transnational interest in their cause which is generally deemed hopeless. Their only real support comes from members of the Dutch 'Red Help' movement.

Achievements With their two train hijacks they have ensured that the world knows about their cause when, previously, most people had forgotten the South Moluccans. They have also forced the Dutch government to take a closer look at this community growing in size and militancy in the heart of Holland. But apart from making life easier for the South Moluccans there is little the Dutch can do for them. Most of this group's achievements are negative. They have aroused a great deal of bitterness among the Dutch who assimilated the other populations from the former Dutch empire. And they have harmed Holland's relations with Indonesia.

Strength The militants have a great deal of support among the community and although Johannes Manusama, 'President' of the self-styled South Moluccan Government-in-exile, does not condone violence, many do. Activists probably number about 250.

Future prospects There seems no chance whatsoever that they will achieve any of their aims. With growing bitterness in their towns and among the Dutch, it seems certain that there will be more trouble.

SPAIN

Euzkadi Ta Askatasuna – Basque Homeland and Liberty (ETA)

Origins This group stems from the struggle for nationhood of the Basques, a struggle which has gone on for hundreds of years. ETA itself dates from 1959 having grown out of a radical group which split from the Basque National Party. It draws its strength from the Basque people who are spread over the border between France and Spain, around San Sebastian.

Ideology and aims The liberation of 'Euzkadi' from Spanish and French rule and the establishment of an independent

Basque Socialist State. Heavily influenced by Marxist–Leninist beliefs.

Activities Acts of sabotage led to the proclamation of a state of emergency in Spain in 1968. Has pursued a campaign of bombing, kidnapping and assassination ever since. Murdered the Spanish Prime Minister, Luis Carrero Blanco, in December 1973, justifying the murder by claiming it was in revenge for the killing of nine Basque militants by the government and to fight repression in Spain. Has carried on its activities despite concessions by the government of King Juan Carlos to Basque nationalism, an amnesty and an easing of the anti-terrorist legislation along with reform of the security forces.

International links There has been contact with the Provisional IRA, including an exchange of revolvers, for training in explosives by IRA experts. The government claims that IRA explosives were used in the murder of Premier Carrero Blanco but ETA denies this. Contacts are also reported with the Breton Liberation Front, Kurdish nationalists and Palestinian groups. There is also some loose co-operation with South American groups, particularly the Tupamaros who, forced out of Uruguay, have been looking for other pastures.

Achievements ETA could claim to have forced concessions on the Spanish government through its campaign of murder and bombing. The government of King Juan Carlos has lifted the formal penalty imposed on two Basque provinces for opposing the Crown during the Civil War; the Basque language has been officially recognised; and the Basque flag is allowed to fly alongside the flag of Spain. It is likely, however, that the King in his search for an 'authentic consensus of national harmony' would have moved in this direction without the killing. Certainly ETA has lost much support by continuing its campaign after these concessions.

Strength Like other nationalistic groups it can draw on a pool of fervent supporters. The Basques have always been hard men and doughty fighters. They take easily to terrorism. But for the reasons set out support is beginning to erode.

Future prospects   There seems little chance that the Basques will give up their struggle to achieve independence. After all they can date their exploits back to the Battle of Roncevalles, where they ambushed Roland. The question is: given that the Spanish government is prepared to make concessions, at what stage would it become unprofitable for the Basques to continue to use the bomb? That time may be approaching, for on 18 January 1978, the government legalised the political arm of the ETA movement and two days later ruled that all fourteen suspects arrested for the assassination of Premier Carrero Blanco would be granted full amnesty.

SPAIN

Frente Revolucionario Antifascista Patriótica (FRAP)

Origins   First reported in 1971, but was not formally constituted until January 1974. It is an umbrella organisation for numerous extreme left-wing groups.

Ideology and aims   Maoist.

Activities   Members of this group have killed policemen and members of the security forces often for no apparent reason other than that they were 'fascist pigs'. Three members were executed in September 1975.

International links   Tenuous connections with the Basque ETA and even more tenuous links with the IRA.

Strength   Small with little popular support. Relying as it does on the ever changing loyalties of volatile left-wing groups it finds it hard to retain a core of activists.

Future prospects   None unless there is a dramatic change in the political situation in Spain. The left-wing groups are now totally involved in a guerrilla war with their opponents on the right. They have little influence with the population in general.

SPAIN

Grupo de Resistencia Antifascista Primo de Octubre – First of October Anti-fascist Resistance Group (GRAPO)

Origins The name of this group refers to the day in 1975 when four Madrid policemen were assassinated in retaliation for the execution of five convicted urban guerrillas.

Ideology and aims Said by a senior police official to be 'the armed wing of a radical breakaway group of the Spanish Communist Party', it has Maoist tendencies.

Activities Kidnappings, murder of policemen, bank robberies and bombings. Suspected of being responsible for a bomb attempt on the life of King Juan Carlos in Majorca. Among its bombings were that of Madrid radio station and the offices of the newspaper *Diario 16*. According to Elvira Dieguez Silveira who admitted to the police that she had bombed the newspaper, it had particularly incensed the terrorists because it claimed that GRAPO was being manipulated by the CIA.

International links None discernible.

Achievements None except to heighten the tension in post-Franco Spain.

Strength Small and severely eroded by police raids in 1977. Fifteen members of its 'executive commission' including its operational commander were arrested in an apartment in Benidorm. The police also seized 100 lb of explosives, 419 detonators, 19 shotguns, 3 revolvers, and scores of false identity cards and number plates. Police arrested Fernando Hierro, said to be the group's leader in a series of raids in Madrid.

Future prospects   Seems to be taking on anarchistic tendencies similar to Baader–Meinhof and could be a threat if new, militant members take over the roles of those arrested. No real political future.

SPAIN

Guerrilleros Del Cristo Rey – Warriors of Christ the King

Origins   First appeared as a right-wing religious group opposed to liberal and left-wing priests. In the past two years has extended its activities to general opposition to all things left of centre.

Ideology and aims   Its leaders would like to see a Fascist International set up to fight both capitalism and Communism. It has connections with the Partido Español Nacional Sindicalista, a neo-fascist syndicalist party. Other extreme right-wing groups which appear to have some identity of ideology are: the Apostolic Anti-Communist Alliance, which is modelled on the Argentine Triple A group and which claimed responsibility for the slaughter of five Communist lawyers in a Madrid law office in 1977; and the Adolf Hitler Commando, which has carried out minor operations of destruction.

Activities   Members like to dress up in Nazi uniforms and beat up bishops, journalists and others who disagree with them. Its leader, Mariano Sanchez Covisa, was arrested in February 1977 when the police uncovered a clandestine arms assembly factory in a flat he had rented in Madrid.

International links   With fascist groups in South America and Italy.

Achievements   None, except to heighten tension in post-Franco Spain.

Strength   Considerable among extreme right-wing religious supporters of the old regime who believe the new regime is drifting towards Communism.

Future prospects In direct ratio to left-wing terrorist groups. The growth of one form of fanaticism inevitably leads to the growth of an opposition group.

YUGOSLAVIA

Hrvatsko Revolucionarno Bratstvo – Croation Revolutionary Brotherhood (HRB) – Ustashe (literally 'Insurgents')

Origins Long-standing Croatian nationalist dissidence within Yugoslavia feeding upon hostility to Serbian dominance in the government of the country. Ustashe agents organised the murder of King Alexander of Yugoslavia at Marseilles on 9 October 1934.

Ideology and aims Nationalist with fascist tendencies. The Ustashe collaborated with the German Army during the Second World War and carried out massacres of the Serbs who mainly supported the Communist partisans of Tito.

Activities They have carried on a campaign of bombing, assassination and hijacking against the Yugoslav government at home and abroad. The Yugoslavs have responded by sending out their own hit teams to kill members of these groups in a small-scale version of the Arab–Israeli war of secret agents. On 10 September 1976, Croatians hijacked a TWA jet on a flight from New York to Canada and forced it to fly to Europe where it made 'bombing runs' over London and Paris, dropping leaflets expounding the Croatian cause. They left a bomb behind in New York to show they meant business. It exploded and killed a policeman but when they finally surrendered in Paris it was found that the bomb with which they threatened to blow up the plane had been assembled on board from an empty cooking pot, paste and putty, all of which had escaped the vigilance of the security men.

International links   None of the usual links, but Croatian emigré communities, particularly in Australia, form the basis of HRB activities outside Yugoslavia. There are also active communities in the United States, Canada, Argentina, Venezuela, West Germany, Spain and Sweden. Soviet-inspired provocateurs are said to be active among Yugoslav workers and students in some European countries.

Achievements   None, except to make the world aware that it has one more problem to face.

Strength   The number actually engaged in terrorist operations is small, probably about thirty. But there is considerable sympathy for them among Croatian communities established all round the world thus giving them the possibility of setting up a widespread web of bases.

Future prospects   Will carry on with their intermittent campaign of terror but they seem hardly likely to achieve any of their goals as long as a Communist government is in power in Yugoslavia.

TURKEY

Turkish People's Liberation Army (TPLA)

Origins   Emerged in the early 1970s as one of a series of violent offshoots of Dev Genc – the Turkish Revolutionary Youth Federation which itself sprang from the student riots in France and Germany in 1968. It has since become the most militant. While most of Turkey's left-wing students engage in campus confrontation with right-wing students and the police, the TPLA uses terror as its weapon.

Ideology and aims   Marxist–Maoist, it has not announced its aims but the intention is clear: the overthrow of the Turkish government by revolutionary violence and the establishment of a far-left regime.

Activities   The usual mixture of murder, bombing and hijacking. On 27 July 1976, the TPLA attempted to kill opposition leader and former Prime Minister, Bulent Ecevit, during his visit to the United States. The most bloodthirsty of their actions was the murder of the Israeli Consul General in Istanbul in 1971 and the kidnapping and murder of three radar technicians, two British and one Canadian. Ten TPLA terrorists were killed in the subsequent shoot-out.

International links   These are strong, especially with the Palestinian movements. Members of the TPLA have been trained by the Palestinians, they killed the Israeli Consul General in Istanbul at the request of the Palestinians, and the French police discovered a close alliance between a foreign cell of the organisation and Carlos when they raided a villa at Villiers-sur-Marne, south of Paris. Also has links with Communist states, particularly East Germany and North Korea. Believed to get financial aid and guidance from East Germany.

Achievements   Internationally, none. But inside Turkey has contributed to the instability of the political situation.

Strength   Estimated at 300 activists. Has suffered losses at the hands of the security authorities – its founder, Mahir Gayan, and several other leaders have been executed or killed in gun battles. It is likely, however, that the fury of the student conflict has thrown up more than enough militants to replace the lost leaders.

Future prospects   The present political situation in Turkey with a failing economy and a weak coalition government allied to fierce conflict between the right and left provides an ideal working atmosphere for terrorism. It would seem that apart from fulfilling its international commitments this group will concentrate on trying to overthrow the government from inside the country. It may well have some success.

ITALY

Brigate Rosse – Red Brigades

Origins Emerged as an extreme left-wing organisation in the early 1970s. Had much the same early history as Baader–Meinhof, springing from the 1968 riots and drawing its members from disillusioned middle-class students.

Ideology and aims The official view, given at the end of a three-year enquiry by public prosecutor, Dr Guido Viola, is that this group seeks to establish Communism through armed struggle. It is doubtful, however, if classic Communism is its true aim. It is both more Maoist and more militant.

Activities Arson, murder, kidnapping, bombings. This group has all the talents of terrorism. It wages war on the extreme right wing and anybody else who opposes its views. Journalists especially are its targets. At first the offending writers were shot in the legs. But in November 1977, Carlo Casalegno, deputy editor of the Turin newspaper *La Stampa*, was shot three times and died a lingering death. A telephone call to a news agency gave the message: 'The servant of the State has been brought to justice by the Red Brigades.' In December 1977 a member of the extreme right wing, Angelo Pistolesi, was similarly shot down in Rome. In addition to these assassinations, this group wounded thirty-seven people during 1977. They were mostly employees of state agencies or large private industrial concerns. The Red Brigades also specialise in sabotage at industrial works, particularly by means of arson. In 1976 the Fiat company in Turin – headquarters of the Red Brigades – suffered four arson fires which caused extensive damage. This group also publishes a clandestine newspaper with the title of *Mai più Senza Fucile* (Never Without a Gun). Care must be taken to differentiate between political kidnappings carried out by the Red Brigades and similar groups and the purely criminal kidnappings which are proving so profitable at the present time.

The 'historic leaders' under Renato Curcio began their

campaign by arresting people they designated 'enemies of the people', such as managers and executives in the industrial north, who were beaten up and then released. From such beginnings they graduated to murder and ransom demands. After the arrest of Curcio and fifteen other leaders in 1974, new and more efficient commanders moved in to launch a sustained campaign to prevent the trial of the original leaders from taking place. They murdered judges, anti-terrorist squad officers and journalists and this violent campaign culminated in March 1978 as the big trial began in Turin. The Red Brigades kidnapped and murdered Signor Aldo Moro.

International links Some contact with the Palestinians but because of geographical and ideological links its closest foreign contacts are with Baader–Meinhof and its successors. One link was through Petra Krause, a holder of both German and Italian nationalities who was arrested in Switzerland in April 1975 on suspicion of directing a gang accused of stealing guns for distribution to both groups. There are many remarkable similarities between the Red Brigades and the West German Red Army Faction. At the time of the Moro kidnap it was reported that one of the terrorist raiders gave orders in German. Already in 1972 Holger Meins of the RAF who later died on hunger strike in prison had killed an Italian police inspector 'as a favour' to the Red Brigades. Weapons acquired by Petra Krause in Switzerland went to Siegfried Haag, the West German lawyer believed to be a second-generation RAF leader. At one stage it was claimed that the RAF and the RBs were almost branches of the same organisation.

Achievements This group has contributed substantially to the terrorism that plagues Italy and has brought the country to the brink of anarchy. It can claim to be approaching the classic terrorist aim of causing the downfall of the established government. It has had, however, a great deal of help with nearly a score of other left-wing groups and half a dozen right-wing groups contributing to the turmoil in Italy's political and industrial life.

Strength   No reliable figure for the number of activists, but a reasonable estimate would be at around 100, for the group has shown the ability to mount operations involving a number of squads in action at the same time. In the aftermath of the Moro affair it began to look as though the Red Brigades had more militants than had been thought. Its leader, Renato Curcio, was arrested but was freed from prison by armed supporters in February 1975, and then recaptured in January 1976 to face charges of kidnapping, multiple theft and arms offences.

Future prospects   Italy's new anti-terrorist inspectorate is conducting a vigorous campaign against the Red Brigades and has made a number of arrests. These do not seem to have affected the group's ability to cause trouble. Far more of a threat to the group are the continuing forces of fission which affect Italy's terrorist groups as much as they do its political parties. One split which has affected the Red Brigades is the breaking away of a group of hardliners who have formed another organisation called the 'Communist Frontline'. It is believed that these professional terrorists have built up their new group by recruiting radical high school students and other young people, who, in their eagerness to prove themselves, have become ultra-violent.

ITALY

Nuclei Armati Proletari – Armed Proletarian Cells (NAP)

Origins   Based largely in Naples, this group emerged as a significant force in late 1974. It is believed to bring together a mixed bag of students, criminals and dissidents from Lotta Continua (an extreme left-wing group which promotes strikes and aims at infiltration of prisons). Linked with the Red Brigades in 1976 to carry out joint attacks.

Ideology and aims   A spokesman described members as

'revolutionaries ... not Marxists; neither Leninists nor Stalinists. We are burying the corpses of the old ideologies' (*L'Europa*, 23 May 1975).

Activities Specialises in attacks on prisons and in 1975 launched a simultaneous attack on three prisons, incited a riot in Viterbo prison and abducted the Rome magistrate, Giuseppe di Gennaro. When two women leaders, Maria Pia Vianale and Franca Salerno, were sentenced to four years' imprisonment after taking part in a gun battle with the police in which their comrade, Antonio Lo Muscio, was killed, they shouted that he 'did not fall in vain, thousands of proletarians hold guns in their hands'.

International links Baader–Meinhof through Petra Krause.

Achievements None, except to contribute to anarchy in Italy.

Strength Membership was considerably reduced in July 1977 when twenty were sent to prison after being found guilty of 'forming an armed band against the state'. Still capable of mounting attacks in co-operation with Red Brigades even though the Red Brigades continue to look down upon them as 'proles', describing them as 'not the right cadres'.

ITALY
Right-wing Extremist Groups

A number of right-wing extremist groups, some of them committed to terrorism, have also been spawned in Italy over the past few years. Some came into being through a revival of old-fashioned fascism and others as a direct reaction to the activities of the left-wing groups. There has also been a growth of right-wing extremism among individual members of the armed forces and the security authorities. The thinking of these men was expressed in an article in *Corriere dell'Aviatore*, October 1975, which said that a *coup d'état* was seriously considered as a 'therapeutic measure' to resolve a 'gangrenous' political situation. As a result of this article a group of high-ranking officers were charged with incitement to subversion.

None of the right-wing groups seems to possess much power. Among the better-known organisations are: La Fenice, Mussolini Action Squads, Revolutionary Action Movement, Rosa Dei Venti, Ordine Nero which has now combined with Ordine Nuovo, and Avanguardia Nazionale. In January 1978, the trial in Rome of 132 members of Ordine Nuovo ended with all but 15 of the defendants being found not guilty. The remaining 15 had their trials suspended until additional evidence could be produced. The trial was held under a post-war law which makes it a crime to promote or reorganise the old Fascist Party which it defines as 'a movement with anti-democratic aims, given over to the exultation of and to the use of violence as a means of political change, and a denigration of democracy and its institutions'. Not a bad definition of terrorism.

10 | The Chronology of Terror

It would be possible to chronicle every known act of terrorism in modern times but the result would be a thick volume devoted to nothing else and of value only to those readers seeking specialised knowledge. So what we have set out to do is to list those acts of terrorism which, over the last ten years, have actually affected the course of affairs. It would be pointless to list every bomb exploded in Belfast, or the murder of every policeman in the Argentine or even every hijack. But where those acts generated an importance outside their own immediate impact and demonstrate the way in which terrorism and counter-terrorism has developed, then we have included them.

We chose 1968 to start our list because it was the watershed year of terrorism. It was the year in which Arab terrorists became active following the defeat of the Arab armies in the Six Day War of 1967. At that time the Palestinian guerrillas were the only forces in the Arab world able to carry the war to the Israelis, and this they did by launching small-scale raids inside Israel – which were quickly stamped out – and then by turning to international terrorism. 1968 was also the year of the student uprising in Europe which failed in its objective of overturning governments but which led, through the frustration of the militants, to the formation of groups prepared to use terrorism to achieve the upheaval which the riots had failed to bring about. In addition, it was the year which saw the emergence of the Provisional IRA and the start of the present round of 'the troubles' in Ireland. Finally, it was the year in which the first tentative moves were made towards international co-operation among the terrorists.

GLOSSARY OF ABBREVIATIONS USED

PFLP	Popular Front for the Liberation of Palestine　*(Palestine)*
ALN	Action for National Liberation　*(Brazil)*
MR-8	Revolutionary Movement of the Eighth　*(Brazil)*
ECLP	Executive Committee for the Liberation of Palestine　*(Palestine)*
PFLP–GC	Popular Front for the Liberation of Palestine–General Command　*(Palestine)*
JRA	Japanese Red Army　*(Japan)*
FLQ	Quebec Liberation Front　*(Canada)*
ETA	Basque Nation and Liberty　*(Spain)*
TPLA	Turkish People's Liberation Army　*(Turkey)*
JDL	Jewish Defence League　*(United States)*
ERP	People's Revolutionary Army　*(Argentina)*
NAYLP	National Arab Youth for the Liberation of Palestine　*(Palestine–Libya)*
PIRA	Provisional Irish Republican Army　*(Ireland)*
UDA	Ulster Defence Association　*(Ireland)*
RB	Red Brigades　*(Italy)*

THE CHRONOLOGY OF TERROR

DATE	PLACE	INCIDENT	GROUP
1968 22 July	Rome	First of Palestinian hijacks. El Al airliner flying from Rome to Tel Aviv hijacked to Algeria.	PFLP
26 December	Athens	Two men attack El Al plane with light arms and grenades at airport. One passenger killed. Two Palestinians captured and imprisoned but released after hijacking of Greek airliner to Cairo on 22 July 1970.	PFLP
28 December	Beirut	First of Israeli retaliatory attacks on Beirut. Commandos landed by helicopter take over Beirut Airport and destroy or damage 13 aircraft.	Israeli Army
1969 18 February	Zurich	Arab terrorists machine-gun El Al airliner preparing to take off for Tel	PFLP

DATE	PLACE	INCIDENT	GROUP
		Aviv. Co-pilot killed, five passengers wounded, one attacker killed by Israeli flying guard. Surviving three terrorists sentenced to prison but released after hijacking of Swissair plane to Jordan on 6 September 1970.	
18 July	London	Marks & Spencers' stores firebombed. George Habash threatens more Jewish-owned stores in all parts of the world.	PFLP
29 August	Rome – Tel Aviv	TWA Boeing 707 hijacked to Damascus. All passengers released except two Israelis, who are exchanged for two Syrian pilots held by Israel. Plane destroyed.	PFLP
4 September	Rio de Janeiro	The first of the diplomatic kidnappings. Charles Elbrick, US Ambassador to Brazil, held until 15 prisoners released and flown to Mexico. Leads to arrest of 4000 leftists and harsh repressive measures.	MR-8 and ALN
8 September	Brussels, Hague, Bonn	Hand-grenade attacks on Israeli offices.	PFLP
6 October	Cordoba (Argentina)	Bombs damage offices of American companies: First National City Bank, Pepsi Cola, Squibb and Dunlop Tyres. Start of three-day campaign of bombing American institutions.	Unknown
12 December	West Berlin	Explosive charges found and defused near the El Al office and 'America House' office block. Third bomb explodes in US officers' club.	Baader– Meinhof
1970 10 February	Munich	Hand-grenade attack on bus at airport kills one El Al passenger and wounds eleven, including Hannah Marron, well-loved Israeli actress. One terrorist is wounded and three others are arrested but freed following the September 1970 hijacks.	ECLP
21 February	Zurich	Swissair plane destroyed by mid-air explosion; 47 people killed. Bomb explodes in Austrian airliner carrying mail to Tel Aviv.	PFLP-GC
31 March	Tokyo	First of Japanese Red Army's international incidents. Armed with samurai swords hijackers force a	JRA

DATE	PLACE	INCIDENT	GROUP
		Japanese airliner to fly to North Korea.	
31 July	Uruguay	A spectacular day of kidnappings (the frequency of which has increased since the abduction of Charles Elbrick): two diplomats taken hostage – Andiel Mitrione, US public safety adviser in Uruguay, and Aloisio Gomide, Brazilian Consul in Uruguay. Mitrione murdered when Uruguayans refuse to negotiate on demands for freeing of 150 prisoners; Gomide released on 21 February 1971. On same day attempts are made to kidnap Gordon Jones, second secretary at the US Embassy in Montevideo, and Nathan Rosenfeld, the cultural attaché. Both escape.	Tupamaros
6 September	Dawson's Field	In a spectacular operation two aircraft are hijacked over Europe and flown to a wartime airfield, Dawson's Field, in Jordan. A third is taken to Cairo and destroyed, but a fourth, an El Al Boeing 707 en route from London to Amsterdam, escapes when Israeli 'sky-marshals' shoot dead Patrick Arguello, a Nicaraguan working for the PFLP, and capture Leila Khaled. A fifth plane, a BOAC VC-10, is hijacked on 9 September and flown to Dawson's Field to provide hostages for Leila Khaled. The 300 hostages at the field are eventually released in exchange for Palestinian terrorists imprisoned in Switzerland, the United Kingdom and West Germany. This incident leads King Hussein to drive the Palestinian terrorist groups out of Jordan, to the formation of Black September, and, because the strain of making peace between Yasser Arafat and King Hussein is so great, to the death of President Nasser.	PFLP
5 October	Quebec	James Cross, British Trade Commissioner for Quebec, kidnapped by French–Canadian separatists and held to ransom for the release of prisoners, publication of political manifesto and payment of	FLQ

DATE	PLACE	INCIDENT	GROUP
		$500,000 in gold. Canadian government rejects demands and on 3 December the kidnappers release him in return for safe conduct to Cuba.	
10 October	Quebec	Pierre LaPorte, Minister of Labour in the Quebec Government, kidnapped and killed because demands made by James Cross' kidnappers were not met. Prime Minister Trudeau invokes emergency powers and breaks the FLQ. LaPorte's kidnappers are sentenced to life imprisonment.	FLQ
1 December	San Sebastian	Basque nationalists kidnap Eugene Beihl, honorary West German consul, and force the Franco government to commute death sentences passed on six Basques accused of murdering a head of the provincial police.	ETA
1971 8 January	Montevideo	Geoffrey Jackson, British Ambassador to Uruguay, kidnapped and held for eight months in a 'people's prison'. Kidnappers demand release of 150 prisoners but government refuses to negotiate. 106 of the prisoners escape and Jackson – later knighted for his courageous behaviour – is released.	Tupamaros
4 March	Ankara	Four American servicemen stationed near Ankara kidnapped and held in exchange for money and publication of political manifesto attacking American imperialism in Turkey. Police capture one of the gang, who talks, and 45,000 soldiers and police mount a search. The hostages are released unharmed on 8 March. The kidnappers are caught – three are hanged, one imprisoned and one killed in a gunfight.	TPLA
14 March	Rotterdam	Palestinian and French sympathisers blow up fuel tanks – the first co-ordinated attack mounted from Paris by Yasser Arafat's organisation.	Fatah
17 May	Istanbul	Ephraim Elrom, Israeli consul general, kidnapped and murdered by gang who demand release of all guerrillas detained by Turkish government.	TPLA

DATE	PLACE	INCIDENT	GROUP
11 June	Bab el Mandeb	Israeli tanker *Coral Sea* damaged by four men who fire rockets at the tanker from a small boat and then escape to South Yemen.	PFLP
20 July	Rome	First of series of attacks mounted by Fatah on Jordanian offices and aircraft in revenge for 'Black September'. Attack is made on Alia, the Jordanian airline office.	Fatah
24 July	Cairo	Attack on Alia plane at airport. Plane slightly damaged.	Fatah
27 July	Paris	Several explosive charges thrown at Jordanian Embassy.	Fatah
28 July	Tel Aviv	Attempt to blow up El Al plane in mid-air by terrorist who gives suitcase bomb to innocent Dutch girl. This is the first in a series of such attempts.	PFLP-GC
1 September	London–Tel Aviv	Attempt to blow up El Al plane in mid-air by terrorist who gives suitcase to innocent Peruvian girl.	PFLP-GC
20 October	New York	Jewish extremists fire rifle shots into apartment occupied by members of Soviet delegation to the United Nations.	JDL
28 November	Cairo	Jordan's Prime Minister assassinated on the steps of the Sheraton Hotel by a team of Black September gunmen. This is the first acknowledged operation by Black September and is carried out against the man they blame for their disaster in Jordan in September 1970. Black September was set up after initial operations mounted by Fatah proved successful.	Black September
15 December	London	Zaid Rifai, Jordanian Ambassador to London, wounded when his car is fired upon by Black September gunman.	Black September
1972 26 January	New York	Offices of the late Sol Hurok, the impresario who manages US tours by Soviet performers, firebombed.	JDL
6 February	Rotterdam	Two gas-processing plants blown up.	Black September
6 February	Cologne	Five Jordanian workers – allegedly Israeli spies – shot to death.	Black September
8 February	Hamburg	Factory making electric generators for Israeli aircraft heavily damaged.	Black September

DATE	PLACE	INCIDENT	GROUP
22 February	Aldershot	Bomb at Parachute Regiment headquarters at Aldershot kills nine soldiers and civilians.	Provisional IRA
22 February	New Delhi–Athens	Lufthansa airliner hijacked to Aden by five terrorists claiming membership of Organisation for Victims of Zionist Occupation. They are in fact members of PFLP. Plane and passengers are released after airline pays $5 million ransom. South Yemen government takes $1 million for 'landing rights'.	PFLP
21 March	Buenos Aires	Berdan Sallustro, president of Fiat of Argentina, kidnapped. Fiat agree to pay $1 million ransom and reinstate 250 workers fired in industrial dispute. Government refuse to release 50 prisoners, launch a hunt for the kidnappers' hideout, find and surround it. Just before they attack the terrorists carry out their threat and murder Sallustro.	ERP
27 March	Ankara	Three NATO radar technicians, two British and one Canadian, kidnapped by terrorists who demand the release of three terrorists who had been sentenced to death. Like Sallustro, the three technicians are murdered when the police surround the terrorists' hideout. In the subsequent battle the police kill ten terrorists.	TPLA
April	Tel Aviv	Israeli police arrest the 'Easter Commando' a group of Westerners led by Evelyne Barge, who had taken part in the attack on the Rotterdam fuel tanks and had been sent to Israel to attack tourist hotels.	Black September/ PFLP
8 May	Tel Aviv	Two men and two women hijack Sabena airliner and force it to land at Tel Aviv, where they demand the release of 317 Palestinian guerrillas. In first successful assault on hijacked plane, Israeli paratroopers disguised as mechanics burst into plane, kill the two men and capture the women. One passenger dies in the shooting.	Black September
11 May		Series of bombs explode at the Fifth US Army Corps HQ killing Colonel Paul Bloomquist and wounding 13	Baader–Meinhof

DATE	PLACE	INCIDENT	GROUP
		others. Bombing is said to be in retaliation for American bombing of North Vietnam.	
31 May	Tel Aviv	Three Japanese 'kamikaze' killers – members of the Japanese Red Army recruited by Wadi Hadad's PFLP – attack passengers at Lod Airport with grenades and assault rifles, killing 26 people and wounding 76. Two terrorists are killed, the other sentenced to life imprisonment. This is the first of the Japanese 'Arab' operations and the first of the transnational murder attacks.	JRA–PFLP
1 June	Frankfurt	Andreas Baader and Holger Meins captured after firefight in which both men are wounded.	Baader–Meinhof
15 June	Hanover	Ulrike Meinhof betrayed and arrested.	Baader–Meinhof
5 September	Munich	The Munich massacre. Seven terrorists take control of the dormitory of the Israeli athletes in the Olympic village, killing two athletes and taking nine as hostages. Israel rejects the gang's demands for release of 200 imprisoned Palestinians but West German government agrees to give the gang and their hostages safe passage to Egypt. At Furstenfeldbruck airport German sharpshooters open fire. In the ensuing gunfight all hostages, five terrorists and one policeman are killed. The incident focuses attention on the Palestinian cause.	Black September
9 September	London	Dr Ami Shachori, agricultural counsellor at the Israeli Embassy, killed by a letter bomb, the first casualty of the letter bomb 'war'. In the next few days some fifty letter bombs sent to Israelis are intercepted – all posted in Amsterdam. Soon afterwards a second batch posted in Malaysia start to arrive. These are followed in November by a further batch posted in India.	Black September
24 October	Belgrade	The Israelis retaliate. A series of letter bombs posted in Belgrade arrive on the desks of Palestinian resistance	Mossad

DATE	PLACE	INCIDENT	GROUP
		leaders in Lebanon, Egypt, Libya and Algeria.	
29 October	Beirut–Ankara	Lufthansa plane hijacked by two terrorists who threaten to blow it up in mid-air if the three Munich massacre terrorists are not released. They are.	Black September
8 December	Paris	Mahmoud Hamshari, the Palestine Liberation Organisation's representative in Paris, is killed by an electronically triggered bomb attached to his telephone. Along with Wael Zwaiter – Fatah's representative in Rome who was shot outside his apartment – Hamshari is the first victim of the Munich revenge killings.	Mossad
10 December	Buenos Aires	Donald Grove, managing director of the British Vestey Industrial group, kidnapped. Released unharmed nine days later after Vestey's have paid a $1 million ransom.	ERP
1973			
		This is the most destructive year of the Provisional IRA's campaign – 467 die in acts of political violence.	
26 January	Madrid	Israeli intelligence officer, Baruch Cohen, shot down in cafe on the Grand Via. Palestinians claim he had taken part in killing of Hamshari and Zwaiter.	Black September
9 February	Amman	Jordanians arrest team of 17 Palestinians led by Abu Daoud, a leader of Fatah, who had been sent to attack the US Embassy and Jordanian government officials. Abu Daoud talks freely under questioning and makes first public admission that Black September is part of Fatah.	Black September
21 February	Sinai	Israelis shoot down Libyan airliner which had strayed over Sinai, fearing it had been taken over and would be used as a flying bomb against Tel Aviv.	
1 March	Khartoum	Eight Black September terrorists take over the Saudi Arabian Embassy during a party for American diplomat George Curtis Moore. Terrorists seize Moore and a number of other diplomats and demand the release of	Black September

DATE	PLACE	INCIDENT	GROUP
		Palestinian and Baader–Meinhof prisoners, Sirhan Sirhan (the murderer of Robert Kennedy) and Kozo Okomoto, surviving member of the Lod killers. President Nixon refuses. The terrorists shoot Moore; US Ambassador, Cleo Noel; and the Belgian chargé d'affaires, Guy Eid. The terrorists are arrested and tried but eventually released. President Numeiry of the Sudan blames Libyan leader Colonel Gaddafi for instigating the attack.	
10 April	Beirut	Israeli commandos attack apartments of leading Palestinian guerrillas and kill 17 people, among them three high-ranking guerrillas, spreading panic through Palestinian ranks. Some Palestinian leaders withdraw to Cairo and Baghdad for safety.	Mossad
6 June	Buenos Aires	Charles Lockwood, a British businessman, kidnapped and held for 53 days until he is ransomed for $2 million. Lockwood later kidnapped by another group. He tells them that it is unfair to expect a second suck at the orange.	ERP Splinter Group
28 June	Paris	Mohammed Boudia, the leading Arab terrorist in Europe – organiser of the Rotterdam attacks, the raids on factories in Germany, and the 'Easter Commando' – killed by a land mine placed under his car seat. His death clears the way for Carlos, the Venezuelan assassin, to be called from London to take over the European operations of the Palestinians and to build a truly transnational terrorism incorporating Germans, Dutch, Japanese and French terrorists.	Mossad
1 July	Washington	Colonel Yosef Alon, the Israeli military attaché, shot to death by an unknown assailant outside his home. A Voice of Palestine broadcast says he had been executed in retaliation for the murder of Boudia.	Unknown
20 July	Amsterdam–Tokyo	A group of three Arabs and one Japanese, led by an unidentified woman, hijack a Japan Air Lines	PFLP–JRA

DATE	PLACE	INCIDENT	GROUP
		Boeing 747. The woman kills herself accidentally when she drops the grenade she is carrying. The aircraft flies around the Middle East for four days until it arrives at Benghazi, where passengers are released and the plane blown up. The hijackers are arrested and some of them spend a year in jail before being released.	
21 July	Lillehammer	A Moroccan waiter killed in error by a 'Wrath of God' team who thought they were on the trail of Ali Hassan Salameh, one of the leaders of Black September and a planner of Munich. Several of the hit team are arrested and jailed. This is the last operation carried out by the Israeli assassination teams in Europe.	Mossad
5 August	Athens	Five passengers killed and 55 wounded in machine-gun and grenade attack on passengers from TWA plane which had just landed from Tel Aviv. Two Arabs sentenced to death are released as ransom in subsequent hijacking on 2 February 1974. Killers claim to be members of Black September but are disowned. Later identified as members of breakaway National Arab Youth for the Liberation of Palestine.	NAYLP
18 August	United Kingdom	Fire and letter bomb campaign launched in London, Birmingham and Manchester. In six weeks some 30 people are injured by 40 bombs. Many other bombs are safely defused.	Provisional IRA
5 September	Paris	Saudi Arabian Embassy seized by five Palestinians – members of a Black September Splinter Group, the Punishment Squad – who demand the release of Abu Daoud. Hostages released and terrorists surrender in Kuwait three days later.	Black September Splinter Group
5 September	Rome	Terrorism adopts electronic aerial warfare. The Italian police arrest five Arabs armed with two Soviet Strela heat-seeking, ground-to-air rockets (SAM 7). The terrorists had taken a house on the flight path to Rome Airport and were planning to shoot down an El Al airliner.	Black September

DATE	PLACE	INCIDENT	GROUP
28 September	Vienna	Two Palestinians claiming to be members of yet another splinter group, the 'Eagles of the Palestinian Revolution' seize a train and take three Jewish emigrants from Russia hostage. They are released after Chancellor Bruno Kreisky promises to close the transit camp for Jewish emigrants at Schonau Castle. The terrorists are later shown to be members of Saika, the Syrian backed group.	Saika
6 December	Buenos Aires	Victor Samuelson, American executive of Exxon, kidnapped and ransomed for the huge sum of $14.2 million. Released on 29 April 1974.	ERP
17 December	Rome	Five armed terrorists set fire to a Pan Am plane with thermite bombs, burning 32 passengers to death and injuring 40. They then hijack a Lufthansa plane, murder an airline worker, and fly to Damascus and Kuwait with hostages. Surrender at Kuwait and are arrested by the PLO, which says that they will be tried by a revolutionary court for carrying out an 'unauthorised operation' detrimental to the Palestinian cause. Said to be carried out by the National Arab Youth for the Liberation of Palestine, it marks the emergence of Abu Nidal, a renegade from Fatah and Black September, as a most ferocious splinter group leader.	NAYLP
18 December	London	Bombs in two cars and a parcel bomb injure 60 people in reprisal for jailing of IRA terrorists who exploded car bomb outside the Old Bailey in March 1973.	IRA
20 December	Paris	Sabotage HQ discovered in a villa outside Paris. Used by international group comprising members of PFLP, Algerian and Turkish terrorist groups. Cache of arms, propaganda and bomb-making equipment found. Discovery is setback to Carlos' attempts to rebuild Boudia network, but confirms international nature of terrorism in France.	PFLP

DATE	PLACE	INCIDENT	GROUP
20 December	Madrid	Premier Luis Carrero Blanco assassinated by explosion which blows his car over a church. Basque militants claim responsibility saying it was in revenge for the killing of nine of their comrades.	ETA
31 December	London	Leading British Zionist Teddy Sieff, President of Marks & Spencer, is shot by an intruder, later identified as Carlos, but escapes owing to malfunction of assailant's gun.	Carlos
1974 24 January	London	In his second act of terrorism, Carlos throws a bomb based on a Russian grenade into the Israeli Bank Hapoalim in the City of London and wounds a woman.	Carlos
31 January	Singapore	Two Palestinians and two Japanese attack Shell fuel installations; later they seize a boat and five hostages, holding out for a week until five more terrorists take over Japanese Embassy in Kuwait. All nine are picked up by Japanese Airline plane and flown to South Yemen.	PFLP–JRA
3 February	England	A 50 lb suitcase bomb hidden in the luggage compartment of a bus carrying soldiers and their families back from leave explodes and kills 11 people.	Provisional IRA
3 March	Amsterdam	British VC 10 hijacked en route from Bombay to London. Blown up at Amsterdam. Another operation by Abu Nidal's splinter group.	NAYLP
11 April	Qiryat Shemona	Three guerrillas storm a residential building in northern Israel town, killing 18 and wounding 16. Attackers are killed in battle with Israeli troops. Next day the Israelis mount a series of revenge raids across the Lebanese border. This is the first major ground attack carried out by the splinter group Popular Front for the Liberation of Palestine–General Command.	PFLP–GC
26 April	Dublin	Rose Dugdale arrested for the theft of Sir Alfred Beit's art collection, which she threatens to destroy unless four convicted IRA terrorists are	IRA

DATE	PLACE	INCIDENT	GROUP
		transferred from English to Irish jails. Dugdale is later sentenced to nine years in prison. The pictures are recovered unharmed.	
26 July	Paris	Yoshiaka Yamada arrested at Orly Airport carrying Japanese Red Army treasury – $10,000. Most of the money is counterfeit.	JRA
3 August	Paris	Car bombs explode outside the offices of *L'Aurore*, *Minute* and *L'Arche*. A fourth unexploded car bomb is discovered near the French radio and TV offices.	Carlos–PFLP
13 September	Hague	In an operation partly planned and financed by Carlos, three Japanese take over the French Embassy and successfully demand the release of Yoshiaka Yamada, their currency courier.	JRA–Carlos
15 September	Paris	Carlos throws hand grenade into the Drug Store, killing two and wounding twelve, in support of the demands of the Japanese occupying the French Embassy in the Hague.	Carlos–PFLP–JRA
8 October	Greece	TWA airliner which had arrived in Greece from Israel is blown up in flight over the Aegean. All 88 on board killed.	NAYLP
11 October	Rabat	Attempted assassination (led by Abu Iyad, Black September leader and Arafat's second-in-command) of King Hussein and possibly other 'moderate' Arab leaders gathered at the Rabat summit is foiled by Moroccan authorities, who arrest 15 after Israeli tip-off.	Black September
22 November	Dubai	British Airways airliner hijacked to Tunis by members of Abu Nidal's group. In exchange for the release of passengers, two terrorists imprisoned in Holland for a previous hijack of a British plane, and the prisoners from Rabat are freed.	NAYLP
1975 13 January	Paris	Members of Carlos' gang try to destroy an El Al plane at Orly using hand-held rocket missiles. They miss but hit a Yugoslav plane and one of the airport buildings.	Carlos–PFLP

DATE	PLACE	INCIDENT	GROUP
19 January	Paris	Carlos' men make another attempt with RPG missiles at Orly, but are spotted before they can fire and in ensuing gunfight seize hostages and bargain their way to a flight to Iraq.	Carlos–PFLP
27 February	Berlin	German politician Peter Lorenz kidnapped and ransomed for the freedom of five Baader–Meinhof terrorists. The West German government capitulates to the terrorists' demands, freeing the five and giving them DM 20,000 each.	Baader–Meinhof
24 April	Stockholm	Six German terrorists, former patients of the Neurological–Psychiatric Clinic of Heidelberg – the crazy brigade – occupy the German Embassy and murder two diplomats when their demands are not met for the freeing of 26 Baader–Meinhof members. The Embassy is blown up as police prepare to attack. One of the terrorists is killed, another dies later and the other four are arrested and deported to Germany.	Baader–Meinhof
21 May	Stammheim	Trial of the Baader–Meinhof leaders begins.	
27 June	Paris	Carlos' identity is revealed when French police are led to his flat on the Rue Toullier by Michel Moukharbel, his liaison officer with the PFLP. Carlos kills Moukharbel and two of the police officers and wounds a third before escaping to Algeria. Until now no one had known of his existence or his involvement in terrorism in London and Paris. From now on he boasts, 'I am the famous Carlos'.	Carlos–PFLP
4 August	Kuala Lumpur	American Consulate and Swedish Embassy seized to secure the release of seven imprisoned terrorists. Two refuse to go. Remainder flown to Libya.	JRA
21 December	Vienna	OPEC's headquarters seized by Carlos and a mixed gang of Palestinian and Baader–Meinhof terrorists. Three men shot and 11 oil ministers kidnapped and held hostage, among them Sheik Yamani of Saudi Arabia and Dr Amouzegar of Iran. The	Carlos–PFLP–Baader–Meinhof

DATE	PLACE	INCIDENT	GROUP
		Palestinians and Germans want to kill them both, but Carlos holds out for ransom – and gets it. The hostages are released in Algeria. Up to the time of writing this is the last operation in which Carlos has been involved 'in the field'.	
2 December	Holland	South Moluccans seize a train at Beilen and the Indonesian Embassy in the Hague in pursuance of their hopeless cause to wrest an independent republic from Indonesia. They kill three and are given heavy prison sentences.	South Moluccans
1976 8 January	Ireland	Detachment of SAS deployed in Armagh. They effectively wrest control of what was 'bandit country' from the Provos.	Provisional IRA
11 March	Dublin	Eddie Gallagher jailed for 20 years and Marian Coyle for 15, for kidnapping Dutch industrialist Tiede Herrema in an attempt to force freeing of Gallagher's mistress, Rose Dugdale.	Provisional IRA
4 May	Stammheim	Gudrun Ensslin admits the Baader–Meinhof gang's responsibility for three of the lethal bombings with which they were charged.	Baader–Meinhof
8 May	Stammheim	Ulrike Meinhof hangs herself from the bars of her cell window.	Baader–Meinhof
23 May	Assen	South Moluccans seize a train at Assen and children's school at Bovinsmilde. The school children are released after four days when they fall ill with a stomach virus; the train is captured in a dawn assault by Dutch marines after a siege which lasts 20 days. Two hostages and six terrorists die in the assault.	South Moluccans
18 June	Buenos Aires	General Cesareo Cardozo, Chief of Federal Police, killed by bomb exploding under his bed. Believed to have been placed there by a friend of his daughter. He is the second police chief killed in less than two years.	ERP

DATE	PLACE	INCIDENT	GROUP
27 June	Entebbe	A mixed group of German and Palestinian terrorists hijack an Air France airbus to Entebbe where they separate the Jews from other passengers and threaten to kill them unless their demands for the release of imprisoned terrorists are met. At least three governments are involved on the terrorist side, those of Uganda, Somalia and Libya. The hijack is brought to an end by the spectacular assault on Entebbe airport by Israeli paratroops. It is the first great defeat of international terrorism. The Israelis kill the two German terrorists involved – one of them Wilfried Bose, one of Carlos' Paris gang – and five members of the PFLP.	Baader–Meinhof–PFLP
19 July	Argentina	Robert Santucho, overall leader of the ERP, is killed in battle with the authorities. His death is a severe blow to the movement.	ERP
31 July	Dublin	British Ambassador to Ireland, Christopher Ewart-Biggs, assassinated by culvert bomb.	Provisional IRA
28 October	Belfast	Maire Drumm, violently anti-British Provisional leader, shot to death in hospital while recovering from an operation.	UDA Splinter Group
1977 24 January	Madrid	Five Communist lawyers killed when two men with sub-machine-guns attack left wingers meeting in Madrid lawyer's office.	Warriors of Christ the King
9 February	London	Balcombe Street siege terrorists found guilty of multiple murders and sentenced to life imprisonment. Up to time of writing no further 'Active Service Units' of the Provisional IRA have gone into action in London.	Provisional IRA
7 April		Siegfried Buback, West Germany's chief public prosecutor, shot to death in revenge for Ulrike Meinhof's suicide.	Baader–Meinhof
10 April	London	Former Yemeni Prime Minister Abdullah al-Hejiri, his wife and the Minister at the Yemeni Embassy assassinated by Palestinian hit man.	PFLP

DATE	PLACE	INCIDENT	GROUP
		Killer later commands Mogadishu hijack. The murder was committed because Hejiri was working for the Saudis to form a Western orientated alliance of Arab countries in Southern Arabia and the Horn of Africa.	
31 July	Frankfurt	Juergen Ponto, one of Germany's most influential bankers, murdered by terrorists who are led into his heavily protected home by his god-daughter, Susanne Albrecht.	Baader–Meinhof
5 September	Cologne	Hans-Martin Schleyer, a powerful West German businessman, ambushed by terrorist gang who kill his driver and three bodyguards and kidnap him. In return for his life they demand the release of 11 Baader–Meinhof prisoners, who are to be given £25,000 each and flown to the country of their choice. This kidnapping virtually brings governmental life to a standstill in Germany.	Baader–Meinhof
28 September	Bombay	Japanese Red Army hijack Japanese Airline plane and demand release of six Red Army prisoners and a $6 million ransom. Japanese government capitulates. The Japanese make their way to Baghdad to join the international group being built up by Wadi Hadad and Carlos.	JRA
13 October	Majorca–Frankfurt	Lufthansa airliner with 79 passengers hijacked by Palestinians – two men, two women – who demand the release of Baader–Meinhof leaders and a £9 million ransom. Terrorists threaten to kill Herr Schleyer and passengers and crew on board airliner. After wild flight around the Middle East and the Horn of Africa during which the terrorist leader, 'Captain Mahmoud', shoots the pilot, Jugen Schumann, the plane lands at Mogadishu. There, the plane is assaulted by members of the German GSG9 commando and all the passengers released. Two British SAS soldiers take part in the assault using special 'stun' grenades. Three of the terrorists are killed and the fourth, a girl wounded. The terrorist	PFLP on behalf of Baader–Meinhof

DATE	PLACE	INCIDENT	GROUP
		leader is identified as one of Wadi Hadad's professional killers, Zohair Akache, who had murdered the three Yemenis in London six months previously.	
19 October	Mulhouse	The body of Herr Schleyer is found in the boot of a car. He has been shot through the head.	Baader–Meinhof
20 October	Stammheim	Andreas Baader, Gudrun Ensslin and Jan-Carl Raspe, who had expected to be freed through Schleyer kidnapping and Mogadishu hijacking, commit suicide in their cells.	Baader–Meinhof
7 December	Cairo	Murder of David Holden, *Sunday Times* Middle East expert.	Unknown
31 December	London	Two Syrian diplomats killed by a car bomb in Mayfair. Victims are members of Syrian Intelligence and it is thought that they are killed by scoring an 'own goal' with a bomb they are taking to plant.	Syrian Intelligence
1978 4 January	London	Said Hammami, the PLO's representative in London, is shot dead in his office. Killing causes furore in the Arab world: Hammami, a moderate, was being used by Yasser Arafat to conduct negotiations with Israelis. Killer is thought to be a member of one of the rejectionist groups, either Wadi Hadad's PFLP or, more likely, Abu Nidal's 'Black June'.	PFLP or Black June
18 February	Nicosia	Two Palestinian gunmen murder Egyptian editor Yusuf Sebai then hijack Cyprus Airways jet. Jet returns to Nicosia where Egyptian commando mission to seize terrorists tragically misfires and 15 men die in fight with Cyprus National Guard.	PFLP
9 March	Turin	Trial of Red Brigades leader Renato Curcio and 47 members begins. They appear caged and manacled in court.	
10 March	Rome	In reprisal action Red Brigades murder Judge Rosario Berardi and prison official.	Red Brigades
16 March	Rome	Aldo Moro kidnapped, five bodyguards slaughtered.	Red Brigades

DATE	PLACE	INCIDENT	GROUP
25 March	Rome	Communiqué announces Moro to be tried by 'People's Court'.	Red Brigades
30 March	Rome	Italian Communist Party join Christian Democrats in refusing to negotiate or to free prisoners.	Red Brigades
1 April	East Berlin	Wadi Hadad, operational commander of PFLP and allies, dies of cancer and is buried in Baghdad.	
7 April	Vatican	Pope appeals to terrorists to spare Moro's life.	
13 April	New York	David Graiver, Argentine terrorist banker indicted in absence. 'He may still be alive.'	
15 April	Rome	Red Brigades announce that Moro has been condemned to death.	Red Brigades
18 April	Rome	False announcement that Moro has been 'executed by suicide'.	
24 April	Cairo	Egyptians smash terrorist ring which they claim is masterminded by Abu Nidal and the 'Corrective Movement' of Al Fatah. Twenty-four arrested including German woman and three Swiss said to be linked with Italian Red Brigades.	
10 May	Rome	The body of Aldo Moro found in the back of a car in Rome. He has been murdered.	Red Brigades
15 June	Kuwait	PLO representative assassinated.	Black June
23 June	Turin	Renato Curcio sentenced to 15 years' imprisonment. Another founder member of Red Brigades, Pietro Bassi, also sentenced to 15 years. Of the 47 on trial, 16 are acquitted.	Red Brigades
24 June	Brussels	Iraqi Embassy bombed. No casualties but bomb signals start of mini-war between Iraqi 'Rejectionists', spearheaded by Abu Nidal's Black June group, and Yasser Arafat's PLO.	PLO
9 July	London	General al-Naif, former Iraqi Prime Minister, is assassinated outside Intercontinental Hotel.	Iraqi secret service: al Mukhabarar
26 July	London	Britain expels 11 Iraqi diplomats because of their involvement in acts of terrorism. Iraqi Embassy has become centre of terrorism.	

DATE	PLACE	INCIDENT	GROUP
28 July	London	Grenade thrown at Iraqi Ambassador's car. No casualties.	PLO
31 July	Beirut	Unsuccessful machine-gun attack on Iraqi Ambassador.	PLO
31 July	Paris	Gunmen invade Iraqi Embassy and take eight hostages. Gunmen surrender but are ambushed by Iraqi secret servicemen as they are taken from the building. Firefight ensues between Iraqis and French police. French police inspector and Iraqi diplomat are killed.	PLO
2 August	Karachi	Two gunmen attack Iraqi Consulate. One of them is bayoneted to death by police guard despite being wounded by four shots. One diplomat wounded.	PLO
3 August	Paris	PLO representative, Ezzedine Kalak, assassinated.	Black June
5 August	Islamabad	Three PLO men and police guard killed when four gunmen attack PLO office.	Black June
7 August	Lebanon	Fierce inter-Arab battles break out in refugee camps between PLO and Iraqi-backed groups.	
20 August	London	El Al aircrew bus attacked outside Europa hotel. One Israeli stewardess is killed and another wounded.	Black June
6 September	Dusseldorf	Peter Stoll, believed to have played major part in the kidnapping and murder of Hans-Martin Schleyer, killed by police attempting to arrest him in restaurant.	Baader–Meinhof
13 September	Milan	Corrado Alunni, prime suspect in the murder of Aldo Moro, arrested in apartment filled with guns, explosives and false documents.	Red Brigades
15 September	London	Astrid Proll arrested at a Finchley Road garage, where she had been working for ten months. West German government asks for her extradition on charges of attempted murder of two policemen. Believed to have links with Carlos.	Baader–Meinhof

DATE	PLACE	INCIDENT	GROUP
24 September	Dortmund	Angelika Speitel and Michael Knoll wounded and arrested after shoot-out with police while target-shooting in wood. Speitel is wanted in connection with murders of Siegfried Buback, Jurgen Ponto and Hans-Martin Schleyer.	Baader–Meinhof

As the year 1978 ended the German security forces were bringing more and more pressure to bear on the remnants of the Baader–Meinhof and Red Army Factions while Red Brigades terrorists in Italy and ETA terrorists in Spain continued their assassination campaigns. At the same time the new liberal regime in Spain was threatened with terrorist action from an extreme right-wing 'Patriotic Justice Committee', composed of the Anti-Communist Apostolic Alliance, the Warriors of Christ the King and ATE, the anti-ETA organisation.

Bibliography

Becker, Jillian, *Hitler's Children* (London: Michael Joseph, 1977).

Begin, Menachem, *The Revolt* (Tel Aviv: Steimatzky, 1977).

Bianco, Mirella, *Gadaffi, Voice from the Desert* (London: Longman, 1975).

Burns, Alan, *The Angry Brigade* (London: Quartet, 1974).

Clutterbuck, Richard, *Living with Terrorism* (London: Faber, 1975).

Conrad, Joseph, *The Secret Agent* (Harmondsworth: Penguin, 1967).

Crozier, Brian, *Annual of Power and Conflict 1976, 1977, 1978* (London: Institute for Study of Conflict).

Debray, Regis, *Revolution in a Revolution* (Harmondsworth: Penguin, 1968).

Debray, Regis, *Strategy for Revolution* (Harmondsworth: Penguin, 1973).

Dobson, Christopher, *Black September* (London: Hale, 1975).

Dobson, Christopher, and Payne, Ronald, *The Carlos Complex* (London: Hodder and Stoughton, 1977).

Fanon, Frantz, *The Wretched of the Earth* (Harmondsworth: Penguin, 1967).

Gott, Richard, *Guerrilla Movements in Latin America* (London: Nelson, 1976).

Guevara, Che, *Guerrilla Warfare* (Harmondsworth: Penguin, 1969).

Hidalgo, Orlando Castro, *Spy for Fidel* (Miami: Seemann, 1971).

Horchem, Hans Joseph, *West Germany's Red Army Anarchists*, Conflict Studies No. 46 (London, 1974).

Jackson, Geoffrey, *People's Prison* (London: Faber, 1972).

Johnson, K., *Guatemala: From Terrorism to Terror* (London: Institute for Study of Conflict, 1972).

Kitson, Frank, *Low Intensity Operations* (London: Faber, 1971).

Laqueur, Walter, *Terrorism* (London: Weidenfeld and Nicolson, 1977).

Marcuse, Herbert, *Five Lectures* (Harmondsworth: Penguin, 1970).

Marcuse, Herbert, *One Dimensional Man* (London: Routledge and Kegan Paul, 1968).

Marighella, Carlos, *For the Liberation of Brazil* (Harmondsworth: Penguin, 1971) – especially the chapter entitled 'Handbook of Urban Guerrilla Warfare'.

Masters, Anthony, *Bakunin* (London: Sidgwick and Jackson, 1974).

O'Brien, Conor Cruise, *Herod, Reflections on Political Violence* (London: Hutchinson, 1978).

Phillips, David, *Skyjack* (London: Harrap, 1973).

Stevenson, William, *90 Minutes to Entebbe* (London: Corgi, 1977).

Tabbora, Lina, *Survivre dans Beyrouth* (Paris: Oliver Orban, 1977).

Thadden, Adolf von, *Die Schreibtischtater, Das geistige Umfled des Terrorismus* (Hanover: Greiffen-Verlag, 1977).

Thomas, Hugh, *Cuba, or the Pursuit of Freedom* (London: Eyre and Spottiswoode, 1970).

Tophoven, Rolf, *Fedayin, Guerrilla ohne Grenzen* (Munich: Bernard und Graefe Verlag für Wehrwesen).

Trotsky, Leon, *The Defence of Terrorism* (London: Allen and Unwin, 1921).

Wilkinson, Paul, *Political Terrorism* (London: Macmillan, 1974).

Wilkinson, Paul, *Terrorism and the Liberal State* (London: Macmillan, 1977).